101
SUCCESS
SECRETS
for Women

SUE AUGUSTINE

HARVEST HOUSE PUBLISHERS

EUGENE, OREGON

Cover by Left Coast Design, Portland, Oregon

Cover Photo © mother image / Digital Vision / Getty Images

101 SUCCESS SECRETS FOR WOMEN
Previously published as *Turn Your Dreams into Realities*
Copyright © 2007 by Sue Augustine
Published 2011 by Harvest House Publishers
Eugene, Oregon 97402
www.harvesthousepublishers.com

Library of Congress Cataloging-in-Publication Data
Augustine, Sue.
 [Turn your dreams into realities]
 101 success secrets for women / Sue Augustine.
   p. cm.
 Originally published: Turn your dreams into realities. © 2007.
 ISBN 978-0-7369-3034-5 (pbk.)
 1. Dreams—Religious aspects—Christianity. 2. Visions. 3. Success—Religious aspects—Christianity. 4. Self-actualization (Psychology)—Religious aspects—Christianity. I. Title.
 BR115.D74A94 2011
 a 248.8'43—dc22

                                                                              2010028942

Printed in the United States of America

       11 12 13 14 15 16 17 18 / VP-NI / 10 9 8 7 6 5 4 3 2 1

To everyone who desires success,
and, most of all,
to the Source of all true vision.

Acknowledgments

This book could not have been written without the prayers of countless friends and family, and for that I am eternally grateful.

Beyond that, I thank God for the privilege of being able to share with others about the miraculous way He first gave us the desires of our hearts, planting them deep within us, and then, in His perfect timing, He brings them to fruition. This book belongs to God, and my prayer is that He will turn the dreams of all who read it into realities like only He can!

Contents

INTRODUCTION

*God can do anything, you know—far more
than you could ever imagine or guess
or request in your wildest dreams!*
EPHESIANS 3:20 MSG

Take a minute to think about what would have to take place in order for your life to be more fulfilling. What would have to happen for you to feel truly purposeful and contented at the same time? What would satisfy you more than anything else? These are questions that will start you on your journey, on the pathway to discovering your purpose and turning goals into realities.

Many people start out with a grand sense of purpose. They tackle a project, launch a new venture, embark on a journey, enter a profession, marry someone special—and then are overcome by the pressure of their own striving to make it a success. Eventually, the reason they began the project or goal eludes them. Their original inspiration may have been genuine, altruistic, and self-sacrificing, but it gets superseded either by a desire for perfection, the fear of a setback, worry over losing it all, or sheer force of habit.

This is a book about achieving success with no limits. You'll find 101 effective approaches and practical concepts that are proven to help you succeed if you put them into practice. It doesn't matter if your particular goals concern your health, spiritual growth, relationships, career, finances, sports, hobbies, education, travel, social change, or politics. The same principles and concepts for success apply in your home, on the job, at school, at church, and in your community. As you read, I pray you will gain inspiration and insights, implement the techniques presented, and trust the one who is the source of all dreams—God. If you ardently desire to make changes, are willing to apply the strategies presented in this book, and seek to be within God's will, then persevere—you will achieve your goals. Start right now to dream big dreams. Expect God to act and get ready!

PART 1
Getting Started

1 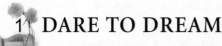 DARE TO DREAM

The poor man is not he who is without a cent,
but he who is without a dream!
HARRY KEMP

Keep thou thy dreams—the tissue of all wings
is woven first of them; from dreams are made
the precious and imperishable things
where loveliness lives on and does not fade.
VERA SHEARD

C an you imagine the tragedy of having the ability to go anywhere you choose, but not having the faintest idea where you'd like to go? This happens to many people. They never experience the joy or benefits of using their full potential because they don't have a vision for their lives. They're not exactly sure what they'd like to see happen. Perhaps they don't know they have a choice. Maybe they aren't aware that having a dream and being a visionary is what makes the difference between merely living and being fully alive.

Many of us spend more time watching television, writing to-do lists, and organizing a party than we do dreaming constructively about our lives. Other times we dwell on past memories or center on our hopes for a better future, but we have no current aims or definite objectives. When this happens, our activities turn into a blur of dealing with day-to-day tensions, handling problems, or coping with crises rather than moving toward worthy goals. We say we'd like to change careers, take up a new hobby or sport, start our own business, be healthier and have more energy, improve our relationships, earn more money, or contribute to a worthy cause, but our desires at this stage are only vague wishes. We dream about making changes, but we hold back from defining it in clear and compelling detail.

Inside every one of us is the seed of the person we were meant to become. If we have hidden this seed as a result of what we were told by others—our parents, teachers, coaches, group leaders, role models, or mentors—we've never had a chance to blossom. When we lose touch with what we really want, we end up becoming numb to our own desires. We don't dare dream because somewhere along the line someone told us not to. We may have heard:

> Get your head out of the clouds.
>
> Daydreamers don't amount to anything.
>
> Be logical. Use your brain.
>
> You don't really want that.
>
> You should be ashamed of yourself.
>
> You don't really feel that way.
>
> Don't you think of anyone but yourself?
>
> Stop acting so selfishly.
>
> How could you do that to me?
>
> You shouldn't expect too much from life.
>
> How can you believe that? Nobody else does.

When we accept such limitations, we soon lose touch with our heart's true desires and get caught in living up to what others think is right. Longing for approval, we act in ways to get it. The result is that we do things we may not want to do, trading our dreams for the more immediate gratification that comes from pleasing others. For example, you may have taken over the family business because it's what your dad wanted or you married and had children right away because your mom wanted grandkids. Some people get stuck in a "real" job rather than pursuing their dream of becoming an artist or musician or an entrepreneur. Some have passed up the opportunity to change careers altogether or relocate to another part of the country in order to appease someone else. For the sake of appearing sensible, we live with our "shoulds," "have tos," and "musts."

How do we reclaim our true self and get in touch with our heart's desires? God is the one who, from our very conception, has placed our dreams within us, along with the seeds of talent and natural ability. He has a purpose for each of us. Along with reconnecting with our hopes and dreams, it is wise to ask the Giver of Dreams for guidance and direction. It is a mistake, however, to believe God will magically make our way clear. Instead he sends reminders and chances to act upon our desires, but he allows us the freedom to choose—and that is where our responsibility comes in. We must *choose to act* upon the opportunities that arise in response to our request for guidance.

God has promised to give you the desires of your heart: "Delight yourself in the LORD, and He will give you the desires of your heart" (Psalm 37:4). Perhaps more than giving you everything you wish for, that verse is saying that he places those desires within your heart! Your heavenly Father knows better than anyone what you were created to do on this earth. Begin today to pay attention to what really matters to you by honoring your personal preferences in small ways. When you're presented with a choice, quit saying "It doesn't matter" or "I don't care." Allow yourself to choose from your heart. Purpose that starting today you are going to dare to step out of a life of mediocrity, routine, and repetitiveness. Leave the average behind and go after your dreams!

> *Dream lofty dreams and as you dream,*
> *so shall you become. Your vision is the promise*
> *of what you shall one day be.*
> JAMES ALLEN

 # 2 ALWAYS HAVE *TOO MANY* DREAMS

Give yourself something to work toward—constantly.
MARY KAY ASH

The truth? It's not possible to have *too many* dreams! Since God is the original visionary and you are made in his image, generating an abundance of dreams is a natural function. By continually creating more than enough dreams for yourself, you'll always be focused on possibilities and opportunities rather than problems and obstacles. Then your inborn creativity will be stimulated, and you'll find your imagination brimming with inspiring, effective, and useful ideas.

Here's a fun and valuable exercise you can do. Sit quietly with a large sheet of paper or journal and a pen or some colored markers. Make a list of dreams you have for your life. Let your imagination go and dream without restricting yourself. Ignore obstacles, limitations, and barriers. Don't inhibit this dreaming exercise by concentrating on the reason something might not happen, focusing on why it looks impossible, or directing your attention toward the hurdles that stand in the way. For now, make a list that includes *everything you can imagine* becoming, accomplishing, or attaining at some point in your life. Here are some ideas to get you going:

Develop a new habit

Let go of a bad habit

Improve family communications

Improve work communications

Contribute to a worthy cause

Build a new friendship

Renew an old friendship

Restore a broken relationship

Get involved in a community or church project

Travel to a new and exciting destination

Go on a mission trip

Found a charitable organization

Start a new hobby

Become debt free

Learn new skills for your job

Learn new skills for personal interests and concerns

Join a committee or sit on a board of directors

Start walking every day

Take up a new hobby

Read more books

Write a book

Join a choir

Learn to play a musical instrument

Improve your eating habits

Go back to school

Learn another language

Perfect an invention you've been working on

Complete a project

Get good at telling jokes and funny stories

Learn to paint, sketch, or draw

Compose a song or poem

Entertain guests in your home more often

Sponsor a child in a Third World country

Become a Big Brother or Big Sister

Get your photographs in an album

Organize your home or office

Clear out the clutter in your garage, basement, or attic

Purge your filing cabinets or kitchen cupboards

Start journaling

Design your own jewelry

Start an exercise program

Plan for your retirement

Make your funeral and burial arrangements

Make a will or update one

Renovate or redecorate your home

Plan a surprise party

Go on a dream vacation

Spend more time with family and friends

Take your kids (and grand-kids) on a cruise

Learn a craft

Take cooking classes

Start a personal Bible study or join a group

Take up a new sport

Build your personal library

Volunteer at a soup kitchen or shelter

Become an expert on a topic

Treat someone you admire to lunch

Start an interesting collection

Change jobs or careers

Start your own business

Keep a diary

Spend more time with God

One incredible truth about taking a dream and turning it into a reality is that once you decide *what* it is and which direction you want to head, you'll be inspired and soon discover *how* to go about accomplishing it. With your dreams in writing, you'll begin to see God at work, miraculously unfolding a progression of events that will place you in a position to go beyond the dream and make it a reality. You'll start to notice the people, circumstances, skills, and finances coming into your path that will activate the dream and help you see it through to fruition.

As you dream, know that God is at work. Your responsibility is to consider the various areas of your life and the lives of others that will be transformed once your dreams become realities.

3 WHY HAVE A DREAM?

To be what we are, and to become what we are capable of becoming, is the only end of life.
ROBERT LOUIS STEVENSON

You are a person of destiny. You may not realize it, but you have God-given dreams inside you right now...along with all the potential you need to bring them about. Dreams start as small flickers. Throughout your life you must constantly fan the flame and add fuel to get them blazing. As you turn to God and continue to grow in your relationship with him, he will reveal himself and his dreams and plans for you in ways you never thought possible. He not only plants the desires in your heart, but he will show you ways to bring them to pass.

Dreams are just as important in your everyday living as they are in the big picture of your life. Think about it. Without a dream, you would not have goals. Without goals, you would not make plans. Without plans, you would not:

Exercise regularly

Eat right and drink plenty of water

Have regular checkups at the doctor and dentist

Save for your children's education

Go on a family vacation

Volunteer in your community or church

Pay off your mortgage and other debts

Make investments for your future

Save for retirement

Pay your bills on time

Get to work each day

Find time for prayer, meditation and Bible study

and on...and on...and on!

Having a plan makes it possible to survive on this earth. With dreams, you stay in good health, enjoy happy relationships, and keep your finances in order. Dreaming makes it possible to go beyond the mere "wants" and "wishes" of life and concentrate on what's really important. Sometimes we are like children in a toy store. Our minds keep vacillating with so many choices, and when we can't make a decision, we get stuck in one place. We see too many options, and that keeps us from moving forward with any one of them. We are robbed of the inner peace and joy we are searching for. But when someone comes along and says, "Make up your mind. You can have one thing," we finally settle down and focus on the most significant one. Start today and begin asking God to show you the most significant things in your life.

Living your dreams involves every aspect of your life. The apostle Paul says, "So whether you eat, drink or whatever you do, do it all for the glory of God" (1 Corinthians 10:31). We bring glory to God when we are an example of the freedom we have in Christ. As you live out your heart's desires and your innermost dreams become realities, you will be a testimony of God's love because his Spirit manifests itself through you.

Why should you have a dream? When you do, you'll stay focused on what matters most while living a life of purpose and integrity. You'll be motivated and inspired to strive toward excellence while fulfilling your destiny. Your life will go from ordinary to extraordinary, from average to exceptional, and you'll experience victory in ways you never imagined. You will let go of the past, develop a healthy self-image, reach your potential for greatness, and create brighter futures for yourself and those around you. You will discover more fulfillment in your life, more satisfaction in your relationships, and a deeper intimacy with your creator. With a dream, you'll enlarge your vision and start believing in all you can become.

God, who created us, put our innermost dreams within our hearts. He calls us to draw out those dreams, to be people of vision, and to walk in faith. He calls us to ask for his wisdom and to rely totally on him to guide us through our journey. Dreams are one of the most intimate ways you will ever work together with God to fulfill his plans here on earth.

4 ORDINARY PEOPLE, EXTRAORDINARY DREAMS

Do what you can, with what you have, where you are.
THEODORE ROOSEVELT

Whatsoever your hand finds to do,
do it with all your might.
ECCLESIASTES 9:10

During the 25 years I've been in business, I have always been fascinated by the difference in the quality of people's lives. Why do some people have seemingly insurmountable odds to overcome and still manage to reach their dreams, while others appear to have it made yet struggle through each day, never feeling satisfied?

Many times the people who have everything going for them—looks, money, health, education, opportunity, a great heritage, and a positive upbringing—are the least contented, achieve mediocre results, and feel disappointed with their lot in life. On the other hand, quite often those who have had the biggest obstacles to conquer and the most challenging difficulties to overcome, are out in front, leading the way for the rest of us. What makes the difference between achieving average results and exceptional ones? And how do we take our lives from ordinary to extraordinary?

When we make a study of successful dreamers, we find that they have certain commonalities and characteristics. Success leaves clues, and winners are recognizable. They tend to do specific things consistently. The pioneers in life—the trailblazers, the entrepreneurs, the innovators, and the inventors—have resolutely determined that they will be the best they are capable of becoming. Colonel Harland Sanders, of KFC fame, said, "I made a resolve that I was going to amount to something if I could. And no hours, nor amount of labor, nor amount of money would deter me from giving the best that there was in me."

Dreamers have no fear of breaking new ground, initiating new ventures, and forging new paths because they know that success is no more than hearing from God, doing what you do well, and always giving your best. In doing so, they tend to enjoy their lives, jobs, and relationships. They are generally happy, healthy, and energetic. Being forward thinkers, they are often ahead of their time…and sometimes pay the price by being criticized or misunderstood. They are the dreamers, the far-sighted, the imaginative, the creative thinkers, the visionaries.

Their main desire is to become all they were created to be. They accomplish that by having a dream bigger than what would seem realistic to the rest of us. Their vision goes beyond what they could reasonably achieve by their natural abilities. Most of all, the dreamers I know who are making a difference in this world, pray for and believe they'll receive God's supernatural guidance and strength. They expect the Father to empower them once they are willing to take risks and do what he wants done. When they've done everything they can to create the desired outcomes, they let go. With absolute trust, they know sometimes God has other plans, and often those are better than what they had in mind.

When ordinary people achieve extraordinary results, it isn't that they are leading ideal, problem-free lives. They have merely discovered innovative ways to soar over the obstacles. Success to them means getting up one more time than they fall down.

What are you doing to actively discover the extraordinary in yourself? To raise yourself to a higher level of excellence and achievement? Orison Swett Marden, founder of *Success* magazine, put it this way:

> When a man feels throbbing within him the power to do what he undertakes as well as it can possibly be done, and all of his faculties say "amen" to what he is doing, and give their unqualified approval to his efforts—this is happiness, this is success!

5 EXPECT MIRACLES

Life is largely a matter of expectations.
HORACE

You'll never exceed your wildest expectations if you don't have some wild expectations to begin with. What you expect in life makes a difference! Expecting something great to happen energizes you and gives your dream momentum. To feel in your innermost being that what you set out to do will happen opens the way for miracles. When you dream, expect positive outcomes every step of the way. "There is no medicine like hope," said Orison Swett Marden, "no incentive so great and no tonic so powerful as the expectation of something tomorrow."

Some people don't expect much on purpose. That way they won't be disappointed. Others go through life being paranoid and believing Murphy's Law, that if anything can go wrong, it will. I know a fellow who chooses to live the opposite way. He calls himself an *inverse* paranoid. He is confident that the world is scheming to enhance his well-being and increase the probability for his success. He approaches every experience expecting everyone he meets to be part of a great plot to make his life more pleasant and enjoyable. And guess what? That's just what happens. He always manages to find a parking space exactly where he needs one. He gets in the right lane at the service station and the bank. When he needs to purchase something, he goes directly to the right aisle—and discovers that it's on sale. If he knocks a crystal glass off the counter, he catches it just in time. He begins each day expecting something good and can't wait to go out there and discover it.

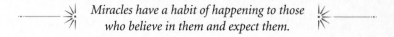

> *Miracles have a habit of happening to those who believe in them and expect them.*

Imagine how your life would be different if you were constantly expecting to be assisted, encouraged, and supported by others and the world around you. We are self-fulfilling prophecies; we very often get what we expect.

Think about how much easier it would be to pursue your dream if you expected to see new opportunities and possibilities open up before you. Successful dreamers do that. Not only do they expect a miracle, they tend to see stumbling blocks and negatives as chances to change and grow toward their success. Rather than complaining "Everything and everyone is against me" when something goes wrong, they believe something good will happen as a result. If their company has downsized and they find they no longer have a position, they view it as a chance to find their dream job with better pay and benefits or to turn their hobby into a business. They believe that regardless of what has happened, God has something better in store for them. If they are diagnosed with an incurable disease, they see it as a wake-up call to discover their true priorities, focus their remaining time and energy on what is really important to them, and create a healthier and more balanced lifestyle for themselves and their families. They may even believe in a miracle cure.

Have you ever had one of those experiences that I call the "best–worst" times of life? That's when something terrible happens but later, when you look back on it, you recognize it was a blessing in disguise. It seemed like the worst thing that could happen, but it turned out to be for the best because of the person you became and where you are now as a result. When bad things happen, get in the habit of asking yourself, "How can I turn this experience around to be beneficial and bring me closer to my dream?" or "What opportunity is hidden in this obstacle?"

Take the approach that good and bad are not accidents. Everything and everyone is put in your path for a purpose, and every experience is moving you along a pathway toward the achievement of your ultimate destiny and your greatest vision.

Miracles have a habit of happening to those who believe in them and expect them. So go ahead with great expectations and have the highest vision possible for yourself.

6 DISPELLING MYTHS OF PROSPERITY

> *I pray for good fortune in everything you do,*
> *and for your good health—that your everyday*
> *affairs prosper, as well as your soul!*
> 3 JOHN 2 MSG

> *But prosperity is the reward of the righteous.*
> PROVERBS 13:21

Before we go further, let's clear up one vital issue. This book is not about offering you a get-rich-quick scheme. It does not support the popular gospel that you should be able to have your every whim fulfilled. While I do believe we are to ask for and expect to receive God's blessings, doing it for purely selfish motives will not bring lasting joy, satisfaction, or peace. Achieving success is not about asking God for a yacht, a Porsche, a six-figure income, or any other sign or material symbol that you have tapped some supernatural reservoir of wealth. Having a dream and achieving your goals is not about cashing in on God's promises to you. Some prosperity teaching has led some people to believe that if they pray intensely, speak in certain ways, or use particular words, God will make them rich. The truth is the Scriptures teach that being faithful does assure abundant spiritual blessings and the promise of great reward in eternity, but it also shows us that we may have to endure hardship and poverty while we receive those blessings.

While I believe our heavenly Father does want us to ask for blessings and that he will bless us immensely, there is so much more he wants to do for us than merely meet our material wishes and self-centered desires.

Although there are no magical phrases or simple formulas that will guarantee that your dreams will meet with success, the principles taught here will inspire you to dream bigger dreams, expect miracles, make the powerful changes and choices that can transform your life, keep you motivated, and encourage you to persevere through the tough times. The wisdom in this book will help you be a more creative problem-solver, master new skills, conquer the fears that hold you back, and strengthen you to face the challenges that go along with reaching for the stars.

When it comes time to write out your goals, think first about your motives. When I was a single mom and hoped to remarry someday, I wrote out a list of the qualities I would look for in a future mate. I didn't do it as some magical wish list, nor was I putting in my order for a man. Instead, I prayerfully itemized the godly qualities I desired in a man as a way of assuring I would only be attracted to someone who was God's best for me. In time, I met Cliff and knew on our first date he was God's choice for me because of that list. In spite of any challenges we've endured over the years, I always rest assured that this is God's plan for us. Later, when we wanted to buy our first home together, we listed the features we would appreciate in a house. We did this not because it was part of a mystical formula, but because we believed God had the ideal home in mind for us, and being specific in our prayers meant we would recognize it when we came upon it.

God has already let you know you can have answers to your prayers and expect miracles. The Bible says, "Be delighted with the Lord. Then he will give you all your heart's desires" (Psalm 37:4 TLB). Think about this. Let's say you are a child who wants to go to Disney World for spring vacation and your parents have told you they are taking you. Yet every day you go to them and ask, "Please, *please* can we go to Disney World?" How do you suppose they will respond, knowing they've already promised you this? How do you suppose God responds when we ask him to help us do and be more for him, to be blessed and be a blessing, and to increase our influence out there in the world? Since we are his children, those are the very things he has already promised. Take him at his word. Let your greatest expectations be from God, and you will surely go beyond a dream!

PART 2
Go a Little Higher

7 DREAM BIG WITH NO LIMITS

Big thinking precedes big achievement.
WILFERD PETERSON

God can do anything, you know—far more
than you could ever imagine or guess or
request in your wildest dreams!
EPHESIANS 3:20 MSG

D uring my career with a large, direct-sales company, I was exposed
to many exceptional success strategies and powerful concepts for
setting and reaching goals. These techniques set in motion a brand-new
pathway in my life, one that eventually led to career success, spiritual
growth, and personal freedom. One technique that impressed me
immensely encouraged me to dream—and dream big with no limits. At
first this was hard for me to do since, with my habitual "poverty mentality," it was more natural for me to focus on the reasons I couldn't
achieve something rather than believing it was possible. So to make the
dream more realistic, I turned my dream into a sort of *mental movie* that
I played over and over in my mind. It is a well-known principle that the
more times you rehearse an experience or event in your imagination,
the more realistic and believable it becomes and the more acceptable it
is. (A good example is doing the opposite, using the destructive power of
worry, which is like a negative mental movie.) To intensify your healthy
mental movie, fill in as much detail and emotion as possible, drawing on
all five senses. How would the dream look, and what would it feel like?
How would it taste? What would be the sounds? And what about the
smell? The idea is to make the dream as genuine and feasible as possible.

My deepest longing was to be an inspirational speaker so I could offer to others the same principles and guidelines that had transformed my life. As a salesperson, I had been exposed to some of the finest sales training and motivational messages in the business. I was also attending church and hearing life-transforming sermons and discovering God's purpose and power in my life. As a result, I made some dramatic choices and changes in my personal life, as well as in my career. I wanted to share those steps with others so they could benefit. So, after much prayer, I settled on a dream: to become the national sales trainer for the company I was working with at the time. Well, that was quite a stretch since there was no such position in that company. Talk about limitations! But my trainer had said "no limits," so I went on dreaming. Next, I started to draw on my five senses and visualized myself wearing a red business suit, carrying a black leather briefcase, and boarding an airplane to travel across the country. Then I pictured myself on stage in front of large audiences, inspiring them with success principles, along with my personal life example of dreaming big. In my imagination I could even hear the applause and see the standing ovations! During that whole exercise, there was always the temptation to say "It can't happen. There are too many obstacles and limitations." Eventually I was living the dream! And it was as if I had been there a thousand times. You may struggle with the same challenges. See if any of these statements sound familiar:

- There's not enough time.
- I don't have the proper education.
- I have no experience in that area.
- I can't afford it.
- I'm too old/young.
- I don't have what it takes.
- It's never been done before.
- I don't know where the funds will come from.
- It's probably not meant to happen.

We can easily sabotage our dreams by coming up with all the reasons why they can't work or won't happen. If we aren't able to see how they're possible, we'll never allow ourselves to dream big. Don't limit yourself that way! With God, all things are possible.

What are your perceived limitations? Are you willing to let them go? An incredible power is released when we dare to step outside our comfort zones, when we learn to genuinely pray, "God, show me your big dream for me!"

8 STRETCH YOURSELF

You want to set a goal big enough so that in the process of achieving it, you become someone worth becoming!
JIM ROHN

God hides some ideal in every human soul. At some time in our life we feel a trembling, fearful longing to do some good thing. Life finds its noblest spring of excellence in this hidden impulse to do our best.
ROBERT COLLYER

A h," said Robert Browning, "but a man's reach should exceed his grasp, or what's a heaven for?" His statement reminded me of an old hymn titled "Awake My Soul, Stretch Every Nerve." I think most of us are reluctant to stretch that far when it comes to dreaming big dreams. We are more likely to put limitations on ourselves and our dreams because we feel stretched to the max as it is. But anyone willing to break through that barrier will discover that life is best and more rewarding when we live out God's adventure for us. Helen Keller said, "Life is either a daring adventure or it is nothing." I agree.

People with the highest ideals, those who have accomplished great works, are those who are never content with mediocrity. They won't settle for average, middle-of-the-road attempts at anything they choose to be involved in. They've never been satisfied with doing things just as others have done them, but they always do them a little different or a bit better. Whatever they do, they push a little higher up, a little farther on. Orison Swett Marden, founder of *Success* magazine said, "It is this little higher up, this little farther on that counts in the quality of life's work. It is the constant effort to be first-class in everything one attempts that conquers the heights of excellence." One thing I have discovered is that we will always achieve excellence when we ask more of ourselves than others ever would.

One benefit of allowing yourself to have a big dream is that you are required to stretch and grow in order to achieve it. In fact, in the long run, expanding your horizons, broadening your knowledge, honing your talents, sharpening your abilities, and perfecting your skills are the greatest benefits you will receive from pursuing your dreams. While you may attain recognition, promotions, a bigger house, a newer car, or a bigger bank account along the way, genuine success is all about who you are becoming in the process. As we all have seen many times over, the outer symbols of success can easily vanish. Houses are lost in a storm, buildings burn down, businesses go bankrupt, marriages end in divorce, friendships fade away, cars get in accidents, clothes wear out, bodies age, and fame vanishes. But who you are, what you have learned, and the valuable expertise you have gained will always be there. These are the true rewards of achieving your dreams!

In the process of developing a career as an international speaker and writer, I've had to stretch and expand in many areas. First I had to conquer the fear of rejection when prospecting and approaching potential clients. Then I had to conquer stage fright and handle the fear of public speaking. It was also a stretch discovering ways to develop new material for my programs while customizing the content to meet the needs of a wide variety of audiences. As new opportunities opened up, I needed to learn how to better balance family, work, and home priorities. When I began writing books, I had to stretch again and learn to work with publishers, marketing teams, and the media, while becoming proficient at doing television and radio interviews. When I thought I had learned enough and couldn't stretch anymore, I started doing talk shows where people called in with questions. I found out you never know what surprises are in store! It was also a stretch to invest in my personal and professional growth by attending seminars, reading books, taking courses, listening to CDs, and asking for advice from those who had gone before me. Through all that stretching, I gleaned valuable wisdom, honed my skills, and learned many lessons.

One of the biggest principles I learned was that while there is no limit to the ways God will ask us to stretch, there is also no limit to how he will supernaturally equip us to do what he's called us to do. He will never take you beyond where he knows the two of you can reach the dream. Just imagine a lifetime of experiencing the wonder of walking hand and hand with your Father through a glorious life of new adventures.

9 STRIVE FOR EXCELLENCE

It's never crowded along the extra mile.
WAYNE DYER

You will always achieve excellence if you risk more than others think is safe, care more than others think is wise, dream more than others think is practical, and expect more than others think is possible.
CLAUDE T. BISSELL

If you really want to see your dreams become phenomenally successful, decide to excel at what you do and always give more than is required. Lee Iacocca made this statement: "The kind of people I look for to fill top management spots are the eager beavers, the mavericks. These are the guys who try to do more than they're expected to do— they always reach." To ensure that you reach your dream, be on the lookout for ways to go the extra mile in every area.

The true hallmark of people who have achieved their dreams, whether they are operating a business, raising a family, leading a team, contributing to a worthy cause, or volunteering their services, is that they consistently go the extra mile and over-deliver on their commitments and promises. They are not content with mediocrity. They're not satisfied to do things just as others do them, but they always strive for a little better. Excellence is the consistent effort to be first-class in everything you attempt.

By sheer force of habit, successful people do more and give more. They never consider themselves as having "arrived." High achievers routinely strive to be set apart from the ordinary and to exceed their past achievements. When Pablo Casals reached 95, a young reporter threw him this question: "Mr. Casals, you are 95 and the greatest cellist that ever lived. Why do you still practice six hours a day?" Mr. Casals answered, "Because I think I am making progress." When renowned artist Robert Bateman was asked which of his paintings he thought was his best work, he answered, "The one I am painting now."

As a result of striving for excellence, you will probably achieve greater material and financial rewards, and you will also experience a transformation in your personality. You'll become more confident, composed, and influential when dealing with others. When you exceed the expectations of others, you will always earn greater respect and stand out from the crowd. People will appreciate what you are attempting to accomplish, have high regard for your dreams and goals, and may even come on board with unexpected support.

Someone once said, "If you are willing to do more than you are paid to do, eventually you will be paid for more than you do!" With an attitude of excellence, you'll be the first to be hired and the last to be fired. You will most likely be the one to receive promotions, bonuses, raises, and other benefits. If you are in business for yourself, you'll have higher sales, earn more money, and attract loyal customers who are glad to provide referrals. Besides all that, at the end of the day you'll feel more satisfied and fulfilled. Here are some examples of going the extra mile at work:

- An auto mechanic says, "Since your car will be here longer than planned, may I give you a lift somewhere?"
- A waitress says, "Since you're sharing your dessert, I'll cut it in half and bring you two plates and an extra fork."
- A receptionist says, "To avoid getting lost on the third floor, may I draw you a map?"
- The gift shop clerk says, "If you need a pen to sign that card, you may use mine."

I know of a hotel that serves complimentary warm, fresh-baked cookies with milk to guests at bedtime; a fast-food restaurant that offers a drive-through windshield washing service; a taxi driver who provides a basket of fruits, snacks, and bottled water and asks you what type of music you prefer; and a service station attendant who will hand-vacuum the floor of your car while you fill up. Whether you sell someone a used car and detail it before you deliver it or sell someone a home and offer a gift certificate to have it professionally cleaned before they move in, one way to give more value to your company, clients, or students is to surprise them with more than they expect. How can you *"wow"* the people you serve? Look for ways to be memorable and knock their socks off!

If you are focusing on your own desires and needs, you may be thinking that giving more than is required is unreasonable. It may seem unfair to be expected to give extra effort without additional reimbursement. Why should you exceed expectations without proper acknowledgment, compensation, or appreciation? There's an old saying that says the cream will always rise to the top. When it does, the greatest benefit is that you will earn an impeccable reputation for going the extra mile—and that is one of your most valuable assets in moving ahead with your dreams.

Orison Swett Marden put it this way: "It's just the little touches after the average man would quit that make the master's fame." Going beyond the call of duty, doing more than others anticipate—this is what excellence is all about. And it comes from maintaining the highest standards, looking after the smallest detail, and going that extra mile.

10 AIM FOR THE STARS

*The greater danger for most of us is
not that our aim is too high and we miss it,
but that it is too low and we reach it.*
MICHELANGELO

*Ah, but a man's reach should exceed his grasp,
or what's a heaven for?*
ROBERT BROWNING

I n a well-known university experiment, a professor gave a test to his class. There were several sections and each one had questions in three categories. The first category was the most difficult and worth 50 points. The second was not as hard, for 40 points, and the third was the easiest for 30 points. Each student had the option of choosing one of those categories for the entire test. When the tests were completed and handed in, here's how the professor graded them. The students who had chosen the hardest questions earned A's, those who had chosen the next level down received B's, and those who picked the easiest got C's, regardless of whether or not their answers were correct.

Understandably, the students questioned the professor's grading system and wanted to know why he had marked them that way. With a grin, he answered, "More than your knowledge, I was testing your aim!" The true measure of success is not whether you reached all your goals, but where you set your target in the first place. It doesn't take any more energy to aim high than to aim low, so set your sights high and you just may surprise yourself.

An inscription on a building in Washington, D.C., says, "They build too low who build beneath the skies." It's been my experience that the main difference between high achievers and the rest of the world is that high achievers simply dream bigger dreams. If you limit your dreams to only what seems doable or possible, you curb your creativity, your imagination, and your natural abilities. You'll never even come close to reaching your full potential. "A hero," said Betty Deramus, "is simply someone who rises above his own human weaknesses, for an hour, a day, a year, to do something stirring." Instead of striving to merely increase your sales, determine to be the top salesperson in your region. Rather than simply going back to school, aim to earn a degree. If you like attending home Bible-study groups, try leading one yourself in the future.

I know someone who kids, "I am wealthy beyond my wildest dreams. Unfortunately my dreams weren't very wild!" Sadly, that is true of a lot of people. Aiming high can be scary. It requires responsibility, accountability, and action. But aiming for the stars isn't about who you are or what you can accomplish. It's about what God wants to do through you. He is saying, "Take courage! I'll be with you. Now, let's go!" He enables you to fly high in spite of your fears.

Do you reach for the stars? It's rare these days, but it's the hallmark of top achievers. Very few people aim high enough. Choose now to leave the commonplace behind and exceed your own expectations. "Ideals are like stars," said Carl Schurz. "You will not succeed in touching them with your hands; but like the seafaring man, you choose them as your guides, and following them, you will reach your destiny."

> *Reach high, for stars lie hidden within your soul.*
> *Dream deep for every dream preceded the goal.*

11 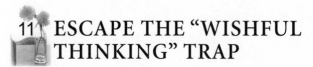 ESCAPE THE "WISHFUL THINKING" TRAP

What most people need is less wishbone
and more backbone!

O ne reason people do not see their dreams turn into successes is that their dreams never go beyond a vague wish or an idea of what they might like to do "someday." They don't realize that having a dream is only the *seed*. Dreaming about what you hope to accomplish or want to become is a good place to start, but to be successful, your dream needs to grow and branch out from mere wishing into solid goals, strategies, plans, and action steps.

For example, what if you dreamed of someday volunteering at a downtown shelter, or starting up a soup kitchen, or sponsoring children in a Third World country, and you talk about it often but never make the effort to investigate what is involved, check out your options, or request information? Or imagine your dream is to learn to ice skate or play the steel guitar or become skilled at woodworking, but you fail to check into which lessons are available, what equipment is needed, or when you could begin? The same is true if you say you'd like to lose weight but never go on a specific weight-loss plan, or you wish to tone and firm your body but don't start an exercise regimen, or you want to go to college but fail to send away and request applications from specific schools. Whether you'd like to open a restaurant, teach a fitness class, sing in a choir, write a novel, or learn to water ski, your success or failure depends on whether or not you get beyond your dream and turn wishful thinking into practical planning.

Imagine if I were to say to you, "We should get together for lunch" and you say, "Great! When and where would you like to meet?" If I reply, "Oh, any place and any time is fine," do you think we would ever meet? Not likely. That's too vague. Your dream, too, must be more specific. It also needs to be supported with plans and backed up by action steps. Successful dreaming requires that you make a decision, do your research, and take that first step. You'll always be stuck if you dwell in the lukewarm zone of wishful thinking.

Many people's dreams never take shape because they waver and can't make up their minds. They're stuck in indecision, not saying yes or no, but maybe. You hear them jokingly saying things like, "I haven't decided what I want to do when I grow up!" While it's not said seriously, the truth is the longer they prolong indecisiveness, the more it robs them of the true joy of accomplishing their dreams. Some people stay trapped in wishful thinking by coming up with excuses. It's more convenient to say "When my life gets back to normal," "When things calm down," "Once I feel more confident," or "After I pray about it some more." Do you know that life is never going to get back to normal? Things aren't going to calm down. You may never have more confidence until you start to take action. And you can pray while you are moving in one direction or another. It's time to place your feet on solid ground. Set your destination, and God can guide you while you travel.

Some wishful thinkers start to move ahead with their dreams but then fail to see them through to the end. For example, they have projects that they began ages ago and never finished, but they keep starting new ones. They never completely finish reading a book. They jump from one new undertaking to another, always believing this is the one they will stick with to the end. The problem is everything left unfinished has a way of haunting their lives and discouraging them from completing other projects.

Dreaming may start with wishful thinking, but it goes far beyond mere desire. Is there something you've been wishing you could do for years, but you haven't taken action yet? Is fear or worry holding you back? They will fade into the distance when you set your sights on your dream and stay committed to the end.

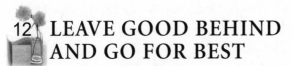

12 LEAVE GOOD BEHIND AND GO FOR BEST

*Doing things right is not as important
as doing the right things.*

There's a big difference between a good dream and the best one. It's possible to be pursuing a lot of good things, yet miss the excellent ones you were destined to do. Some goals and activities may not be harmful or detrimental in any way. In fact they may produce positive results. They simply aren't the right ones for you to be investing your valuable time or energy in because they don't contribute to fulfilling your ultimate destiny. Once you've captured your vision, you can prioritize the activities in your life by determining which things are beneficial to your dreams and which are not.

Your greatest challenge is not in choosing between good or bad, but between *good* and *best*. Most of us know the difference between right and wrong, moral and corrupt, just and unjust, honest and dishonest. So we would naturally choose the good without hesitation. But people who pursue the best and go after excellence rather than settling for good enough, are the ones who capture the greatest opportunities for astounding success. It sounds simple, yet it's surprising how many people, including some of the world's most influential leaders, professionals, and entrepreneurs, get caught in the trap of pursuing merely good goals while the pathway to the best goes ignored.

If you have given in to the habit of chasing after mediocre opportunities and pursuing average dreams, misguided proposals, or your own hasty plans, you could be holding yourself back from fulfilling an incredible destiny. With a crystal-clear dream and a distinct vision, you won't get bogged down with just doing acceptable things. You will do things that are the most beneficial for the accomplishment of the dream you've been given. Having a rock-solid dream gives you a firm foundation and protects you from being led astray by those average alternatives and mediocre activities. It keeps you focused on the most excellent opportunities and allows you to say no to the lesser ones. If we make the mistake of concentrating all our efforts on achieving what is acceptable and satisfactory, there's no time or energy left to go after excellence. Besides, adequate and sufficient results that are "good enough" quite often take the same amount of time and effort as producing exceptional ones.

Many people choose between good and bad, and feel they made the right choice because they opted for the good. That will work if all you're after is a middle-of-the-road existence, but you won't see your highest visions come about. It's no wonder the Bible clearly says the greatest commandment is to love God first with all your heart, mind, soul, and strength (Mark 12:30). Once you do that, he is able to impart his desires into your heart, revealing to you the positions, responsibilities, and missions you were born to fulfill. God doesn't want us to start any project, including doing good works for him, until we consult with him. Once you capture that wisdom and truly commit to it, a lot of irrelevant "good" things will drop off on their own. You can concentrate on only those tasks and activities that will result in the finest and most valuable results.

In the story of Mary and Martha (Luke 10:38-42), we see a profound yet simple illustration of the principle of *good* versus *best* priorities. Martha had welcomed Jesus and his disciples into her home, and while she was fussing over the big dinner she was preparing, her sister, Mary, sat on the floor and listened to Jesus talk. Martha made a very good point when she expressed to him that what she was doing was important and she needed help. After all, what could be more noteworthy than preparing a meal for Jesus? But listen to what Jesus essentially said to her: "Martha, dear friend, you are so upset over all these details. There is really only one thing worth being concerned about. Mary has discovered it—and I won't take it away from her." Jesus didn't say the details Martha was concentrating on were bad things. In essence he said Martha was doing what was good, but Mary had chosen what is better. Notice that in this story it doesn't even say Jesus was hungry! Many of us have our own ideas about what we want to do for God. We get preoccupied doing things *for* him rather than finding out what he has specifically told us to do. Have you been chasing after the good over the best? Have you been satisfied with average and acceptable? Just imagine what could happen if you said *no* to the mediocre dreams and *yes* to the great ones.

 13 PRACTICE IMPECCABLE INTEGRITY

> *A person who is dishonest in little things isn't really honest in anything.*
> CHARLES FINNEY

> *If you must choose, take a good name rather than great riches; for to be held in loving esteem is better than silver and gold.*
> PROVERBS 22:1 TLB

In her book *My Father's House,* Corrie ten Boom says her father was so honest he wouldn't allow her to have a pacifier as a baby. "They think they are getting a drink," he would say, "and that is fooling a child to put something in her mouth which is a lie." He knew the value of being honest even when an idea was acceptable to others.

Although I must admit I do not regret giving my babies pacifiers when they wanted one, integrity is about being above reproach. It's a crucial ingredient when it comes to turning your dreams into realities. Through your conduct, deeds, and choices, you will either gain trust or lose credibility with your family, friends, coworkers, employees, boss, or clients. Trust has to be earned, and you can win confidence by doing the right thing. When you do, others will more readily adopt your dream and become willing supporters.

Integrity is not what you *appear* to be when others are watching. It's who you are even when no one else is around. Integrity is all about the decisions, actions, and behaviors you practice when only you and God will ever know. That's the difference between reputation and character. *Reputation* is the person you are when all eyes are upon you. It's who others *think* you are, and to be honest, we can pretty much get people to think whatever we want. Most of us are good actors and can say and do the right things in public. And some people have become proficient at swaying others with charm and captivating them with charisma.

While reputation is your public life, *character* is your private life. Who are you when no one else will ever find out? For example, what do you do when a salesclerk accidentally gives you too much change, you find a wallet full of money on the sidewalk, or you're in a hurry with 15 items and tempted to sneak into the "10 items" lane at the grocery store? These may seem like small, incidental matters, but when you make the right choices in these areas, you'll be more likely to retain your integrity in trickier situations. You'll be prepared to handle them the right way if you're ever tempted to lie on your income tax return, cheat on an exam, be unfaithful to your spouse, or steal from the company. It's a good idea to think about these things ahead of time so you won't be caught off guard when the temptations arise.

A person of integrity says something and means it. He will keep his word even if it costs him something to do so. He builds a reputation for being reliable, dependable, and trustworthy, and by today's standards, that's something that will surely stand out in a crowd! Many times when I have committed to speaking at a charitable event for an honorarium, a corporate client will come along and offer me my full fee to speak on the exact date. Because I have already committed myself, I have to turn down that opportunity to earn income. Sometimes, I admit, it makes me say "Ouch!" but in the end, I can live with myself and I believe God honors my decision by bringing even greater rewards.

Integrity is a high standard of morality you keep no matter what's going on all around you. It's about having dignity and living by your highest principles at all times. When you're at work, it means doing your best regardless of how much you receive for your services, the number of people you serve, or the class of people served. In the business world today, integrity's becoming a rare commodity. It's reported that many small companies go out of business because of employee theft. A pervasive attitude in the workplace today seems to be "a little here, a little there. Who's going to notice?" Numerous anonymous surveys reveal that large percentages of people admit to regularly stealing, telling lies, and cheating on exams. One university instructor told me that because the Internet has made cheating very tempting and easy, many students now copy and paste together passages from various articles and hand in the work as their own. Although we might think the computer has made cheaters out of our students or that cheating is understandable given the pressures and deadlines they face, no amount of justification makes it right. Here are some questions you can ask yourself when being tempted with tough choices:

- Would I be happy to have my actions aired on the six o'clock news or printed on the front page of the newspaper?

- Would I be proud of my decision if my family, friends, and coworkers knew about it?

- Would I be willing to have a videotape of my life's choices used as a training device for others?

By asking these questions, you'll soon be very clear as to which choice is the right one. Many situations will come along to make us waver, but God hears our prayers when we ask for strength to stay strong in the face of temptation (see 1 Corinthians 10:13). No matter what you've done in the past, it's true you cannot go back and make a brand-new start to your life. But you can begin now to make a brand-new ending!

Don't just pretend to be good!
Be done with dishonesty and jealousy
and talking about others behind their backs.
1 Peter 2:1 tlb

14 THE POWER OF PURPOSE

The secret of success is consistency of purpose.
BENJAMIN DISRAELI

You, LORD, give perfect peace to those who keep their
purpose firm and put their trust in you.
ISAIAH 26:3 TEV

Two men were working on a construction site when someone asked about their jobs. The first man replied, "I'm laying bricks. I earn minimum wage and double for overtime." The second man said, "I am building a cathedral, the spires of which will reach the highest heavens. It will stand out in this community, and people will be drawn to it. Lives will be changed as a result of what I am doing!" It is easy to see that one man merely had a job while the other one had a magnificent purpose.

There's a big difference between simply working and working toward your purpose. When I consider the "job" aspect of my business, I think of the hours I spend at my desk doing paperwork, filing, handling correspondence, and returning phone calls or email messages. Other times I am researching and developing material for new programs and future books, following up with clients, or sending out promotional materials. Probably 80 percent of my time is spent doing those things. The other 20 percent of my time is spent doing what I love to do— putting all that background work, research, and information together in such a way that when I go out to deliver it to an audience or mentor a young speaker or author, they are challenged to make the powerful changes and positive choices that will transform their lives. That's where I believe I am fulfilling my purpose. Although both aspects are neces- sary and must be done, I don't think I could endure the *job* part of my business without having the greater *purpose* to spur me on and keep me passionate. Purpose is the fuel that enables us to keep working day after day. Nothing energizes like clear purpose.

Henry David Thoreau observed that many people live lives of quiet desperation. A better description today might be to say people are involved in pointless diversions, meaningless pastimes, and purposeless pursuits. Many people have busy lives but never accomplish much or go anywhere. They either spin out of control in one spot or keep changing direction. They change relationships, jobs, churches, cars, hobbies, or neighborhoods, always hoping they will find fulfillment in their next endeavor or the next location. The peace and genuine contentment they search for continues to elude them because they're not getting to the real problem—a lack of purpose. There's a big difference between being active and being productive.

Here's an interesting concept. Hundreds of years ago you wouldn't have heard people saying they were "going to work." Instead, each person had a skill they perfected or a craft they honed that could improve a situation, a product, or a life. Then they would go into the community, the marketplace, or someone's home to offer their ability or talent in exchange for money, grain, or goods. Today, many people have the mentality that they are owed something, that by showing up at work for 40 hours each week they should receive a paycheck plus benefits. They have forgotten what it means to offer themselves and their gifts in order to make a difference in the workplace, the community, and the world. George Bernard Shaw wrote, "This is the true joy of life: the being used up for a purpose recognized by yourself as a mighty one, being a force of nature instead of a feverish, selfish little clot of ailments and grievances, complaining that the world will not devote itself to making you happy."

What are you doing with your life—with all your God-given talents, gifts, opportunities, and resources? Everyone has a purpose; it's the reason we exist. What is your life's mission, your objective, your calling? On the whole, we are here to honor God and to prepare ourselves and others for eternity. But how that translates in our individual lives is unique to each of us. Your life is not an accident. You are here by design, and you were made for a definite purpose. Are you fulfilling it? The psalmist said, "May He grant you according to your heart's desire, and fulfill all your purpose" (Psalm 20:4 NKJV).

PART 3
It's Up to You!

15 MAKE A DECISION

Nothing will be impossible for you.
MATTHEW 17:20

In order to achieve what you want, you must first decide what it is. Now that sounds obvious, yet so often people overlook this most crucial step. It usually happens because, at the end of most days, we fall into bed totally exhausted, feeling mildly satisfied if we managed to cross off a few items on our to-do list while surviving a flurry of new activities and managing our normal daily expectations, never mind considering the future. We can get so caught up in the busyness of life's daily demands that we don't even realize we have the option to make decisions about a better tomorrow...or we believe that if it's meant to be, it'll just happen. We fail to recognize the tremendous power in making clear decisions about exactly which direction we'd like to take.

If you want to learn sign language, go on a family vacation, take music lessons, or go back to school to earn a degree, you won't get around to it until you decide to go for it. You'll never move into a different neighborhood, get a better job, replace the old vacuum cleaner, get a newer vehicle, learn a new hobby, or take up gardening if you never make the decision. Many people fail to see dreams happen simply because they haven't decided what they want to accomplish. Indecision is a dream-killer. It drains the joy right out of us. Is this one of the primary stumbling blocks keeping you from living beyond your dream?

Rather than deciding on a goal, most of us find it easier to go on complaining about what we don't have; regretting the opportunities we have missed; remembering past mistakes, offenses, or injustices; or noticing how others appear to be living their dreams while we cannot seem to make ours happen. It's a trap we fall into.

49

For years I griped about our small kitchen and even smaller dining room, until I got serious about deciding to renovate and combine those rooms. Soon afterward, we were tearing down walls, gutting floors and windows, and designing and creating our dream kitchen. The one thing that had been holding back this project was deciding to do it. Miraculously, once the decision was made, my speaking business took a new and exciting turn and funds gradually became available to support the dream.

Similarly, when I was dissatisfied with always having dinner in front of the television, I decided that once or twice a week we'd prepare and serve a proper sit-down meal with candles and linens, and occasionally fresh flowers and the good china and crystal. These days there's no more discussion or complaining, and a dream has been realized. Likewise, whenever I feel exhausted and close to burnout from business responsibilities, writing deadlines, speaking schedules, and career pressures, I know I have a choice. I can keep pushing myself to work harder or decide to have a mini-vacation, weekend retreat, or spa day to regain my sanity and joy and get reenergized. Interestingly, once the decision is made, things begin to fall into place.

Whatever is keeping you from living a life beyond your dreams, decide what you'd like to change. Rather than whining about your current job position, take action either by meeting with your boss to discuss ways to improve the situation, applying for a promotion, seeking out new employment, or checking into the possibility of starting your own business. If you'd like to begin a foundation for a worthy cause, decide what you want to support, how the organization would function, the best venue, and who else would be involved. When you are struggling within a relationship, decide what you'd rather see happening between you and the other person and what you are willing to do to bring it about. With those decisions made, you'll be surprised at how quickly changes will be set in motion.

Deciding exactly what you'd like to experience is probably the most profound, influential, and often the scariest action you can take when it comes to getting unstuck and moving into your dreams. It can be frightening because once the decision is made, you are committed to seeing it through. But with dedication, work, prayer, and God's guidance, you will also discover the resources necessary to turn your dreams into realities.

16 THE IMPACT OF YOUR CHOICES

God asks no man whether he will accept life. That is not the choice. You must take it. The only choice is how.
HENRY WARD BEECHER

The choice is yours. You hold the tiller. You can steer the course you choose in the direction of where you want to be—today, tomorrow or in a distant time to come.
W. CLEMENT STONE

If there is one key to unlocking your dreams more than any other, it is knowing you can choose. In this world, you have been given complete, absolute power over only one thing and that is your choices. Yet that alone is enough because it's always choice, not chance, that determines your destiny. Your future is not left up to chance. It is in your hands through the very choices you make each day.

We decide what we think, what we believe in, what we say, where we go, and what we do. We choose our responses to most situations, including which emotions we will experience and for how long. No one can make us feel a certain way. Nor can they take the power to choose away from us. It is ours alone. No person can get inside our heads and determine where we will focus our thoughts and energies. We can think what we want and do what we want concerning any circumstance life puts in our pathway. Because of that, we can be who we want to be. We can dream any dream and take the necessary steps to see it become a reality.

Every day, all day long, you are making choices. From the time you wake up in the morning, before you even get out of bed, you can think, *Good morning, Lord,* or *Good Lord, it's morning!* Then, depending on your choice, your day will get better or worse from there. Likewise, at any time, you can decide to alter the course of your life. The choice is yours. No one can take that away from you.

Sometimes we feel stuck in a situation and don't even dream about a better way because we believe we really don't have any choice in the matter. The truth is that you don't *have* to do anything or stay anywhere. Everything is a choice. You don't have to buy anything from anyone, no matter how persistent he or she may be. You don't have to work at any particular job, continue participating in any relationship, stay on the phone longer than you want, eat foods you do not enjoy, or attend functions when you don't want to be there. In fact, you don't have to go to work every day as long as there is government assistance available nor do you have to raise your children. There are agencies who will take them. You don't have to pay taxes either, although jail is the consequence. You don't even have to get out of bed in the morning. I am sure that if you chose to stay there long enough, someone would eventually come to your rescue. We may say that we had to do something, or that we were forced into it, but truthfully, whatever you do, you do by choice, unless you are being held at gunpoint.

So the reason we do most things is because we don't like the consequences of not doing them. Sometimes, sadly, that is our highest motivation. An even greater motivator is to focus on the consequences and outcomes of doing something that will bring us closer to the realization of our dreams and aspirations. But in order to do that, we must have dreams and aspirations in the first place.

Understanding that the choices we've made in the past have brought us to where we are today helps us know the significance of making right choices for tomorrow. By taking a good look at where we are now and the options that brought us to this place, we'll be inspired to make positive choices.

Each of us has many more choices and alternatives than we've ever considered. The greatest key to turning goals into realities is to know that you can choose the best alternatives available to move you toward your dreams.

> *Our lives are songs; God writes the words*
> *And we set them to music at pleasure;*
> *And the song grows glad, or sweet or sad,*
> *As we choose to fashion the measure.*
> ELLA WHEELER WILCOX

17 IF IT IS TO BE, IT IS UP TO ME!

As human beings, we are endowed with freedom of
choice, and we cannot shuffle off our responsibility
upon the shoulders of God or nature. We must
shoulder it ourselves. It is up to us.
ARNOLD J. TOYNBEE

It's a simple thought: *If it is to be, it is up to me.* Yet I believe these could be the ten most powerful two-letter words in the English language. The saying really means that you are responsible for all your choices, decisions, actions, and behaviors, and they in turn determine all your outcomes. The bottom line is you are the one who is creating your life the way it is. The existence you have right now is the result of your past thoughts, actions, and behaviors. Today you are in charge of what goes into your mind, what dreams you think about and focus on, and how you respond to every situation. You decide what you will say and do, whether you worry and live in fear or trust in God. There is only one person responsible for the quality of life you will experience. That person is *you.*

There's a popular myth that tells us if our dreams are meant to be, they'll just happen. We tell ourselves if God wants us to achieve some goal or have a happy, healthy, prosperous life, he'll work all things out on our behalf. While the Bible tells us "all that happens to us is working for our good if we love God and are fitting into his plans" (Romans 8:28 TLB) and God can take what was meant to harm us and turn it around for his glory, we actually make our life the way it is by our daily choices. Think about it. Depending on the choice of foods you eat, the amount of exercise and rest you get, the way you spend your money and time, who you associate with, and how you react to events and people, your life is either one you are satisfied with or one you're disappointed in. The choices you make minute by minute are determining your outcomes.

If you want to accomplish your dreams, then you have to take respon-sibility for your life. No more excuses. Give up all your victim stories, all the reasons why you cannot achieve something, and all the explanations as to why you haven't succeeded with your dream up until now. Blaming outside circumstances will have to go. It's true some things might be easier if certain people or circumstances changed, but you are only in control of your own thoughts and actions. You cannot change others. You have to take the position that your dream can happen regardless of what others are doing. To achieve those things in life that matter most to you, you must assume total responsibility for your outcomes.

Even in Scripture, there are so many verses that start with some action required of us before the promise can be fulfilled. In other words, if it is to be, it is up to me. For example, when God says to "love your neighbor as yourself" (Luke 10:27), whose choice is it to love? When we are told to "be joyful always, pray continually, give thanks in all circumstances" (1 Thessalonians 5:16-18), who is it that must take action? We know when we "draw nigh to God," he will draw nigh to us (see James 4:8 KJV), but we must make the first move. Scripture says, "Submit yourselves therefore to God. Resist the devil, and he will flee from you" (James 4:7 KJV), so we know we are the ones who must do the submitting and resisting. Again, if it is to be, it is up to me.

Obviously we have many choices available to us that will affect our outcomes. Granted, there are many promises that let us know God will protect, guide, and strengthen us to do those things as we take the initiative. He never leaves us alone. But if we are going to eat healthier, get fit, be happier, enjoy better relationships, volunteer our time, pay off our debts, produce better results, save for the future, attend church regularly, plan a vacation, make changes in our families and homes, spend more time seeking God, and make any other improvements to our lives, those things are up to us. George Washington Carver said, "Ninety-nine percent of all failures come from people who have a habit of making excuses."

We alone have the responsibility to shape our lives, "not that we are sufficient of ourselves to think any thing as of ourselves, but our sufficiency is of God" (2 Corinthians 3:5 KJV). Once we understand that God has already done all he will do for us, we'll know that we are the ones propelling ourselves forward or holding ourselves back. The decision to take what he has given us and use it wisely toward our dreams is ours alone.

18 DEVELOP THE HABIT OF "ACTING AS IF"

Act as if everything depended upon you,
and pray as if everything depended upon God.

G rowing up, I often heard my dad say, "You don't always whistle when you're happy, but you'll always be happy if you whistle." What a simple yet profound statement. How we loved to hear Dad whistle because we knew that, regardless of his mood, he would trigger a cheerful state of mind by choosing to act it out. The same holds true with smiling, singing, laughing, or walking tall. When we act out certain states, we soon experience them.

Actors do this all the time. In order to simulate a particular emotion, they first take on the posture, stance, and facial expression of someone feeling that way. Then shortly afterward, the emotion starts to come. I have heard actors explain that this is how they are able to sob, produce tears, or act out anger so realistically and "on demand."

The technique of "acting as if" can work for you too. What you act out physically and mentally can become your actual experience. Imagine choosing to drag yourself around in a slumped posture, shuffling your feet, with a sad, gloomy expression on your face, dressed in your "help me, Jesus, I'm a total failure" sweat suit. In no time at all you would be feeling downhearted, disappointed, and miserable. Likewise, when you stand tall, walk with gusto, focus on your grandest dreams, and put a big grin on your face, you use certain muscles that send messages to your brain, which proceed to send out endorphins (and a lot of other neurotransmitters, some of which are stronger than morphine) through your entire body. In a short time, these simple acts not only make you feel happy, but they may reduce pain as well. Our bodies are so miraculously designed that by changing our posture and facial expressions and acting happy and healthy, we soon start to feel that way.

The same holds true when you need to feel confident, energetic, triumphant, positive, or loving in order to reach your dream. One of the great strategies for achieving success is to act as if you've already done it. When you are acting *as if* you are successful, your brain

subconsciously begins to create the right emotions and inspire innovative ways to achieve your goal. You'll start noticing situations and
relationships developing that will help you succeed. If your dream is to
revive a loveless marriage or improve relationships with your teenagers,
you can *act as if* you have unconditional love, choosing to do and say
the things you would if that were a reality. When your dream is to be
fit and healthy, start to do what you would if it were true. Your physical
body will respond to the messages you provide. If you have ever had
the experience of waking up just before the alarm clock goes off, you
know that your body acts in response to what you programmed into
your mind the night before. God has given us this incredible ability.
Why aren't we using it more?

When I started out as a motivational speaker, I knew I wanted to
do training across the country, even though I didn't feel confident or
capable in the beginning. So I started to act as if I was. Even though
I didn't feel ready, I chose to dress the part, associate with successful
people already in the business, and attend the same meetings and events
they did. It was a stretch, but the more I acted it out, the more comfortable I became. Eventually, when I moved into my new role as national
sales trainer, it felt natural to me.

After that I started my own seminar company and decided I wanted
to travel internationally. I actually had business cards made with the
title *International Conference Speaker* printed on them. At that time I
had contracted with an agency that often sent speakers overseas, so I
decided the first place I'd like to work was England. I went to a travel
agency, picked up some brochures, cut out pictures of Big Ben, double-
decker buses, and thatch-roofed cottages, and made a dream collage. I
posted it where I could see it every day to keep the dream alive. Then I
made a list of British terms and started memorizing them. Within a few
months, I was engaged to do a series of workshops in England. Acting
as if is a great tool to prepare yourself for when the dream happens.

You can begin right now to act as if you have accomplished your
dream. Ask yourself how you would act if you already were an outstanding athlete, a renowned artist, an A-student, a famous musician,
a published author, the top salesperson, the editor of a magazine, a

sought-after speaker, or a leading authority on a particular subject. How would you act if you owned your own business, got the promotion, or headed up a worldwide charitable organization? How would you think and talk? How would you dress and carry yourself? What type of friends would you have, and what would your diet consist of? Think about your wardrobe choices, your posture, the way you would treat others, and how you'd manage your money. Flood your mind with powerful images of already having achieved your aspirations. The whole purpose of "acting as if" is to create an emotionally charged image of what it will be like when you have attained your dream. Once you have a clear picture of the person you'll be and trust that your dream is from God, believe he will work out the details. Start being that person now. The rest will follow!

19 THE INFLUENCE OF YOUR DESIRES

Whatever you are doing in life, obstacles don't matter very much. Pain or other circumstances can be there, but if you want to do a job bad enough, you'll find a way to get it done.
JACK YOUNGBLOOD

When dreams come true at last, there is life and joy.
PROVERBS 13:12 TLB

For years, as I traveled internationally speaking to corporations about success principles, I had the persistent desire to write a book on healing for past hurts. I saw it as a book in which I would share my personal story of overcoming tremendous odds, how I learned about the power of forgiveness, and the steps I took to take my life from tragedy to where it is now. My yearning to put this information in writing was so strong that I would sometimes describe it by saying, "I feel as though there's a book inside me trying to get out!" The desire was so intense and unwavering that, through much prayer and contemplation, came to realize this was definitely God's will for me. Eventually, I had the wonderful opportunity to see the dream come true. My book *When Your Past Is Hurting Your Present* has helped thousands of people get beyond the fears that cripple their dreams. And it all began with my own dream that became a clear goal backed by fervent desire.

My initial intent in writing that book was not to sell millions of copies or become wealthy, but to express ideas and concepts that I genuinely believed would enable readers to trade regrets and remorse for joy and peace, bitterness and resentment for genuine forgiveness, and guilt and shame for complete freedom. I believed the book would help those struggling with a difficult past leave behind the baggage of long ago and start to recapture their dreams. Most of all, I had a genuine longing to provide support and direction for those who wanted to take their own lives to where they only dreamed they could go. Today that book continues to sell well, and I receive mail regularly from readers who tell me how much they are blessed by it. Through it all, I've discovered that great desires produce great results.

Now I must admit that I have also said many times that I would love to learn to play the flute or the steel guitar—two of my favorite instruments—and also take oil painting lessons. I've been talking about both of these for a long time yet I haven't accomplished either one. I'd prefer to lay the blame on money or time. With my speaking schedule, I could easily convince myself I really couldn't fit in those new activities. Besides, the equipment, materials, and lessons I'd need are costly. But I have to admit the simple truth. I really don't want those things as much as I wanted to write a book. I know deep down inside that the only thing holding me back is my lack of desire. Perhaps the reason is that God has not placed the desire in me or it is not his timing. I know when the desire to play the steel guitar and paint with oils is as powerful as it was to write that book, God will make a way. Somehow the time, the money, and the capability will be there.

When your desire becomes that intense, you are able to narrow your focus and streamline your thinking to get the greatest results from your efforts. When it came to the book, I knew in my heart that I had to write it because I couldn't *not* do it! When you have that kind of desire in you, when you aspire to do something with such intensity, you will always find creative ways to go about it. That's often the case when we ask musicians or artists why they do what they do. Their answer is the same. They believe it's something inside of them, and they simply can't *not* do it! When you consider your dreams, ask yourself how much you want what you say you want. Imagine how you would desire air to breathe if you were drowning. Think about how much you would want your first meal after a long fast or a drink of cool water after being parched in the desert. Desire that intense is the fuel that ignites your passion. It's the energy that stimulates your imagination and the spark that kindles creativity. When you are impassioned by a strong, heartfelt desire backed with the deep belief that this is God's will for your life, you will generate enough enthusiasm to not only set your dreams in motion but carry them through to completion.

> *May he give you the desire of your heart and*
> *make all your plans succeed.*
> PSALM 20:4

PART 4

*Keys to Unlock
Your Dreams*

20 RELEASE THE POWER OF GOAL-SETTING

If you don't know where you're going,
you'll probably end up somewhere else!

Hold fast to your dreams, for if dreams die then
life is like a broken-winged bird that cannot fly.
LANGSTON HUGHES

Something miraculous happens when your dream makes the transition from being a lofty desire or a whimsical wish to a sound and comprehensible target. Your mind will move you in the direction of achievement once it has been given a clear and established objective. The dreams and aspirations of many people eventually die because they do nothing to turn them into solid goals or neglect to make plans for their fulfillment. Certainly it's a good idea to build your castles in the air but, as Henry David Thoreau reminded us, be sure to put foundations under them.

Some goals are never realized simply because they are not rational. A true goal should lie just outside your reach and cause you to stretch and grow. A viable dream must be realistic and eventually be within your grasp at the same time. In some cases, calling a dream unrealistic or irrational may be just a way of covering up the limits we put on ourselves, so be honest with yourself when deciding. Your goal should always be tough enough to challenge you but not so daunting that it squashes you.

Other dreams are never reached because they are simply not doable or achievable, regardless of how much effort is invested. For instance, it is not a realistic goal to want to be younger, shorter, or taller (unless you are still growing), to be married by next week if you are not even dating, to have different parents, to become a millionaire overnight, or to win the lottery. Dreams and goals that depend on fate or luck or the behavior and actions of others are not practical. It would be futile for you to say your dream is that your spouse would be in better spirits first thing in the morning, that your son would clean his room every day, that there would be an end to all crime, and that your boss would start appreciating all your creative suggestions. You have no control in those areas and will always be disappointed. Make sure your goals are not contingent upon others changing.

Setting goals is a *process*. The first step is to have a long-range dream by imagining what you'd like to see or do or have altered in your life. Your dream might be to become the chairperson of a fund-raising committee, spend more time with your spouse or children, visit with friends more often, improve your eating habits, change jobs, lose weight, enjoy a new leisure-time activity, have a pampering spa day, learn to fly a plane, lead a Bible study in your home, or travel to an exotic place. Allowing yourself to dream is the spark that sets everything else in motion. Make a list of your dreams and rate them according to priority. Then work your way through the list one at a time.

The next step in goal-setting is to get clear about what you want to accomplish. Take your top-priority dreams from vague wishes to definite goals by making them specific, measurable targets you can aim toward. Measurable means how much and by when. If it's vague and unspecific, how will you know when you've achieved it? For example, you might say your dream is to have more free time, but if you were given five extra minutes by yourself each day, it might not be what you had in mind. Sure, you'd have more free time but your dream would probably not be fulfilled. For your vision to become a clear goal, state precisely what you'd like to see change or take place, along with when and where. Change your wish from "I'd like to lose some weight" to "My goal is to weigh 150 pounds by the first day of spring." Likewise, saying you want to be healthy is a vague statement compared with having a definite goal stating you want to increase your strength, energy, endurance, and muscle tone over the next six months. Rather than vaguely wishing for a better job, your goal might be to work as a nature photographer in Africa one year from now. Set goals that have a clear sense of purpose and deep inspiration. You can discover what your best goals are by asking yourself:

- What is my deepest desire?
- What would I attempt if I knew I could not fail?
- What do I feel most passionate about?
- What idea never leaves me?
- What would bring me the greatest fulfillment?
- What is the most important thing I wish I could do in my lifetime?

The best way to set each goal is to clarify your intent—the reason or objective in wanting to pursue the dream in the first place. It's been said that when we give ourselves enough reasons, we will always find a way. What are your reasons? As you determine your goals, remember what the apostle Paul said: "Our goal is to stay within the boundaries of God's plan for us" (2 Corinthians 10:13 NLT). When you ask the Father in faith, he will reveal the goals and plans he has planted in your heart.

21 DESIGN YOUR GPS: A GOAL PATTERNING SYSTEM

*Hike in all directions and explore the
new possessions I am giving you.*
GENESIS 13:17 TLB

If you drive a car, it may be equipped with GPS (Global Positioning System) technology, a navigational technique that helps you get from where you are to where you'd like to go. It works with an onboard computer that receives satellite signals to calculate your exact position. Then, when you type in your destination, it plots an ideal route for you and directs you through the course. I have found that having a dream works in much the same way. Once you identify your vision and values, clarify your goals and objectives, and start moving in the right direction with much prayer and faith, the route miraculously begins to unfold and reveal itself. As you make your way, God will cause the path to become clear. "In everything you do, put God first, and he will direct you and crown your efforts with success" (Proverbs 3:6 TLB).

The GPS I want to introduce is your **G**oal **P**atterning **S**ystem, a personal planning book you can create that will help you identify the precise steps to keep you on track as you move toward the fulfillment of your dreams. It's a tool you can use to stay committed to your goals by devising a specific set of action plans within a systematic strategy. Helen Keller said, "I long to accomplish a great and noble task, but it is my chief duty to accomplish small tasks as if they were great and noble."

When I decided to create my own GPS, it enabled me to focus on the little tasks that eventually led to the fulfillment of the great and noble ones. It altered my life in a way no other goal-setting concept ever has. If you are wondering whether you can add one more task to a schedule that is already full, you will find that having a comprehensive strategy is a powerful way to ensure you *don't* overwhelm yourself. By assembling your own goal planner, you will also benefit immensely by seeing all the pieces of your life puzzle fitting together.

Here's a fun way to assemble an integrated system that's easy to use. Buy a 3-ring binder and fill it with both lined and blank paper, plus a set of dividers. Label the cover your "GPS: Goal Patterning System" for the current year, and put your name, address, and phone number on the inside. If it's ever lost, you'll want to be sure you can recover it since it will contain your personal life dreams and plans. This will be your goal-setting workbook, and it's a good idea to refer to it daily. You will get so much enjoyment from assembling it, updating the pages, and witnessing the speedy and spectacular results that I'm positive you won't have a hard time reviewing it regularly. If you are dissatisfied or disappointed with any part of your life right now, you probably already know it's a good idea to invest whatever time and effort is required to make changes.

Take your GPS, along with some pens, pencils, and colored markers, and find a quiet place where you can be alone to reflect on your current situation. Now you can begin creating the new and improved version of your life. Your system will cover several areas of your life journey, so start by labeling the dividers with these five headings:

1. Core Values (This will include your personal ideals, ethics, and moral codes.)
2. Life Purpose (This will lead you to your mission statement.)
3. Past, Present, and Future (This is a record of what's happened, your current position, and your future dreams.)
4. Strategies (This will include your itemized plans and daily action steps.)
5. Balance (This will be a record of accomplishments and ideas for fun rewards.)

In the following chapters, we will be covering each of these areas in detail so you can begin making entries in your GPS.

Something miraculous happens once you commit your goals to paper! To be sure you are not looking to outside sources for the direction of your life and to stay on track, fully seek God's plan and trust him completely for your future success. " 'For I know the plans I have for you,' says the Lord. 'They are plans for good and not for evil, to give you a future and a hope. In those days when you pray, I will listen. You will find me when you seek me, if you look for me in earnest'" (Jeremiah 29:11-13 TLB). To seek in earnest means to have a deep, sincere, heartfelt longing. Is that how you feel today? Are you earnestly looking for direction from your heavenly Father, who made you and everything in the entire universe? He will direct your path. He has promised to guide you through the twists and turns as you journey toward your dreams. After all, he is the one who planted the dreams in your heart in the first place.

22 GPS #1: DETERMINE YOUR CORE VALUES

What profit is there in gaining the whole world
when it means forfeiting one's self?
LUKE 9:25 TLB

Values give direction and validity to your dreams and goals. In this segment of your Goal Patterning System, determine and write out your core values. Without being clear about what you value most, you may get what you wish for yet never be satisfied or content. Arriving at true success means achieving dreams that are expressions of your core values. My thesaurus says another word for *core* is *essence*. Your core is the epitome of your inner self. It's all that is deep in your heart, at the very nucleus or the center of your being. Your values are the ideals you hold dear and treasure. They reflect what matters most to you in this life, your highest standards and principles, your main beliefs and doctrines, and the set of guidelines you live by. Without knowing your core values, you may find yourself chasing after happiness in all the wrong places, and true joy will elude you. Genuine fulfillment is usually the result of a praiseworthy and admirable goal. Fulfillment is not necessarily found in the goal itself.

Sadly, in our society we have been told a lie that it's not possible to get ahead without sacrificing values. The underlying implication is that attaining true success means forfeiting the things that make life worthwhile: worshiping and communing with our heavenly Father; enjoying ourselves, our families, our friends, and the work we do; investing the time and effort to keep our bodies healthy, rested, and relaxed; and appreciating our homes and other possessions. But once you are aware of your true values, you can make choices as to the dreams you want to follow that will allow you to make the best decisions in order to live by your highest ideals.

One of the easiest ways to determine your core values and identify the principles and standards you want to live by is to consider certain areas of your life and rate them according to importance. When you do, the ideals you treasure will begin to surface. To get you started, contemplate these 14 areas of your life and rank them according to the value you place on them:

___ Faith, spiritual beliefs, and relationship with God

___ Moral principles and ethics

___ Health—mental, emotional, and physical

___ Marriage

___ Children

___ Family

___ Friends

___ Career

___ Financial independence and security

___ Church and community

___ Reputation

___ Home and material possessions

___ Leisure time

___ Hobbies and other interests

Most of us will find the emphasis varies on some of these from time to time. But to realize your dreams, you'll want to create a life of balance that is built around a value system that encompasses all these areas. Your life can get out of balance so easily if you emphasize one aspect over all the others when setting your goals. But when you focus your choices and decisions based on your highest values and a system you have set up for yourself, you will rarely get thrown off balance. Your career, your finances, your family, and even your spouse may change in some ways, but when your values are firmly entrenched, they will provide a point of reference. You will have a solid foundation and a center of balance.

Now, write a statement in your GPS about those areas that are important to you and tell why. True inner values will emerge as you do. They might include inner peace, vitality, energy, laughter, honesty, trust, loyalty, contentment, confidence, creative expression, privacy, a tranquil environment, accomplishment, independence, passion, play-fulness, adventure, or love. You may add to this list. Your goals and values will then work together in perfect harmony. If you are married or thinking of marrying, you may choose to do this exercise with your partner as well as on your own.

If you pursue goals that don't match your values, they'll drain you of mental and emotional energy and leave you asking, "Is this all there is?" The further your dreams are from your core values, the more unrest and inner chaos you will experience. Sooner or later your system will break down physically, mentally, emotionally, and spiritually. It's amazing how many times we betray ourselves by following dreams for ourselves that violate our own principles. Give yourself a *values check* every now and then. When you notice a conflict or incongruity, ask yourself, "How can I alter my dreams and goals to uphold this value?" Naturally, the first thing you will consider is your relationship with your heavenly Father. If you want to know which dreams to follow based on true and lasting values, you can start by reading the Owner's Manual! The Bible says, "Seek first his kingdom and his righteousness, and all these things will be given to you as well" (Matthew 6:31).

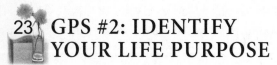

23 GPS #2: IDENTIFY YOUR LIFE PURPOSE

I believe God made me for a purpose but he also made me
fast, and when I run, I feel God's pleasure.
ERIC LIDDELL, OLYMPIC RUNNER

One way to assure your dreams and goals are in alignment with your core values is to determine how you view your life purpose. The next step in your GPS will be to write out a personal mission state-ment, being sure that it addresses the four key elements of balance in your life: physical well-being, psychological growth, emotional wellness, and spiritual harmony.

Every activity you are involved in can be part of fulfilling your purpose. You might think of your purpose as only concerning spiritual matters or some form of ministry such as volunteering at a shelter, serving at a soup kitchen, helping out at church, singing in the choir, teaching Sunday school, going on a mission trip, or sharing your faith. The truth is that you can fulfill your purpose in every detail of your life, including times when you are working, resting, playing, eating, exercising, and enjoying time with friends. Your purpose can be fulfilled on the job whether you are selling insurance, raising a family, running a farm, teaching school, operating a retail store, managing a hotel, doing home renovations, flying airplanes, repairing cars, managing an accounting office, or working in a factory. You are fulfilling your purpose anytime you use the talents, gifts, and abilities God has given you. You may be gifted in the arts, or teaching, or technology, or a particular trade, or dozens of other skill areas. All these abilities enable you to fulfill your God-given purpose.

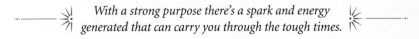

With a strong purpose there's a spark and energy generated that can carry you through the tough times.

There is nothing quite as invigorating or stimulating as a focused life, a life of purpose. It energizes like nothing else. Knowing your purpose motivates you to go beyond a dream. It inspires you with an intensity of desire to take action that you don't normally possess. A greater sense of purpose and mission allows you to see the big picture of your life. It connects you to others and the world around you. It guarantees you will keep moving toward only those goals you feel are worthy and most important, which will also be the most satisfying and rewarding to you.

People who coast through life without a sense of purpose or mission lead empty and disconcerted lives. Their attention is always being shifted, and their thoughts are continually scattered. Their activities and accomplishments are meaningless, and the result is confusion and hopelessness. With a strong purpose, a reason for being, there's a spark and energy generated that can carry you through the tough times and difficulties that are sure to arise when pursuing any dream.

Your purpose will come clear when you write out your personal mission statement. Based on your natural gifts and abilities, the answers to the following questions will help you to discover your mission and help you write a statement of purpose in your GPS:

- Which of your dreams will use your inherent talents, temperament, personality, and character traits?
- If you were given one year to live, what would you want to achieve?
- What three things do you want to accomplish before (or after) you retire?
- What contribution do you want to leave this generation?

As an example, I would like to share with you what I wrote when I did this exercise.

> My mission in life is to serve God according to his Word, to make use of my God-given gifts, to leave this world a better place in some way for having lived here by making an impact on as many lives as possible including my family, friends, readers, and audiences that would encourage them to trust Christ for all things, to inspire others to see themselves as the miracles they are and become all they were created to be, and to always live in the moment, enjoying each day while being ever mindful of eternity.

As I revisit this statement, I am reminded that it is not a guarantee that I will fulfill every aspect at all times. But it does serve as a guide with checkpoints where I can measure my progress and bring myself back on track when necessary.

God has a purpose for your life. You were made for a reason, and your life has profound meaning. We discover that meaning when we make God the primary focus of our lives. "Long before he laid down earth's foundations, he had us in mind, had settled on us as the focus of his love" (Ephesians 1:4 MSG).

24 GPS #3: PAST, PRESENT, AND FUTURE

Your future hasn't been written yet...
so go ahead and make it a good one!

A s you move along in your Goal Patterning System, this is the segment where you will identify what has taken place in the past and what's happening in the present in order to determine where you'd like to go in the future. To start, take one page in this section and itemize your various responsibilities, activities, involvements, and relationships to get a clear picture of your life so far. You can do that by considering these four main categories: work, home, personal, and community. Identify your roles within each category. For example, under "work" you may have sales manager, plant foreman, fashion designer, travel agent, restaurant owner, homemaker, or loan officer. Next to "home," you might include your roles of spouse, parent, chef, chauffeur, shopper, maintenance and repair person, groundskeeper or gardener. The next category, "personal," could say runner, nature lover, reader, friend, artist, or cyclist. And finally, "community" might include chairperson for a charitable association, board member, church usher, or Big Brother or Sister. Include whatever is important and meaningful to you. If you get stuck, think about the many hats you wear during a typical week.

Now take each item and expand on it by identifying all of the various activities, functions, responsibilities, duties, and obligations connected with it. This is a modified version of a brainstorming technique known as mind-mapping and has been used by personal coaches and life-management experts for years. It is a great strategy for viewing your life at a glance and gaining a clear understanding of where you've been and what you've been accomplishing up until now. By analyzing what has taken place in the past, you can more effectively prioritize your activities to make future plans. As you study the results, you will see patterns emerging, and it will become apparent to you what's been missing from your life, which projects you started but never finished, and what you want to do but haven't attempted. These will become your dreams and eventually your goals.

On the next page, write the date and the title "Dreams List." Based on the previous exercise, and keeping in mind the four categories for balance, jot down anything that would have to change or take place in order to improve your future. At this stage, dream big with no limits. Don't think too hard or evaluate how your dream could come about. Just let your creativity soar! Dreams that are not right for you will come to light later when you assess them according to your core values.

Now you'll be able to take your dreams to the next level by turning them into goals. Someone said goals are really dreams that have sprouted wings. While dreams are created in a spirit of casual lightheartedness with a wide spectrum, goals will require commitment and dedication and will encompass definite areas of your life. You will want to have goals that deal with your mental, physical, and spiritual well-being, as well as those in the areas of family and friends, career or occupation, continued education, social and cultural events, finances, leisure activities, and material possessions.

When determining your top goals, select some that are short-term, to be accomplished within the next few months, others that are mid-term within the next year, and long-term goals over the next three to five years. You'll also want to have some lifetime goals, so begin by asking yourself, "When I am 90 and looking back, what would I like to have done with my life?"

You have a starting place and a destination. Now you'll be able to determine what it will cost you to get there. When a computer or a machine is programmed properly, it does the job it was designed to do and gives the right answers, information, or data. When your mind is programmed right—in other words, when it is focused on God's Word and lines up with his purpose for your life—then you will do the things you were created to accomplish. The dreams God places in your heart always go beyond the acquiring of bigger, better, and more. His dreams—the ones that will fulfill who you are in the depth of your being—will be dreams that make you a better person and the world a better place. You no longer will be struggling through life, barely making it. You will prosper and live in health even as your soul soars. You will be going someplace because you have planted a dream.

25 GPS #4: STRATEGIES AND ACTION PLANS

Some people dream of success; others
wake up and work hard at it.

We should make plans—counting
on God to direct us.
PROVERBS 16:9 TLB

In the next segment of your GPS (Goal Patterning System), write out an itemized plan with some action steps. Let's say you enjoy photography, or writing and producing comedy skits, or making stained glass, and your dream is to turn that passion into a business. In the first stage, the dream is more of a vague wish or a distant yearning. It's a mere notion you toy with every now and then. To turn it into a goal, put it in writing by describing it in detail and defining it in measurable terminology. Here's an example: "My goal is to operate a business doing cabinetry and woodworking by January of next year earning $30,000 annually." To develop a strategy for going "beyond" a dream, write out your goals in the following areas of your life, completing them in the present tense as though they are happening now. To maintain balance, you'll want to cover each of the areas of body, mind, and spirit.

My spiritual growth will include _____.

To improve my health I am _____.

To become fit I am _____.

To maintain my ideal weight of _____ pounds, I am

_____.

To spend more time with my loved ones I am _____

_____.

To contribute to my church or community I will _____

_____.

The habits I am letting go of are _____.

The new habits I will develop are   _____ .

My next career goal is to   _____ .

To become debt free I am   _____ .

The debts I will pay off are   _____ .

My next annual vacation is   _____ .

My next weekend get-away is   _____ .

I am reducing stress in my life by   _____ .

My new hobbies include   _____ .

I am taking a course to learn new skills in _____ .

I want to continue my education in   _____ .

To develop your strategy further, write out an itemized plan with some daily or weekly action steps for each statement. As you do, be sure your goals are measurable, backed by your reasons and objectives, and connected to your core values. For example, one of my seminar attendees had a vague dream of someday operating a child daycare center. In this strategy exercise, she wrote out a specific goal that said: "Open a daycare in my home five days a week, with a maximum of six children under the age of five, starting in September of this year." Her reason or objective was to earn extra income while being at home. This supported her core values since she loved children, and especially enjoyed working with those at the toddler stage. She got very excited about using her natural gifts to teach and train them. Another core value was to be able to be home to spend time with her own young family. The next part of the strategy was to make definite action plans that included researching what is involved in starting a business in your home, identifying what certification, training, and licenses are needed, determining the capital requirement, exploring financing sources and options including government grants or funding, applying for appropriate tax numbers, investigating insurance requirements, establishing what equipment she would need and obtaining costs from retailers, doing market research to find out who else offers the same service and how they operate and who would use her services, deciding how and where to advertise, and determining how much profit she would like to earn.

As you begin to write definite plans in your GPS, ask yourself: What skills and expertise do I currently have in this area, and which ones could I acquire? Who do I know that I could approach as a mentor? What research can I do now? How much will my dream cost, and how long should it take? Where can I gain experience? What supplies will I need? Who should I associate with and which organizations could I join? What courses will I enroll in, which books could I read, and who could I talk to for wise counsel? Proverbs 20:18 (TLB) tells us, "Don't go ahead with your plans without the advice of others."

If all these steps sound rather daunting, you may need to reassess your dream, your core values, and your true priorities. When the dream is from God and your values line up with his, then he will give an inner excitement and the endurance to follow through in spite of the hard work. The Bible says, "We can make our plans but the final outcome is in God's hands" (Proverbs 16:1 TLB). It's been said that some people make things happen, others watch things happen, and the rest just wonder what happened! So go ahead with your plans. "Commit your work to the Lord, then it will succeed" (Proverbs 16:3 TLB).

> *If you have built castles in the air,*
> *your work need not be lost;*
> *that is where they should be,*
> *Now put foundations under them.*
> HENRY DAVID THOREAU

26 GPS #5: ACCOMPLISHMENTS AND REWARDS

> *If you observe a really happy man, you will find him*
> *building a boat, writing a symphony, educating his son,*
> *growing Double Dahlias in his garden.*
> W. BERAN WOLFE

Too often after accomplishing our goals and fulfilling our dream, we immediately throw ourselves back into the daily grind or tackle the next project without pausing to enjoy the rewards. When you've worked hard to reach your dream, you have earned the joy that comes as a result of the discipline, dedication, perseverance, and determination you've invested to achieve the goal. Take time to celebrate and savor your success! In this section of your GPS (Goal Patterning System), list your achievements and some ways you can reward yourself.

Whether you've gone back to school to earn a degree, decluttered your basement or attic, learned to downhill ski, coached your sales or sports team through to victory, or submitted a report by its due date, take time to rest, recharge, and celebrate before moving on. "Rest is the sweet sauce of labor," said Plutarch. If you have organized a successful fundraising event or a convention, worked as a missionary for two months or two years, lost ten pounds, learned to play the flute in time for a special function, or coordinated the annual family reunion, be sure once it's done you treat yourself with something pleasurable and fun. Allow yourself the privilege of commemorating your success by doing something enjoyable that you rarely get to do, either alone or with a special someone. Take time out to appreciate and be thankful for your accomplishments. Otherwise you will be stressed and overwhelmed at the thought of continuing.

Rewards come in all shapes and sizes. Choose one that is proportionate either to your investment of time or energy or the significance and magnitude of the end result. When you've completed some of the smaller action steps that are part of the bigger dream, take a break to enjoy a cup of your favorite coffee or herbal tea, get out into nature for a leisurely stroll, read a few pages of a good book, flip through a magazine, do a crossword or jigsaw puzzle, or play a game on the computer. When I have finished an activity, I will often play the piano or get out my sketch pad and pencil to doodle for a few minutes. When I go back to the project, I feel refreshed and invigorated, with an abundance of energy and new ideas.

When you've achieved those intermediate dreams and more involved goals, you may want to reward yourself by taking off for an afternoon or a full day. Go for a country hike, watch a movie you've been waiting to see, or spend time catching up with a good friend. Plan to go fishing, golfing, or play a game of tennis. Unwind with a massage at a spa or spend time on your favorite hobby. Attend live theatre or the ballet or go to hear a philharmonic orchestra. Go shopping for a new CD, your favorite cologne or perfume, a great piece of jewelry, or a new tool for the workbench. Arrange a fun picnic outing with your spouse or the whole family or play with your kids or grandkids—building sand castles, riding a merry-go-round, having an ice cream cone, jumping in autumn leaves, or making snow angels. When our grandkids were small, one way I stayed motivated while working on challenging tasks was to reward myself with a visit once I had completed a few hours worth of work. It made the tasks so much more enjoyable.

When you've accomplished your highest aspirations and dreams, reward yourself with something more substantial. Maybe you've wanted to try something risky like white water rafting, sky diving, or deep sea fishing. You might choose to make a major purchase you've been putting on hold or go ahead with a decorating or landscaping project you've wanted to invest in. Perhaps you could plan a weekend getaway, a vacation at a favorite spot, a camping trip, or time at a cottage. There are five girls in my family, and we live at quite a distance from each other. Although it takes a lot of planning, our annual sisters' weekend getaway is something that makes it easier to stay focused during the year as we each face our individual career challenges. The reward of being together for a girls' weekend is priceless.

Make a joy list for yourself and keep it handy to refer to once each stage of your goal is met. Include some leisurely pastimes for rest and relaxation, as well as a variety of recreational and entertaining activities for celebrating. Whether your treat is to abandon modern technology for a day, escape into a good book, indulge in a midday snooze, spend the day at the beach with the family, or dust off the board games for an evening of fun and laughter with friends, be sure to reward yourself when you achieve each step of the dream.

PART 5
Just Imagine!

27 BE, DO, AND HAVE...
THEN COMES THE DREAM

*You must be, do, and have the dream before you can
actually experience its fulfillment!*

L et's say your dream is to be a ballerina or a golfer. Okay, so maybe
those are the furthest away from what you would actually dream,
but whether your dream is to be an airline pilot, a missionary, a concert
pianist, or anything else, you can fill in yours later on. For now, we'll
use these examples to go through the steps of being, doing, and having.

The first thing you must do is *be* a ballerina or golfer in your mind and
imagination. One primary step in goal-setting is to start seeing yourself
clearly in your mind's eye, picturing yourself as you'd be once the dream
is fulfilled. What would you look like, how would you walk and talk, what
would you wear as a ballerina or golfer? Consider your stance, bearing,
posture, and body movements. What would you think about and focus
on much of the time? What attitudes, viewpoints, and outlooks would
personify you? How would you typically approach each day if you were
living out the dream? Create a mental image and hold on to it.

Next, consider what you would *do* if you were a ballerina or a golfer.
Would you invest in lessons or some other type of training? Would you
rehearse to hone your natural talents and practice new skills? Which exercises would you regularly do to increase your strength and endurance?
What classes could you take to enhance your sense of balance, poise, and
confidence or to improve your posture and carriage? How would you
spend your spare time, and where would you go to get away for a time of
renewal and refreshment? Who would you associate with? What groups

or clubs would you belong to? Are there books you could read or mentors you could enlist to help and encourage you along the way?

Then decide what you must *have* in order to be a ballerina or golfer. Obviously a ballerina would need ballet slippers and a tutu. As a golfer you'd need a set of golf clubs, golf polo shirts, and appropriate shoes. Would you also have an office assistant or a babysitter to free up your time? Maybe you'd have a golf cart? Perhaps a ballet bar installed for doing stretches. Remember when you get to the "be" stage to be specific.

Don't underestimate the power of doing, being, and having ahead of time. Although these steps sound simple, they are powerful and effective. Whether your dream is to own a motorcycle and travel across the continent, do some acting in community theater, be an evangelist, organize events that would double the attendance in your church, write a novel, volunteer on a mission field, play an instrument in a band, become a Big Brother or Sister or foster parent, compose music or poetry, write and produce dramatized sermons, open a bookstore, or turn your woodworking or dressmaking hobby into a full-time business, you can apply these techniques to activate that dream.

Finally, fill in your own dream. Take some time before you go on to the next chapter to choose one goal you want to accomplish. Go through the "be, do, and have" steps. Put them in writing too. Think of it this way: If you are clear on who you want to become through reaching the goal or what you hope to get from it, then being that person—doing and having what he or she would do and have—will make the dream even more believable. Eventually you will become so comfortable with your vision that it will be as though you have always done it. When I made my way up on stage to speak at my first paid engagement, it was as though I had been there a hundred times before. For months I had practiced being, doing, and having all that was involved in being a successful presenter. When my big break came, I had mentally practiced and physically rehearsed so often that I practically knew what to expect each step of the way.

To dream big and have big goals you will need to have a big vision. That's why it's so important to see yourself achieving in advance. "Sooner or later," said Richard Bach, author of *Jonathan Livingston Seagull*, "those who win are those who think they can." See yourself being, doing, and having all that God has created you for, and you'll soon know you can.

28 THE GIFT OF IMAGINATION

Nimble thought can jump both sea and land.
WILLIAM SHAKESPEARE

Imagination is the highest kite one can fly.
LAUREN BACALL

The great thing about imagination is that it is free. You can't go wrong! It doesn't cost a thing to create a mental picture of the successful desired outcome of your dream. And it is one of the most effortless ways to stay focused on the dreams you want to pursue. "I do not like the phrase: Never cross a bridge till you come to it. The world is owned," said Bruce Barton, "by men who cross bridges in their imaginations, miles and miles in advance of the procession."

Imagination comes naturally to us. I believe it is a marvelous gift from our Creator. Whether your dream is to organize an after-school program for teens, landscape your backyard, play drums in a band, coach a Little League team, travel to an interesting destination, start your own magazine, or organize a surprise party, you must clearly see it in your mind before you can accomplish it. Just as an architect must have a design and a fashion designer will have an image in mind, so you must have a clear mental picture of what you want to accomplish.

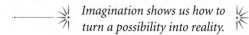
Imagination shows us how to turn a possibility into reality.

Over the years, as I have studied success, I've noticed an almost universal trait among those who have achieved their dreams. They not only see what they want to accomplish, but they can smell it, taste it, hear it, feel it, and imagine the emotions associated with it. They actually *experience* the dream in their imagination *before* it happens. That intense, sensory image becomes a powerful motivating force in their lives. "Go confidently in the direction of your dreams. Live the life you have imagined," said Thoreau.

Seeing all the possibilities, envisioning what can be done in this world and how it can be accomplished—this is what marks the power of imagination. Your imagination is your own personal laboratory. Here you can create events, map out plans, and imagine what the desirable outcome would be. By going over these mental images and describing the details, you can work out problems and make modifications and alterations before you actually move ahead. This is an opportunity to fine-tune your plans and make the necessary changes. You can visualize overcoming obstacles before they occur.

Imagination shows us how to turn a possibility into reality. It is difficult to even think without having a mental image form in our minds. When you think something, you don't just think it in words. You think in pictures that express those thoughts. If you think you can't create pictures and images in your imagination, think back to the last time you worried about something. Worry is a form of negative imaging!

As incredible as your imagination is, it will never be big enough to comprehend all that God wants to do for you, in you, and with you. The apostle Paul wrote, "Now to him who is able to do immeasurably more than all we ask or imagine, according to [Jesus'] power that is at work within us" (Ephesians 3:20). I don't know if we really believe what that verse is saying. It says Jesus' power is at work…in us! This means that what you are able to accomplish has nothing to do with your upbringing, your heritage, your race, or your past experiences. It is not hampered by self-limiting beliefs and conditioning. It also has nothing to do with our own abilities or self-ambitions. As Paul wrote to the Corinthians, "We dare to say these good things…not because we think we can do anything of lasting value by ourselves. Our only power and success come from God" (2 Corinthians 3:45 TLB). What you are able to accomplish has to do with the mighty power of God's Spirit living in you! He has blessed you with imagination, and he will enable you to fulfill your dream.

Start today to imagine things as they could be rather than the way they are. God has endowed us with the capacity to create vivid pictures in our imagination. Let's use that capacity to bring glory and honor to him!

29 ' WALK THROUGH YOUR DREAM

*You will now have a starting place and a destination, and
you will be able to determine what it will cost you to get
there. You will be going someplace.*
H. STANLEY JUDD

D id you know you can actually go on a tour of your dream? Imagine
the fun you could have visiting model homes, attending travel
presentations on vacation spots you'd like to visit, or trying on the
designer suit you'd love to own. Once you get the ball rolling, you may
be surprised at how affordable and achievable your dream really is.

Let's say you want to take a class in photography, study sign language, or learn to play the violin. Take the initiative and call around
to check into lessons in your area, as well as the cost and dates and
times of classes. Note the information you gather in your Goal Patterning System (GPS), and keep it handy for future use. Your dream
may happen sooner than you think.

 *The more real the activity or plan becomes in your
mind, the more likely you will fulfill the dream.*

Perhaps you want to move to a certain vicinity, live in a condo-
minium, or build your dream home. Visit your area of choice. Stroll
through the neighborhod and go to open houses there. Notice how the
places are landscaped or decorated and then redo them in your imagination to your taste and style. Imagine living there. Hold the feeling in
your mind. Perhaps you'd like to remodel your existing home or add
on a room but feel you don't have time or can't afford it right now. It
doesn't take much time or cost anything to browse trade shows and
furniture showrooms. Check out fabrics and styles and note prices.
Glance through decorator magazines and clip articles or save pictures
of furnishings and accessories that interest you. Call around and get
someone to give you quotes and estimates.

Get quotes for other projects too. Maybe you'd like to restore a
classic car, own a boat, or build a log cabin on a lake. Perhaps you've

been wanting to have some landscaping done in your backyard or simply put in some gardens. When you talk to the experts, they may have additional ideas or alternative methods you can implement to achieve your dream that you hadn't thought of. You won't know until you check into your options and gather prices whether it's within your reach. Even if it's not possible just yet, all dreams that were ever realized started in someone's imagination.

If you'd love to own a new vehicle, why not take your dream car for a test drive or rent one for a weekend? If your dream is to write a book, spend some time in bookstores and libraries. Interview a few published authors. If you want to become a professional golfer, speaker, preacher, musician, comedian, TV host, or tennis player, watch television shows or DVDs of other people doing those things and imagine yourself in their spot.

The more real the activity or plan becomes in your mind, the more believable it is and the more likely you will fulfill the dream. You may not have realized it, but this is how you've been achieving your goals in the past. If you wanted to obtain something, you first had to get the idea, and then you checked out the details, and eventually it happened. The only difference is that now you are doing it before you're actually ready to see it materialize.

Another way to walk through your dream is to put it in a picture book. Start with a three-ring binder, scrapbook, or photo album. If you want to take a vacation, clip pictures from travel brochures and magazines of your favorite destinations. If your dream is to make changes in your home, whether you hope to renovate a single room or remodel the entire house, you can first make a goal book representing the project. Save pictures and images from decorator magazines, catalogs, and brochures. Add your own sketches and photographs from similar projects. Collect actual fabric swatches and paint chips of colors you plan to use and assemble them all in your book. We did this when we wanted to turn two rooms into a large country kitchen and the workmen were happy to have the images to refer to. The finished project became so real in my mind that by the time the renovations were completed, it was as though I had walked through that room a hundred times.

If you want to start your own business, make up some inexpensive business cards on the computer with your name and chosen title, plus the name of your future company. Carry a few with you and post some where you can see them daily. When I was writing my first book, I designed a mock cover and glued a banner across the front with the word "Bestseller!" When you use pictures from magazines, catalogs, and brochures to represent the dream, put yourself in the picture with a personal photograph. Not long ago I chose a picture of two people relaxing at a summer picnic by a pond with swans in the background. I dreamed of a day like that for Cliff and me, so I took a recent photograph, cut our heads from it and pasted them on the people in the picture. The following year we were on the magnificent grounds of a castle in England having a picnic by a pond—complete with swans!

So go ahead and price the piano lessons—and the piano too! Make an appointment at the weight loss clinic for a consultation. Visit the travel agent and check into a cruise, a beach house on an island, or a resort in the mountains. Visit the college or school or performing arts center you hope to attend. Make arrangements to talk with a chef, a horse trainer, or an orchestra conductor if that's the career you want to pursue.

Unlocking the gift of your imagination allows you to focus on possibilities rather than obstacles. Taking a tour of your dream is a fun way to make it more realistic. And it will bring you a little closer to being able to believe in it.

30 PRACTICE MENTAL REHEARSAL

I never hit a shot, not even in practice, without having a very sharp, in focus picture of it in my head.
JACK NICKLAUS

As [a person] thinks in his heart, so is he.
PROVERBS 23:7 NKJV

Jesus taught us to pray believing. This reminds me of times my sisters and I played make-believe as children. When we did, we actually lived out the situation in our imagination and believed it was real. We

didn't merely *wish* we were driving a car or operating our own grocery store. We believed we were doing it! When kids play-act, they are
practicing being schoolteachers, firefighters, nurses, and astronauts. It
becomes their reality at the moment. To truly believe something, you
have to see it in your mind's eye.

Olympic athletes call this visualization process mental rehearsal.
Lee Evans, an Olympic gold medalist runner, said, "I visualized each
step of the 400-meter race until I saw every stride I would take." Mental
rehearsal is using your imagination to try out your dreams, goals, and
plans. When I knew I would have to take my two small children and
leave my marriage to start over after suffering severe physical abuse for a
number of years, it was difficult for me to conceive living without a husband. I wasn't sure how we would survive without someone providing
for us. I spent nearly a year mentally rehearsing what it would be like
to be the only parent, to know no one was coming home at the end of
the day, to sleep by myself, to look after home repairs and car maintenance alone, and to be the sole financial provider. When the time came,
the difficult transition was made a little less stressful because I had
become comfortable with my new situation after mentally rehearsing
the actions I needed to take so often.

Peak performers know the value of using the skill of mental
rehearsal. In their minds, they run through important events before
they happen. My dad played the piano in an orchestra for many years,
and we would often catch him tapping his fingers on a tabletop or the
arm of his favorite chair. When we asked him about this, he'd admit he
was mentally practicing a new number for an upcoming engagement.
My pastor says he often rehearses his Sunday messages while driving in
his car and even finds himself putting in the hand gestures he may use
for extra emphasis. His wife says if you didn't know what he was doing,
it would look very strange indeed. In my career I often mentally practice
doing television interviews and going on stage in front of thousands
of people as I drive to the event. By the time I actually get there, I have
developed a comfort zone for myself.

Mental rehearsal can help you fine-tune and hone the skills you
need to make your dreams happen smoothly. The more vivid the image

in your mind, the freer from doubt and the more at ease you'll be in the actual situation. When our home renovations were going on, I had walked through the completed project so often in my imagination that I felt sorry for those visitors who could only see the current mess and disarray and not the finished results as I did! You can see your dreams in advance just as easy.

Mental rehearsal can also help you overcome apprehension, anxiety, and nervousness. Are you feeling uncomfortable about going to a party or a conference alone? If so, mentally rehearse the event ahead of time and see yourself walking into the room with poise and confidence as you introduce yourself to new people. When you know you'll be dealing with a difficult person or handling conflict or confrontation, you'll be able to stay calm by practicing in advance what you'll say and how you'll respond.

Maybe you're preparing to entertain a larger-than-usual group of friends in your home. Before people arrive, mentally go over all the details and rehearse ways you can be a gracious host, helping to make your guests feel relaxed and comfortable.

The real key is to make the moves in your head first as a way of testing them out. Begin by determining what your desirable outcome would be. Go over these mental pictures and define the details. Play them over and over to yourself.

By practicing your day, your dreams, your vision, and your goals in your imagination before you even begin to tackle them, you can actually start acting out your success right away. After all, dreams are free and so is mental rehearsal. Robert G. Ingersoll said,

> Surely there is grandeur in knowing that in the realm of thought, at least, you are without a chain; that you have the right to explore all heights and all depths; that there are no walls nor fences; no prohibited places nor sacred corners in all the vast expanses of thought.

31 AN IMAGINARY RETREAT

*Many have no more happier moments than those
they pass in solitude…which shifts the scene of
pleasure with endless variety, bids all the forms of
beauty sparkle before them, and gluts them with
every change of visionary luxury.*
SAMUEL JOHNSON

Here's something you can do to activate your ability to dream big. Try this when you've got the boss-is-driving-me-nuts, spouse-let-me-down, new-car-got-dinged, just-ate-a-whole-pizza, and might-as-well-lay-on-the-couch-and-watch-television blues. When everything's gone wrong and you feel you need a break from it all, it's probably the best time for an imaginary retreat. If you feel you need an escape more than ever but you know a real vacation is out of the question right now, try taking a fantasy trip. After all, dreams are free!

You might not think so, but you can benefit from an armchair retreat in many ways. Amazing as it sounds, the therapeutic benefits you gain from taking a fantasy trip can be nearly as powerful as if you had gone on an actual journey. Here's why I'm so sure about that. If you've ever awakened from a nightmare in a sweat, with your body trembling and your heart pounding, you were reacting physically to what was happening solely in your mind. Your body responded as if what just occurred in your dreams was the real thing, even though the experience was imaginary. A fantasy dream vacation works much the same way, but in reverse. Unlike the nightmare encounter, your body, mind, and soul will experience positive outcomes and beneficial results. You'll end up feeling calm, relaxed, energized, and refreshed.

To limber up your imagination, visit the library for books about where you would go on your imaginary vacation. Log on to websites that allow you to virtually visit places you may not have a chance to see otherwise—the Louvre in Paris, a waterhole in Africa, or the outback in Australia. Collect travel brochures, maps, and guidebooks about places that interest you. Borrow or rent travel DVDs of some of your favorite spots. After you've watched them, you will feel as though you've actually visited those places!

Now, start your dream trip by sitting in your favorite chair and closing your eyes. For this particular vacation, put monetary restrictions and physical limitations aside. Why go economy? Make this trip as lavish and extravagant as you want. Imagine that you've been given unlimited resources to plan your dream vacation. You may as well go first-class all the way.

Tell yourself you can take as long as you wish—a weekend, two weeks, a month, or a year—and you can visit anywhere you choose. Consider an exotic or relaxing place you'd like to be right now, such as a rainforest, a white sandy beach on a deserted island, a charming country inn, a cottage by the lake, a cabin in the mountains, a ski resort, a sailboat on the Caribbean. Then imagine you are really there. Observe each detail. Envision yourself strolling through your vacation spot. Fill in the particulars, remembering to appeal to all five senses. What are the smells you'll enjoy—the flowers and trees, coffee brewing, ocean breezes, fresh baked bread, a lobster barbecue? Where would you eat dinner—a picnic on the beach, a small café, a table for two by the edge of the sea, an elegant restaurant? What foods are on the menu? What are the weather conditions? Can you hear waves lapping against the shore or feel the wind in your hair or warm sunshine on your face? The more details you can fill in, the more you'll benefit from your dream trip.

Here's another fun exercise you can do. Gather together a sheet of poster board, a pair of scissors, and a glue stick. Create a dream vacation collage. Post it where you can see it for those times when you need to get away from everything. Sometimes we get so caught up in the demands of daily living that the only fantasy we ever have is that the next light will turn green before we get to it, we'll have one good night's sleep, or that the job jar will someday be empty. We tread wearily through our days, asking what difference a dream would make anyway. It was Henry Ward Beecher who said, "The soul without an imagination is what an observatory would be without a telescope." Our great Creator has made us with incredible creativity. So allow your imagination to take you away from the daily grind, at least temporarily. When you do you will return invigorated. And who knows? Your dream just may turn into a reality someday!

32 ENVISION YOUR GOAL

Vision…it reaches beyond the thing that it is,
into the conception of what can be. Imagination
gives you the picture. Vision gives you the impulse
to make the picture your own.
ROBERT COLLIER

Where there is no vision, the people perish.
PROVERBS 29:18 KJV ·

Helen Keller was asked if there is anything worse than being blind. "Yes," she replied. "The most pathetic person in the world is one who has sight but no vision." For a practical application of vision, let's say your dream is to renovate part of your house, add on a garage, redecorate a living room, purchase a new car, or buy some patio furniture. Perhaps you think you can't afford it right now. In the meantime, what's to stop you from envisioning the completed project just the way you'd like it? Fill in all the details—the color of the carpet, the pattern in the drapes, the artwork you want hanging over the fireplace. Picture the completed renovations or the finished garage. See the car in the driveway or the patio furniture sitting in its place. It's a lot of fun and doesn't cost a thing.

The first year I was living with my two daughters as a single mom, we suffered severely from malnutrition of the wallet, and it was a stretch to simply pay the rent and put food on the table. But this did not discourage us from having a dream. In our modest apartment we started to imagine the furnishings we could use and exactly where we would place them. For example, because we wanted to have a stereo system to play our favorite gospel music, we cleared a spot where it would go and propped our albums (now I'm dating myself!) against the wall. Whenever I passed by, I could vividly imagine the stereo in place. Each time it would remind me to say a prayer of thanksgiving. Eventually the time came when miracles happened and through a series of amazing events, the vision became an exciting reality. Why? I believe God taught us to push beyond the hazy, vague yearnings that so many of us settle for and focus our dreams by actually envisioning the desired outcome. That picture was backed by deep, intense prayer and sincere faith that God would provide. The albums against the wall made the dream more tangible by giving it substance and reality. That in turn produced the ability to ask in faith and gave us the energy, drive, and innovation to work hard as well.

One winter weekend I was asked to babysit for a couple in our church. When they came to pick up their daughter at the end of the day, they asked the kids and me to stay in the other room for a few minutes. We heard some scuffling, and then they called us to come out. We could hardly believe our eyes! There sat a stereo system in the exact place we had envisioned it. It was their personal stereo and a gift to us. They explained that they felt God had spoken to them about giving it to us as a Christmas gift. Although they were not even aware of our vision, they were open to God's leading. He used this precious family to bless us that year. We are eternally grateful and through them we learned much about listening for God's leading and selfless generosity.

At about the same time, my daughters were given the opportunity to take music lessons at no cost if we had a piano for them to practice on. So we bought sheet music and placed it where the piano would sit. Eventually we were able to compile money from various sources—birthday and Christmas gifts, savings from my earnings, and some extra money family members chipped in—and we bought an old upright piano. Your dream may be fulfilled through an incredible miracle or it may require you to go out, work hard, and budget resourcefully. In either case, through clarity, intensity of prayer, and genuine faith, dreams can happen!

Later on, when Cliff and I were married and living in an apartment with the girls, we wanted to move to a family home. We were not sure if we would buy a new home in the city, an older house we could restore, or perhaps a piece of country property where we would build our dream home. We started out with very vague ideas as to what we were looking for, and, although we spent many hours searching, we were not having much success finding a place that met our family's needs. Finally, one day while we were praying about our predicament and asking for divine guidance, we felt God nudging us to be more definite and specific in our description. So we started to visualize our new home very clearly right down to the smallest detail. We described two acres of wooded land, a three-bedroom house with an attached two-car garage, two bathrooms, a main floor laundry room, a den, and a screened-in porch at the back overlooking the woods, complete with deer, raccoons, and chipmunks. One day we drove past a beautiful country home on a treed lot. Our realtor was able to show us through that day. The moment we stepped onto the property, we had the amazing sensation that this was to be our new home. When we saw the inside of the house, we were astounded. It matched what we had envisioned perfectly! We bought that house and have lived happily there ever since, enjoying the beautiful scenery and the wildlife in our backyard. To some, it may seem like sheer coincidence, but one thing seems certain: You and I have been given a most miraculous ability to envision desired outcomes and then watch God turn them into realities. It's time to start believing in this most marvelous gift that can take you beyond a mere dream!

33 CREATE A DREAM COLLAGE

When you cease to dream, you cease to live.
MALCOLM FORBES

I pray that you will begin to understand how incredibly
great his power is to help those who believe him.
EPHESIANS 1:19 TLB

One remarkable yet simple concept that can very quickly move your deepest dreams to astounding new heights is a *dream collage* or goal board. The first dream board I ever saw inspired me so profoundly that it got me started on a fun and fascinating practice that continues to enhance almost every aspect of my life to this day. Early on in my sales career, while attending a national conference, one seminar leader introduced this unique idea. Even now I can vividly recall every distinctive detail as she held up her simplistic work of art on stage for all to see. It was created on a sizeable piece of picture board and dramatically framed with a border of one-hundred-dollar bills. (Fake, I presume!) In the center of the frame was a hodgepodge of pictures, photos, and drawings representing some of what this presenter wanted to take place in her life. The images were actual cut-outs representing her dreams and were clipped from new car brochures, furniture catalogs, travel pamphlets, and magazines. It also included images of a woman working out at a gym, a happy family enjoying a delicious meal around a table, and someone volunteering at a food bank. That day she was excited to tell us that nearly everything she "dreamed" on her collage had become a reality for her. Needless to say, I could hardly wait to get home and begin working on one of my own.

As I started to assemble the supplies for my project, I must have been thinking smaller than she suggested because the mat I chose to work with was the cardboard from inside a package of pantyhose. Nonetheless, I got the scissors and glue and proceeded to cover it with a few unpretentious pictures of items I was in need of at that time. From a catalog, I cut out the image of a basic wristwatch, as well as a set of luggage. I also yearned for a dishwasher and dreamed of owning a fur coat (which, by the way, was a perfectly understandable desire since in those days they were commonly presented as awards to top producers by sales organizations), so I attached pictures of those items too. Shortly after, while shopping at a mall, I spotted a set of luggage on sale for half-price. When I brought it home and compared it to the picture, I was astounded to notice the set I purchased was identical to the one on my dream board. Since the fur coat pasted on my collage was not a style I really wanted, I quickly tore it off and waited until I found a better picture! After a short time I earned a monthly sales bonus that was enough to purchase a coat—just like it!

Another picture was of a square oak coffee table with four panes of glass and some brass trim. Underneath I had written the figure $200, although I'm not sure why. When I showed it to my sales team, they chuckled at the low price and were sure I hadn't been shopping for coffee tables lately. They felt I would end up disappointed. I wasn't discouraged and let them know I believed a $200 coffee table was out there, and God would divinely direct me to it. Shortly after, I was booked to make a group presentation in a client's home. When I arrived, the hostess apologized that her home was not furnished except for the one room we'd be using because her family moved every year and sold their furnishings to buy everything new. As we passed by the near-empty living room, I commented that the one piece she had there was exactly like the coffee table I had on my dream collage. She explained that for some reason, it was the only piece that hadn't sold from the former house and added, "Would you like it? It's yours for $200!" I took it home in the trunk of my car that day and couldn't stop smiling and thanking God!

As you can imagine, I became a regular user of dream boards. Today I use a "dream book," complete with dividers. It's a three-ring binder with segments for travel information, landscaping and decorating, health, family, church, community, career, fashion, home décor, and so on. To make your dream collage, go to any art supply store and purchase a piece of mat board. Then gather magazines, catalogs, brochures, scissors, and a glue stick. Clip a collection of pictures that reflect your dreams and what you'd like to see happen in your future. Whether the pictures are of a restful vacation spot, positive family relations, healthy living ideas, a new career, a fascinating hobby, furniture or clothing styles, and ways to experience inner peace, choose the images that appeal to you. Arrange your cut-out pictures on the mat and leave them overnight. See if you still like your choices the next day. If not, change them. Finally, glue them in place and display your dream collage where you can see it regularly. It will help to keep the dreams alive. Creating a collage is a fun way to turn your dreams into realities!

 ## 34 BE A VISIONARY

It is impossible to even think without a mental image.
ARTISTOTLE

Visionaries see things not as they are but as they could be!

Have you ever noticed how some people can look at an old, dilapidated, ramshackle of a house with crumbling walls and a roof that's in tatters and immediately envision it as a mansion? They see the potential and get excited at the thought of what could be done to transform it. Someone else sees a vacant lot overgrown with weeds, thistles, and thorns, and pictures the possibilities. Instantly he can imagine a beautifully landscaped piece of property with a manicured lawn, flourishing plants, shrubs, and trees, and colorful, lush gardens. One special friend loves to shop at yard sales. What impresses me most is how she can spot a worn-out, threadbare sofa or a table on its last legs and in her mind's eye see what a piece of new fabric, a few nails, some stain, or a bit of varnish could do. She has decorated her home with many of these precious treasures that a nonvisionary person would have passed by. In the same way, a seamstress looks at a tattered piece of clothing and imagines it transformed into the most beautiful garment. Graphic artists, landscapers, architects, playwrights, set designers, painters, sculptors, and crafters of all sorts know the power in mentally seeing the dream as though it were completed. Albert Einstein said, "Imagination is everything. It is the preview of life's coming attractions."

Granted, some people are visual by nature and think in pictures about any new venture that comes to them. But while they have the gift of visualizing spontaneously, others learn to do it through practice. Many peak performers, top-level athletes, and great achievers excel at what they do because they've discovered how to see future events and situations in vivid detail. My mother, who knew the value of visualizing, was a great example. For many years, she saw herself living in a quaint Victorian cottage with a white picket fence and rose gardens. After my dad died, she sold the family home in the country in the hopes of finding her dream cottage. Instead, she went to live in a small townhouse in the city, and eventually, after remarrying, lived with her new husband in an apartment. Through the years, although it didn't look promising to others, Mom continued to envision her cottage and believed one day she would live there. It was so real in her mind that she would get excited anytime she talked about it. At the age of 75, she and her husband had the opportunity to move to Vancouver Island in Canada, an idyllic spot for retirees. Their real estate agent showed them many fine condominiums to choose from, but one day she suggested they take a look at a small house on a corner lot. It turned out to be a small Victorian cottage that had become overgrown with vines, bushes, and shrubbery. Mom took one look and was immediately captivated as she visualized what it could look like with some tender loving care and a lot of elbow grease. They bought the place and immediately after moving in she got to work. Neighbors passing by would stop to thank her for her efforts in transforming this little house on their street. All summer, little by little, she pulled away vines, dug up weeds, cut down dead bushes, and dragged away the brush. She painted the fence and finally planted the rose gardens that she would enjoy the following summer. When fall came, she put in bulbs—daffodils, tulips, and crocuses—to bloom in springtime. Shortly after that, I had the chance to go for a visit and the transformation was a delight to see. Sadly, Mom never saw the final results, as she went home to be with the Lord the day after Christmas that year. By the time my sister Lois and I, along with our husbands, made the trip to retrieve her belongings, it was springtime. There we stood in the midst of Mom's heavenly, peaceful garden, thankful for the wonderful heritage and sense of vision Mom had instilled in us. Although she didn't see the glory of her beautiful gardens, she did get to live in her charming cottage with the picket fence. And best of all, she gave us an incredible gift—believing in the power of dreams.

PART 6
You Are Unique

35 RUN YOUR OWN RACE

Always dream and shoot higher than you know you can do.

Don't bother just to be better than your contemporaries or predecessors. Try to be better than yourself.
WILLIAM FAULKNER

My husband, Cliff, has an interesting hobby: drag racing. For those who don't know a lot about it, you're like me. However, I do know that two cars race each other side by side down a quarter-mile track and the cars reach exceptionally high speeds in a matter of seconds. That means both drivers must stay incredibly focused. Although I don't understand a lot about the dynamics of racing, and attending drag races is not where I'd choose to spend a beautiful, summer weekend, I support Cliff by being there occasionally. One time, after watching an exceptionally close race, I asked him how it was possible to stay focused while driving at such high speeds, especially when he could clearly see the other driver was gaining on him and at times, possibly about to overtake him. His reply is something that comes to my mind often. It's a powerful reminder and a good life principle: "When I race, I don't think too much about the other car. Instead, I predetermine how fast I want to go and how quickly I want to get to the finish line, all the while concentrating on how my own car is performing. Then I simply run my own race." What a great concept for each of us to use as we set goals and live out our plans to achieve our dreams!

Basically, what Cliff is saying is that if he is going to compete with anyone, it's himself. "Our business in life," said Maltbie Babcock, "is not

103

to get ahead of other people, but to get ahead of ourselves." Rather than trying to be better than your colleagues or those who have gone before you, strive to surpass yourself. Instead of spending useless energy and precious time analyzing others' dreams, how they go about achieving them, and where they stand with their personal targets and plans, we can concentrate on improving our own performance with personal goals and objectives. "Let everyone be sure that he is doing his very best, for then he will have the personal satisfaction of work well done and won't need to compare himself with someone else" (Galatians 6:4 TLB).

People are also hindered from running their own races when they try to keep up with the Joneses. The media today supports this harmful practice by convincing us that unless we drive a specific vehicle, have a certain number of vacation days each year, dress a special way, brush with a particular brand of toothpaste, or wear the latest fragrance, we must be missing out on the best that life has to offer. It's no wonder we are tempted to compare ourselves and what's happening in our lives with others.

Running your own race eliminates the comparison trap. I have a small sign in my office that reads: *Comparison equals depression!* Anytime we compare ourselves with others, we're setting ourselves up to feel like failures. The reason is that we normally compare our very worst trait, characteristic, or part of our life with the best of others. Even if we were to come out the winner, comparison is never fair since we are all at different levels, with very personal values, dreams, and priorities. Yet most of us compare everything from our appearance, career success, and financial status to relationships, education, physical fitness, and material possessions. It's not surprising we can be left feeling inadequate and unsure of our ability to attain any dream.

The solution is to know clearly where you are headed and what would make a satisfying life for you—and then stay focused on that target. Try redefining success and see the difference it can make. To run your own race means not looking over your shoulder at the other guy. It means escaping the comparison trap and avoiding unfair assessments based on another's perceived judgments of you. Every time you perform a task, try to outshine your last performance. Very soon you will notice your dreams coming true!

36 BELIEVE IN YOUR WORTH

*Look inside yourself, Simba.... You are more
than what you have become.*
THE LION KING

O ne thing that could be holding you back from achieving your
dreams is that deep down inside you don't truly believe you are
worthy of experiencing your heart's desire. Whether your dream is to
have good health, a fulfilling marriage, meaningful family relationships,
great friendships, financial independence, a job you love, or opportunities to make a valuable contribution, when you doubt your worth you
hold yourself back. When it comes to following your dreams, it probably isn't as much about achieving success as it is about *receiving* it. A
person who feels unfit or undeserving will never fully accept all God has
in store. Most of us don't realize that we are a great work of art, brimming with potential and bursting with possibilities to turn our lives
into the masterpieces they were meant to be. You were not intended to
fail; you were not created for defeat. At this very moment, extraordinary
possibilities lie dormant within you.

In the sixth story of the Narnia series by C.S. Lewis, *The Silver
Chair,* Prince Rilian was abducted by a witch, taken to her underground
kingdom, and placed under a spell in which he believed the witch was
good and he was a no-good wretch. He lived as her slave except for
two hours each day when he would awake from the spell and realize
who he really was. During those two hours the witch chained him to a
silver chair, but the rest of the time he was free. There was no need to
restrain him, since during most hours he saw himself as a grateful slave
of the witch. Eventually two schoolchildren with the aid of Puddleglum,
the Marsh-wiggle, found the prince and freed him from the power of
the spell. When they did, he recalled that enchanted life and realized that
while under the spell, he couldn't remember his true self. Most of us
are like that. We don't see ourselves clearly. It's as though a veil has
been placed over the eyes of our hearts. But we have been set free. The

apostle Paul said when anyone turns to the Lord, the veil is taken away (2 Corinthians 3:15-16).

You were made in God's image. That means you are his reflection, his likeness. Is there anyone more glorious than God? Is there anyone more creative, more caring, more thoughtful, more courageous, or more faithful? You were created to reflect his glory! Notice in the story of creation, when God made the heavens and the earth, he said, "It is good." But when he made us, he said "It is *very* good!" (Genesis 1:31). The Living Bible puts it this way: "Then God looked over all that he had made, and it was excellent in every way." Isn't it interesting that we can go out into nature and stand in amazement when we view God's creation, yet we, who were endowed with such splendor when he created us that all creation pales in comparison, don't see ourselves that way. We may be awed by a magnificent sunset, a cascading waterfall, a majestic oak tree, the brilliant colors of autumn leaves, a rainbow, or a butterfly's wings, but what do we think of ourselves? Not much sometimes. Listen to some of the personal put-downs we use when talking about God's creation. Do they sound familiar?

I'm nothing to look at.	I'm such a klutz.
I'm not very creative.	What a dummy I am.
How could I be so stupid?	I haven't got what it takes.
I'm a born loser.	I have no talent.

We justify this negative self-talk in the name of humility. However, all this self-deprecation and scorn is false modesty if we truly believe we are God's creations. How can we bring God glory when we are weighed down with this outlook? We convince ourselves it's not godly to love ourselves or have healthy self-esteem. Yet to *esteem* something merely means to hold it in high regard. The Bible clearly teaches: "Love your neighbor as much as you love yourself" (Matthew 22:39 TLB). I don't know about you, but there are some people I wouldn't want to love me as they love themselves. They obviously don't esteem themselves, and their low self-worth is one of their greatest detriments. Doubts about their true worth have cast a giant shadow over any success they do achieve and block them from experiencing the joy that could be theirs. Maybe this sounds familiar? Reaching your dreams, then, will be more about healing your heart, setting it free, and restoring your life to become all you were meant to be. Today, look deep inside yourself. You are more than you have become!

37 APPRECIATE YOUR VALUE

*It's a funny thing about life; if you refuse to accept
anything but the best, you very often get it.*
W. SOMERSET MAUGHAM

*You'll never achieve your dreams until you see the value
in what you are doing.*

Early in my career, I was privileged to speak at a unique event in California. It was a weeklong conference for entrepreneurs, and I had been invited to share my area of expertise at that time: presenting a powerful professional image inside and out. Delegates came from around the world, some to offer their insights and others to learn or be mentored. This was a diverse crowd with many faiths and beliefs represented, including Christians, Jews, atheists, agnostics, New Age advocates, and secularists. I soon realized that of the 16 presenters speaking on various aspects of success, not only was I the only woman, but I might be the only Christian. The setting was a huge auditorium with seating for thousands of attendees. There was a giant screen above the stage, and television sets lined the aisles so every person had a clear view of the speakers. The stage was flamboyantly decorated and the lights were dazzling. As an "up and coming" speaker, I was awed by the magnitude of this event and felt both exhilarated and scared.

Although it was a business event and I was not there to share my faith, I had prayed so much about this opportunity that when I got up to speak I was immediately overwhelmed by an incredible sense of God's presence. I thought, *God is going to do something miraculous today!* During my presentation, I was able to creatively share biblical principles, parts of my own faith experience, and some encouraging Bible verses. People laughed, cried, and applauded. Later, I was deeply moved as many people lined up to speak with me, offering their sentiments and thanking me for sharing my faith, which they said had spoken to their hearts.

Afterward, my client said he needed to talk with me. My first thought was, *Uh oh, what have I done?* Isn't it interesting how we assume the worst? But instead, what he told me that day became a major turning point in my career. He reminded me that I had just shared the platform with some of North America's greatest speakers, that my message was as inspiring, practical, and beneficial as theirs, and that we had all received standing ovations. Since I was not charging nearly what the others speakers were, he said I would be wise to double my fee. I could hardly believe what I was hearing. (I forgot to ask him if it would be retroactive!) He told me by not keeping my rate competitive, I was lowering the value of what I had to offer. His point was that I needed to highly regard the gift I had and not underrate it by charging too little.

I remember thinking, *Is it right to charge that much? Who would hire me at that new rate?* Then I was reminded how we always draw into our lives events and people that support our deepest perceptions of what we have to offer. Charging a rate more in line with other speakers of my caliber would be one way to ensure I would be taken seriously in this business and, consequently, have the opportunity to speak more often and offer inspiration and encouragement to larger audiences. Although it was difficult for me at first, I started to get used to the new amount and eventually accepted it. I determined in my heart that whatever fee I charged, I would always give double of myself, of my information, and of my energy. That's one thing that continues to make it easy for me to state my fee with confidence, knowing audiences will be getting twice what they paid for. In essence, it's a bargain at half price! I also decided that, regardless of my fee, I would continue to donate part of my time each month to speak for charitable and nonprofit organizations.

When that international event was over, I was standing in the hotel lobby arranging a taxi ride to the airport when I noticed some stretch limousines. I remember thinking, "Anyone who earns as much as I now do can afford to have a little fun riding in a limo!" So that's exactly what I did. Even though I hadn't actually earned it yet, the amount had become a reality in my mind. After all, that's where dreams begin.

Shortly after that, a potential client called my office to invite me to speak for a small professional group. I knew I'd have to state my new fee and started to choke up at the thought. But when she asked me if I *had* a fee, I nearly fell off my high heels! When I told her, she apologized and said since she'd never heard me speak, she didn't know I was a speaker of "that caliber." How did she know now? Because I had just told her my rate! She admitted her budget was too low, but recommended I contact her organization's head office since they regularly hire speakers like me. I followed through and was hired to speak at their annual international convention. That same company continued to engage me for other conventions year after year, and also at their regional events across the country.

Too often we hold ourselves back from achieving our dreams because we don't recognize the value of what we offer. If we sell a product or charge for a service, we're tempted to apologize for the price or surrender when customers object to our fees. Then we grudgingly negotiate special rates because we feel what we do or sell may not really be worth the cost. We end up feeling taken advantage of and usually regret giving in. Start today to see the true value in whatever you have to offer, whether it's a service, a product, or your God-given talents. When you determine to give twice the value, it'll be a good deal at any cost.

38 DISCOVER YOUR UNIQUE GIFTS

*There is someplace where your specialness can shine;
somewhere that difference can be expressed. It's
up to you to find it, and you can!*
DAVID VISCOTT

*God has given each of us the ability
to do certain things well.*
ROMANS 12:6 TLB

Y ou are one of a kind! There has never been and never will be anyone else just like you. Your personal flair, your capacity for brilliance, and your special talents are gifts that are yours alone. Every person was created to be unique and distinct and to accomplish what no one else on earth can accomplish. Bruce Barton said, "When you have anything really valuable to contribute to the world, it will come through the expression of your own personality—that single spark of divinity that sets you off and makes you different from every other living creature." You have been endowed with unique gifts, special abilities, and a distinct vision that is designed to accomplish your designated purposes. You begin to realize the true significance of your life once you discover this truth.

You've probably noticed there are certain things you do that come easy to you, things you love to do. Take a good, candid look at what you're good at and what you're not so good at. Ask others for their honest opinion and let them know you are not just fishing for compliments. The feedback you get will help you assess and confirm your natural talents and abilities. Some of your gifts have been evident since childhood. One TV host I know has been curious about human nature, and her inquisitive mind was evident from a very young age. She has always been intrigued by the opinions and perspectives of others, so questioning them on her show comes naturally to her. My husband has had a fascination with cars, engines, and speed since school age, and he now gets to live out his passion as a race car driver. Many famous comedians were once class clowns. No matter what your gifts, seek out ways to adapt your outstanding abilities to your dream.

I love speaking and writing and believe I am gifted to do them because people report that they are blessed by them. I wonder if it would have happened that way had I not been encouraged to step out and develop my unique gifts by a very special mentor. Years ago, I had the privilege of working for a boss who saw a particular strength in me that I hadn't seen in myself. He was the president of the company that hired me to do sales training, and after working for him for a short time, he suggested I start my own business. He pointed out that by working freelance as a speaker, I could make an impact on many more lives and earn more too. Although I rejected the idea at first, I have always been thankful for this man who spotted my talents before I did and dared to play the role of a mother bird pushing me from the nest. We often don't recognize what we're good at until someone points it out. There could be dozens of gifts and abilities still hiding inside you. Be receptive if others spot them in you.

Whether or not someone else notices your unique talents and abilities, you are responsible for stirring the gifts within you. When you do, your success will never depend on the condition of the economy or the job market or which careers are currently in demand. When your God-given abilities come alive, you will be able to transcend current trends and conventional wisdom. You won't be held back by others' opinions, including what they think you can or cannot accomplish. You won't be hindered by your past experiences or the apparent lack of resources, income, training, or education. Instead, you will be empowered to fulfill your purpose regardless of who you are or what your background has been.

Many highly effective people have similar qualities and common denominators; however, it's the particular combination of your individual characteristics that makes you unique. You have been endowed with distinct qualities, mannerisms, and personality traits that can contribute to your dream.

Successful dreamers don't want to be like anybody else. They recognize and appreciate their uniqueness. To clarify yours, list the activities that occupy your time, including personal pursuits, home activities, career responsibilities, and community involvement. From this list, choose three things you are particularly accomplished at, and the unique talents and abilities that make it so. Romans 12:3 TLB says to "be honest in your estimate of yourselves." Ask yourself: "When do I feel most alive? What do I enjoy doing more than anything?" Those are the areas you will focus on when following your dream. That is where you will want to concentrate the most time and energy.

Next, list people you know who have realized at least one dream in their lives. What did they do to get started, and how did they carry out their plans? What personality traits do you notice about them? What do you have in common? What makes you different from them? Part of using your unique attributes is recognizing your limitations. No one is good at everything. You are called to fulfill a particular purpose, and God wants you to use the unique abilities he has given you.

> *Be sure to do what you should, for then you will enjoy the*
> *personal satisfaction of having done your work well, and*
> *you won't need to compare yourself to anyone else.*
> GALATIANS 6:4 NLT

39 RECOGNIZE YOUR POTENTIAL FOR GREATNESS

> *We all have possibilities we don't know about.*
> *We can do things we don't even dream about.*
> DALE CARNEGIE

In the Old Testament there's a story of a man named Gideon. He was someone who didn't believe in his potential. He was without a dream. Rather than making plans for the future, he was merely trying to make a living. He saw himself as weak, poor, and trapped by his circumstances. One day he was hiding while threshing wheat to make bread for his family because he was afraid his enemies, the Midianites, would find him and take away what little he had. The angel of God came to him and said, "The LORD is with you, *you mighty man of valor*" (Judges 6:12 NKJV). Well, this was completely contrary to the way Gideon saw himself and his life. In his mind he had never been a winner or a champion. He did not see himself as brave, courageous, and fearless, or as a man of honor and influence. He was merely trying to endure his situation in life.

Gideon argued with God that he was not mighty but inadequate, a loser, and a failure. But God would not allow him to stay in this meager mind-set. Through a series of events, Gideon eventually saw the purpose for his life and changed his view of himself...and his future. Through these changes, he was empowered to defeat the Midianites, deliver his nation from bondage, and become one of the greatest judges of Israel. When the angel of the Lord had come to him and called him a "mighty man of valor," it was because he had the *potential* for greatness in him all along. God did not make him something he was not, but led him to overcome the things that were holding him back and to go on to accomplish his destiny.

You have what it takes to realize your dreams, to prosper, and to succeed. You have seeds of greatness inside of you to make a difference in your family, your church, your community, and the world. You will prove God's perfect will only as you are prepared to go beyond the dream and be empowered by the inner potential he has placed in you. You are a mighty man or woman of valor. It's time you uncovered the genuine you! Many people live out their entire lives without really knowing the full range of their potential. William Shakespeare said, "We know what we are, but know not what we may be." Each of us can achieve far beyond our limited natural horizons. There are avenues of life most of us have never even explored. Too often we limit ourselves to what we've been able to do in the past rather than believing we have unlimited potential for future achievements.

It's been said that compared to what we are potentially capable of being, we are merely half awake. We are only making use of a small part of our physical and mental resources. Research and studies have long revealed that each of us uses only three to ten percent of our natural inborn potential. Considering that, there is virtually no limit to our untapped capabilities. Once we comprehend our full potential, our vision expands and we capture the dream. Our lives become full, and we will effortlessly reach out beyond the limits of our natural possibilities.

Some people are easily deceived into believing the ticket to attaining their dreams is limited to good fortune or luck, such as winning a lottery, being born into the right family, or inheriting riches. Others believe that with the right education they are guaranteed success. If that were the case, all teachers and professors would be living their dreams, and according to the ones I've spoken with, that's not always true. Although education can be a principal key in achievement, it's still necessary to draw on your inborn potential while following your heart, regardless of how many degrees you have earned. If you truly want to reach your dreams, believe that the potential for greatness is inside you. Begin today to look at yourself as you *can* be! You don't know what you can do until you try. When you think about your highest aspirations, ask yourself, "Why not me?"

40 WHY NOT ME?

If we did all the things we are capable of doing,
we would literally astound ourselves.
THOMAS EDISON

One of the things I loved to do as a young homemaker was sew clothing for myself and my family, even though I never thought of pursuing it as a career. When I found myself in a position where I wanted to earn extra money without leaving my children, I wondered about starting a business as a seamstress. Although it would be a challenge working around two toddlers, the best part was that I could do it from home. After deciding I'd like to give it a try, doubts and fears flooded my mind. My inner, critical voice reminded me I had no formal education or training to start a business. The only experience I had was making my own clothes and home décor items, plus sewing for members of my extended family and close friends. Besides, I had no idea how much to charge or where to find clientele. I nearly abandoned the whole idea until one day I found myself musing, "Why not me? If anyone else can build a successful business as a seamstress in her home, can't I do it too?"

Although I didn't have the best workplace conditions, I did have the necessary equipment and, most of all, sewing was something I enjoyed. So I placed a small ad in our local newspaper and in a short time I received a call from a woman who eventually became one of my best clients. I will always have fond memories of Mrs. Stevens and the ways God used her to bless me and my family beyond the financial compensation. When purchasing fabric, she always bought too much. When I suggested she cut costs by getting only the required yardage, she'd reply, "Never mind, dear. You can use the leftovers to make dresses for your little ones." It took me a while to catch on to her plan, and my girls were the best-dressed kids in the neighborhood. Mrs. Stevens and my daughters had the cutest matching outfits for quite some time! This kindhearted lady graciously recommended my services to her friends, and soon business was flourishing.

Too often we focus on our limitations and lack. We think about why something can't be done. While it's true I lacked money and business experience, by focusing on the desired outcome and my personal objectives, the obstacles gradually disappeared. Refuse to base your future success on your present circumstances or past results. To attain your greatest victories, seek out your gifts and nurture them. Why settle for a JOB—Just Over Broke—when you could be fulfilling your utmost potential? Richard Byrd said, "Few men during their lifetime come anywhere near exhausting the resources dwelling within them. There are deep wells of strength that are never used."

No matter what your level of ability, you have more potential than you can ever develop in a lifetime. Commit to expanding your dreams by exercising your talents and challenging yourself to discover new sources of imagination and energy. When it comes to thinking "Why not me?" children are great examples for us. They have unlimited vision and tend to believe everything is possible unless shown otherwise. As a toddler, you believed you could do anything. There was no stopping you. You would climb up on things and think nothing of it. You knew there was a world beyond the playground and no barrier was too big for you. Your goal was always to get beyond the fence and out of the yard. But gradually your confidence was eroded by messages you received, whether from parents, teachers, coaches, or friends. Today you can't expect to reach beyond the horizon if your vision is limited to your own backyard. Take responsibility to believe in yourself. Decide that you are capable of achieving your dreams and start climbing that fence now. If anyone can do it, then why not you?

Of the hundreds of people I interviewed for this book who have achieved high levels of success in various life situations, almost everyone said that although they felt they may not be the most gifted, talented, or knowledgeable in their field, they chose to believe, "If it's possible for anyone to succeed in this particular endeavor, then why not me?" Of course, they also admitted to studying, practicing, working hard, and expecting more from themselves than anyone else ever would. But they claim it was the belief that they are just as capable as anyone that got them where they are today.

"Everyone has inside of him a piece of good news," said Anne Frank. "The good news is that you don't know how great you can be. How much you can love. What you can accomplish. What your potential is!" If you are going to be successful in living out your dreams, you have to know you are made of the right stuff. As one little boy remarked, "God doesn't make junk." Your Creator has called you to a higher purpose. After all, God doesn't call the equipped; rather he equips the called. You have been chosen for a purpose, and you'll be given what it takes to accomplish it—the skills, the talents, the gifts, and the inner resources. Believe in yourself because you can trust your heavenly Father.

41 DEVELOP SOARING CONFIDENCE

*If one advances confidently in the direction of his dreams
and endeavors to live the life which he has imagined, he
will meet with success unexpected in common hours.*
HENRY DAVID THOREAU

Confidence comes when you know who you are and which dreams you've been created to accomplish. You may not think so, but your greatest strength—and your greatest vision of your contribution to the world—lies in who you already are. You don't have to strive to be someone you're not. And you don't have to rely completely on yourself. We have been conditioned to believe confidence means self-assurance, self-reliance, and self-sufficiency. Now to me, that's pretty scary. It sure puts the pressure on us to perform and live up to certain expectations. What happens, then, is our security becomes dependant on knowing it all. Our confidence is based on never being wrong. Then we lose our inquisitiveness and don't ask questions anymore because we're supposed to have all the answers.

As children we asked lots of questions, but as we grew older, we began to think we must know everything. As a result, we try to understand all that happens to us in terms of what we already know. Yet all of our dreams lie in the area of the unknown. Growth and change strengthen our confidence, and they can only happen when we step out in faith to seek out new opportunities, new information, fresh approaches, and innovative ways of perceiving ourselves and the world around us. That comes from having God-confidence over self-confidence—faith in the one who made us and trust in his plans for our lives.

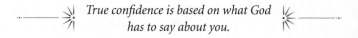

True confidence is based on what God has to say about you.

Sometimes we fall into the trap of believing our confidence is based on what other people think of us. In reality, what others think about you is none of your business. If your confidence is suffering because of the opinions of others, remember what Eleanor Roosevelt said: "No one can make me feel inferior without my permission." Often it's those with the least confidence who criticize us and try to bring us down a notch in order to elevate themselves.

Confidence is not based on what you think of yourself either. If it was, you'd be all over the place, feeling confident one day and not the next, based on how you felt about your life and circumstances at the time. True confidence is based on what God has to say about you. He says you are more valuable than precious gems. He knew you before you were born, and while you were still in your mother's womb he called you by name (Isaiah 49:1). You are on God's mind 24 hours a day: "How precious it is, Lord, to realize that you are thinking about me constantly! I can't even count how many times a day your thoughts turn toward me. And when I waken in the morning, you are still thinking of me!" (Psalm 139:17-18 TLB). Those truths alone should boost our confidence.

Maybe when you grew up you never heard the words "Great job!" "I love you!" or "You're special to me." Maybe you never had the assurance that you were loved unconditionally and appreciated for who you are. Insecurity is a *learned* behavior coming from negative experiences. Lack of confidence is an invalid belief based on what happened in our past. Today you can know you are loved and then choose to start acting like a secure person. Confidence will come naturally. Emotions always follow behaviors.

To dream great dreams, you will need to concentrate on your greatest strengths rather than your limitations. If you were asked to itemize your faults, you may not have a problem coming up with a list. But what about taking inventory of your strengths and most valuable qualities? Start keeping a success journal to record your accomplishments at the end of each day and reward yourself, even in small ways. Start an "appreciation file" where you can save notes, letters, and thank-you cards to reread on days when you need a lift. Develop an expertise in something unique by reading books and taking courses on the topic. Set goals that require you to take risks, and never verbalize that you are lacking confidence. Take God at his word when he says, "You've got what it takes to finish it up, so go to it" (2 Corinthians 8:11 MSG).

Moving beyond your limiting beliefs is a crucial step in fulfilling your potential for greatness. Are you facing some challenge in reaching your goals so you doubt your ability to carry on? Do old insecurities keep resurfacing to hold you back from moving ahead? Are you battling indecision because you're not sure you have what it takes to succeed? Whenever you doubt your ability to reach for your dreams, see yourself in your mind's eye meeting that challenge or solving the problem. Give thanks for the solution in advance. Then picture yourself filled with a surge of confidence and energy that releases all doubts and fears. Imagine your mind coming alive with fresh, new energy, crackling with new concepts, teeming with new ideas. "'For I know the plans I have for you,' declares the LORD, 'plans to prosper you and not to harm you, plans to give you hope and a future'" (Jeremiah 29:11). Equipped with this kind of confidence, you'll dare to follow your dream!

PART 7

*Condition Yourself
for Success*

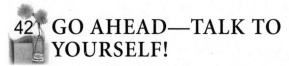

42 GO AHEAD—TALK TO YOURSELF!

*We must talk to ourselves, instead of allowing
"ourselves" to talk to us!*
MARTIN LLOYD-JONES

*A word out of your mouth may seem of no account,
but it can accomplish nearly anything—or destroy it!*
JAMES 3:5 MSG

D o you ever talk to yourself? You do if you're like most of us. But do you listen to what you are saying? A great part of following your dreams involves talking to yourself with encouraging, optimistic words rather than listening to the negative or critical messages that come as the result of years of pessimistic programming. The Bible says, "Be careful how you listen" (Luke 8:18 TLB). We can easily fall into the trap of unintentionally hearing all the incessant and damaging chatter that goes on in our heads on a subconscious level. When you want to pursue your dreams, you've got to address yourself on purpose: question yourself, preach to yourself, lecture yourself, and give yourself a good sermon now and then. Too often we don't reach for our dreams because we choose to pay attention to our own feeble reasons and excuses for not succeeding rather than taking ourselves in hand and speaking God's truth into our lives. Listen to what some of us say when it comes to reaching for our highest aspirations:

I've never accomplished anything.
I don't have what it takes.

I'm lacking the education/money/support.

I'm not too bright.

I could never handle it.

It's not worth the effort.

Nothing will work anyway.

Even if it works, I'll probably mess it up.

I can't take the pressure.

Poor me! Everything's against me.

It's difficult to take action when you are wallowing in this type of self-defeating talk and self-pitying behavior. Whether you are stuck in a state of hopelessness, or don't think you have the capacity to get beyond the stumbling blocks, or feel overwhelmed with piles of work, or think it's useless to try to focus on your dreams, you may be looking at your goals and seeing red circles with diagonal lines drawn through them. If you've fallen and you can't get up or you think something outside yourself is holding you back, remember that it's what you say about yourself and your dream that is forming your reality.

The Bible tells us our words do impact us, since there is life and death in the power of the tongue (Proverbs 18:21). In the Old Testament, Job said that what he greatly feared came upon him. If you are always saying "I'm going to go bankrupt," "This relationship just won't work," or "We'll never be able to save for a vacation," you begin to subconsciously search for ways to bring it about. When you say, "I have no energy" or "Everything I eat goes straight to my hips," your body says, "Okay, I can do this!" and then sets about finding ways to make it happen. Watch your words!

Imagine the success you'd have in achieving your dreams if you always talked to yourself like a winner instead of a loser. What if you transformed your negative self-talk into positive confessions? What if you replaced your victim language with the language of a victor? With some awareness, attention, and effort, it is possible! Here are some steps that can make it happen:

1. Say "Stop" or "Delete" when you catch yourself saying something negative and self-defeating.

2. Replace negative statements with positive ones. Instead of "I have a terrible memory," say, "I have been given a great memory with excellent recall." Rather than reinforcing "My life is full of clutter," say, "I am becoming more and more organized in every way." Tell yourself, "I am happy, healthy, and energetic; I enjoy my life, my job, and my relationships; and I'm thankful my dreams are becoming realities!" You may smile as you say these things because they're so far from the truth right now, but nonetheless, your spirit receives the seeds you've planted. Because we always reap what we sow, you begin to grow what you desire rather than more of what you don't want.

3. Learn what God's Word has to say about you: "I can do all things through Christ who strengthens me" (Philippians 4:13 NKJV); "my God shall supply all your need according to His riches in glory by Christ Jesus" (Philippians 4:19 NKJV); "for the Lord GOD will help Me; therefore I will not be disgraced" (Isaiah 50:7 NKJV); "for God has not given us a spirit of fear, but of power and of love, and of a sound mind" (2 Timothy 1:7 NKJV).

As a believer, based on who you are in Christ, get into the habit of speaking positively about yourself, to yourself. Practice daily. One of the most powerful tools in building confidence and faith is the repetition of affirming thoughts until they become a natural part of the way you talk to yourself.

> *There has never been the slightest doubt in my*
> *mind that the God who started this great work*
> *in you would keep at it and bring it to a flourishing*
> *finish on the very day Christ Jesus appears.*
> PHILIPPIANS 1:6 MSG

43 WATCH YOUR LANGUAGE

Do you want a long, good life? Then watch your tongue!
PSALM 34:12-13 TLB

I once heard a comedian say, "I accidentally played my motivational tapes backward and now I'm a failure!" While I had to smile, the truth is that words do have power. When you speak to yourself, the words you use are programming your mind, either positively or negatively. Then what you say is quite often what you get. That's why positive affirmations are so important to having a dream. To affirm is not some mystical New Age practice. It simply means to declare something and verify it. When you affirm a condition or a particular state, you validate and reinforce it. With your words, you endorse what's happening in your life, whether it's something you'd like to see happen or something you don't want.

Some people find it difficult to affirm something before it happens. It might be hard for you to say, "I've successfully overcome my obstacles and achieved my dream" while you are still struggling because you think that would be lying. Likewise, you may feel it's not right to say you have a happy marriage when you're still at odds, or that you're fit and full of energy when you feel lethargic all the time, or that your finances are flourishing while you still have debt. It may seem futile to state positive affirmations if you are experiencing one setback after another, or life's disappointments are overwhelming you, or your doctors have given up on you. But the Bible says there is a way that seems right to man but the end is going to destroy him (Proverbs 14:2). It's actually the result of your words that may kill you more than the circumstances or the diagnosis. Start speaking what you would like to see happen rather than confirming more of what you don't want. When you are weak, say you're strong (Joel 3:10). You may not feel strong at first, but if you continue to say you are weak, you will surely stay that way. What you say does influence your experience, and there is life and death in your words (Proverbs 18:21).

Even if you are not successful in attaining your goals just yet, you can plant seeds of success by the words you choose. Some people feel they are not being truthful if they don't speak what actually exists. But choosing words as a positive influence is not a method of self-deception. Instead, it is a principle God gave us for new direction.

To remove the mountain, you must speak *to* the mountain, not *about* it. Before I learned about turning dreams into realities, I used to talk a lot about my devastating and harmful situation as a battered wife. Then someone suggested I positively affirm a new and better life. That's when things began to change. Proverbs 15:23 NKJV tells us: "A man has joy by the answer of his mouth." If you don't have joy, keep check on what's coming out of your mouth. It's been said that when you get bumped, whatever you're full of will spill over!

There was a crippled man sitting at the pool of Bethesda when Jesus approached him and asked, "Would you like to get well?" (John 5:6 TLB). What a strange thing to ask a man who is crippled! He had been lying there for years waiting for a certain movement of the water so he could go down to the pool and be healed. Yet when Jesus asked him if he wanted to be healed, the man responded by talking about his problem: "I can't…for I have no one to help me into the pool at the movement of the water. While I am trying to get there, someone else always gets in ahead of me" (verse 7). Jesus was trying to get his mind off his problem and have him speak words of faith about his healing. But the man complained and kept focusing on the problem instead. Does this sound familiar? It's a trap many of us fall into.

Whenever you are experiencing challenges and roadblocks as you pursue your dream, you will be tempted to talk about the dilemmas that come along to hold you back. When that happens, you get to decide how you'll talk about it. Instead of giving in to the temptation by verbalizing what's wrong, say with Paul, "And my God shall supply all your need according to His riches in glory by Christ Jesus" (Philippians 4:19).

The words you speak are more than words. Exercise diligence over the words you use, and when it comes to your dreams, never speak anything that is not your ultimate desire for your life.

44 GOOD THINKING!

Don't believe everything you hear—
even in your own mind.
DANIEL G. AMEN, M.D.

Do not be conformed to this world, but be
transformed by the renewing of your mind.
ROMANS 12:2 NKJV

One reason many people don't pursue their dreams is because their thought lives need to be renewed. To change your life, you must change the way you think. God addressed this long before psychologists and self-help gurus understood and promoted it. "Be careful how you think; your life is shaped by your thoughts" (Proverbs 4:23 TEV). When doubt, apprehensiveness, indifference, and hopelessness seep in, they control our minds and prevent our lives from being transformed. We think about why something could not happen and the reasons our dreams are too far-fetched or impossible. We dwell on why we're not able to fulfill our goals and plans. Those thoughts soon take over and determine the direction we're heading—unless we get control over them first.

Your thoughts, and the mental images and self-talk they produce, have power. Behind every action is a thought, and behind every behavior is an attitude. If you saw Steven Spielberg's classic movie *Jaws,* you no doubt can still remember how you reacted when the great white shark was attacking everything and eating people. Just thinking about it or picturing it in your mind may cause you to stiffen with fright. I was shocked to hear that thousands of people who saw that movie reported being unable to swim in the ocean. If watching a movie can produce such a strong reaction in our minds, think about the power we have with our own thoughts.

Most of us are not even aware of the incessant chatter that goes on in our heads. You may have to play detective and "tap the phone lines" of your mind. Listen in and notice what you are thinking about yourself, your life, and your dreams. You may hear words like "impossible," "failure," "it's no use," or "why bother?" Choose to replace them by focusing on words like "possibility," "opportunity," "success," "health," "prosperity," and "fresh start." Henry Ford, back in the early 1900s said, "Whether you think you can or think you cannot, you are always right."

The results of some interesting research experiments showed that when people's thoughts were monitored, more than 80 percent of what they thought about on an average day was negative. That's on an *average* day, so can you imagine what that percentage is on a *bad* day? Where does all this negativity come from? Some is the result of what we read or hear from others, such as on the daily news. Mostly it comes from what we allow ourselves to focus on and mull over. What you dwell on creates your emotional state and eventually determines your actions and outcomes. We have a guideline in our home for controlling at least some of these negative messages. We do not listen to the evening news or read the newspaper just before going to bed. According to psychologists, the subconscious mind works while we are asleep, and the last prevailing conscious thought we have simmers there during the night. If it is a negative one, is it any wonder we wake up the next morning feeling more exhausted than when we went to bed? Be sure to program some positive thoughts into your head before going to sleep by reading something inspiring, such as a passage from God's Word, or saying a prayer of thanksgiving.

God says he has not given you a spirit of fear, but of power and of love and of a *sound mind* (2 Timothy 1:7 NKJV). A sound mind is one that is healthy, levelheaded, unwavering, and sensible. With a mind like that, you are clever, resourceful, and imaginative. You can have thoughts that are wise, rational, intelligent, and full of good judgment. A sound mind means you think in a composed and orderly fashion. Decide that you will receive the promise of that sound mind at all times. As a child of God, it is your birthright. As believers, we have the mind of Christ (1 Corinthians 2:16). He wants us to have his thoughts. What an honor to share what God is thinking! Once you realize this, you can think more clearly and decide what you will and will not allow into your mind. Then you can confidently pursue your highest aspirations and greatest dreams.

45 FOLLOW YOUR HEART

Whether you turn to the right or to the left,
your ears will hear a voice behind you saying,
"This is the way; walk in it."
ISAIAH 30:21

Whatever you call it—a hunch, intuition, a gut feeling, or your heart's desire—God has many ways of getting your attention. If you're like most of us, you usually ignore that still small voice within. Instead, we'll more often choose to listen to what our heads tell us. We can easily get caught in the snare of trusting logic and what makes sense rather than inner nudgings. When that happens, we tend to trust outside sources or believe others know more and have better ways to reach a dream than we do. But if you listen to your heart, you'll discover that you can know better than anyone else what's best for you. That's because your heart is usually God speaking to you, and through prayer and faith it is possible to hear clearly as he directs and guides you.

When it's the voice of God, following your
heart will always be empowering and beneficial
for your life and others.

It takes practice and courage, and it isn't always easy, but following what God plants in your heart will not lead you astray. You may be so used to listening to your head rather than your heart that it may be scary at first. Yet your heart can reveal the answers you are seeking. Those "holy hunches" and "divine promptings" are God's way of getting your attention. His Spirit is always ready to guide, direct, and protect. He can provide an answer when you thought there wasn't one and solutions where there didn't appear to be any. Be assured that you can know what's right for you as you dream and set goals. Here are some steps you can take:

1. Make a decision to listen to your heart when it comes to improving your life. Once you recognize that God speaks

to you that way and there is a spiritual source of super-natural direction available to you, you'll have more assur-ance when it comes to altering what's been taking place.

2. Learn to distinguish between your head and God's voice. For example, when you have a decision to make, your head may tell you to trust only common sense and what you have learned from past experiences. On the other hand, through your heart, God's Spirit will give you inner hunches and promptings that may seem unconven-tional or peculiar at times. "I advise you to obey only the Holy Spirit's instructions. He will tell you where to go and what to do" (Galatians 5:16 TLB).

3. Don't confuse *following your heart* with impulsive behavior. Although acting impulsively now and then may enable you to be less rigid and loosen up to pursue bigger dreams, some spontaneous decisions result in reckless and irresponsible conduct. When it's the voice of God, following your heart will always be empow-ering and beneficial for your life and others. Your dreams can be achieved as you act in trustworthy and conscientious ways.

4. Become familiar with how it *feels* to follow your heart. Rather than being panicky, anxious, uneasy, or stifled, when you are truly hearing from God in your innermost being, you will feel calm, confident, joyful, energized, and free—even though your dream may pull you from your comfort zone.

5. Know that few things in life worth striving toward are risk free. Following your heart may mean taking a posi-tive risk. That means doing your homework, weighing the pros and cons, understanding the outcomes, and making your decision to take a risk based on a combi-nation of faith and fact finding. In nearly every instance, when you make a choice based on your core beliefs, true values, and inner ideals, you will not regret it.

So don't shush that inner voice. Go to the Word and test it to see if God is trying to get your attention. Listening to the true message of your heart—verified against God's principles in his Word—ensures you will follow a path that is just right for you. And that makes it easier to leave your comfort zone when you want to achieve your dreams.

46 TAP YOUR CREATIVITY

*When I was six, I made my mother a little
hat—out of her new blouse!*
LILY DACHE, HAT DESIGNER

[O God,] you are the God of miracles and wonders!
PSALM 77:14 TLB

People who know how to create new ideas are the ones who will turn dreams into realities and prosper regardless of the future of this world. Most of us use our minds to contemplate and store the ideas of others. But creative thinkers have discovered that the human brain is capable of so much more. As human beings we have been blessed with the amazing ability to generate new ideas—ideas that can take our dreams to the highest level.

There really is nothing mystical about creativity. It's not some unexplained power available to a select few. If you can think, you can imagine; and if you can imagine, you can create new ideas. In order to fulfill your dreams, you'll need to use your inborn creativity. Your success depends on your ability to formulate innovative solutions, to creatively overcome obstacles, and to devise imaginative new ways to do things.

Start by asking God to stir your creativity. After all, he is the original creator of all things in heaven and earth. Long before man ever designed and built suspension bridges, the spider demonstrated engineering feats of amazing brilliance. The development of radar and sonar systems is seen as a miracle of science, yet bats can fly around a room without hitting anything because they emit supersonic sound pulses. Bird nests display high levels of skill in masonry and weaving, bees air condition their hives with their wings, beavers build dams from trees and mud, and wasps manufacture a type of paper. God's creatures are evidence of his incredible creativity. Since we are made in his image, that creativity is an inherent trait in us too.

The starting point in activating creativity is when you get that basic idea. Maybe it occurs to you that you want to write the script for a play or compose a song for the piano. Or perhaps you have an idea for a cost-cutting measure for the company you work for, a way to encourage and inspire students with special challenges in the school where you teach, or a business concept for starting your own company. This initial insight can come to you years before you actually take action. Next, you'll want to investigate the possibilities and examine all your options. Then let the idea sit for a while.

Creative insights will eventually come to you, and they usually happen at the least-expected times. Many creative people claim their most innovative thoughts come to them in the bathroom, whether showering, bathing, or shaving. I call these ideas "bathroom inspirations" and tend to get them while I'm styling my hair or brushing my teeth. People are not sure why this happens except that perhaps it's because we are isolated from most of the outside influences that distract us, leaving our thoughts to flow freely. When I am traveling by car, plane, or train, I like to use my commuting time for generating new ideas. Being alone and away from the demands of my perpetual to-do list, I have the freedom to pray, dream up new projects, devise better approaches to personal or business challenges, brainstorm ideas for a client, or come up with inspiring concepts for my next seminar or book project. My travels end up being more pleasant because I have something ready for my imagination to work on as I pass the time. Rather than feeling bored if I'm stuck in traffic or waiting for the next flight, those spare minutes become immensely constructive. I carry a notepad and pen or small tape recorder with me at all times for capturing those ideas.

The creativity needed to fulfill our dreams is within each one of us. The Bible says, "Now glory be to God who by *his mighty power at work within us* is able to do far more than we would ever dare to ask or even dream of—infinitely beyond our highest prayers, desires, thoughts, or hopes" (Ephesians 3:20 TLB). That power is God's Spirit, and he is working within you for the fulfillment of your dream. He promises to do *immeasurably* or *exceeding abundantly* beyond all that you can ask for, think about, or imagine. As incredible as your inborn creativity is, you cannot possibly dream a dream as big as the one God has for you.

47 STIMULATE INNOVATIVE THINKING

I turned my mind to understand, to investigate
and to search out wisdom.
ECCLESIASTES 7:25

During one long flight overseas, I said to my husband, "It always amazes me how these huge jets, with all these people and their baggage, can stay up in the air. It's incredible." Being the left-brained logical one, he replied, "Not really. It's the very nature of a plane because of the way it's designed. Planes are created to fly, and it would actually be difficult for one not to stay up in the air. That's just the way they are put together." Being the right-brained creative one, his comment got me thinking about how our imagination and innovative abilities are very much like that. It's the way we are put together. There's nothing magical or mystical about it. Using your innate creativity is not some form of mental gymnastics or New Age philosophy. Sometimes I think we forget that our imaginative, creative self is God-given. It's our very nature and an intrinsic and natural function. It's not abnormal for us to soar on our dreams. This creative feature is what gives birth to our dreams. Once our dreams are planted in our hearts, God can use our creativity to bring them to our attention. Creativity is an incredible gift. Let's not take it lightly. Being innovative allows us to advance and progress with our dreams, making changes for the better.

Our thoughts come to us in two ways. People who study the human brain tell us that when we think, we use both logic and imagination.

In logical thinking, we're drawing on the left side of our brains. So you want to have "wisdom—that is, knowing and doing right—and common sense" (Proverbs 3:21 TLB). The right side is where we do creative processing. Of course, logic is crucial because it allows us to tell right from wrong and separate good ideas from bad ones. With that side of our brain, we reason, analyze, evaluate, contemplate, investigate, scrutinize, and probe into any new ideas and concepts. That's what enables us to make healthy choices and wholesome decisions. With right-brain thinking we are exposed to the wondrous part of us that goes beyond what is rational and explicable. The creative self is unrestricted by logic. It stays untouched by all our doubts, inhibitions, and narrow thinking, those obstacles that hold us back from using our innovative and artistic abilities. Logic and analytical thinking are extremely important when you are dreaming big dreams, but they can take you only part of the way. Before you even get to analyzing and dissecting your ideas, there has to be a dream. Your dreams are put in your heart by God and are not usually found through systematic, diagnostic thinking and reasoning.

As children, before we fully developed our logic, it was easy to draw on our intrinsic creativity. But as we grew, we became conditioned to trust only what we could prove logically. Even our education system, as good as it is, encourages linear thinking over creativity and imagination. Now it's up to us to return to God's plan, to recapture and nurture the innovative side of us, and to begin dreaming once again.

Creativity is like a muscle. The more you use it, the stronger it becomes. There are many ways to kindle your creativity, to jump-start your imagination, and to strengthen your inner resourcefulness. When a new idea comes to you out of the blue, read about it, talk to others, ask questions, browse the Internet, take notes, and explore as much as you can. When you have done that, take a break and allow all the information you've gathered to ripen. Leave it alone and forget about it for a while. When you return to it, you will find things suddenly falling into place. This happens to me all the time when I am working on a writing project, doing a crossword or jigsaw puzzle, or trying to think of the title of a movie or a person's name. If possible, get out into nature and enjoy a brisk walk, have a snooze, or work on another project. When you can't get away, take a moment to read something funny or a few pages of fiction, listen to classical music (which is very inspiring!), glance through a magazine or a photo album, or doodle with some fluorescent markers. Doing something technical like puttering on your car or learning a new computer program, will also spark creative juices. You'll see answers you didn't notice before. Get in the habit of recording your ideas. Always be prepared with a notepad and pen or mini-recorder. I have even called home and left my ideas on my voice mail for later retrieval.

Associate with other creative people and brainstorm new ideas together. Get in the habit of doing crosswords, number games, brainteasers, and jigsaw puzzles. Play group games such as charades and word games. Travel to different places and meet new people. Take up a new hobby or sport or try some form of art, for instance drawing, sculpting, painting, woodworking, or needlework. All of these will arouse your senses and invigorate your creativity. You'll see new opportunities for creative expression all around you. Remember, God wired you to be creative so that your dreams can come true. It's up to you to nurture that gift.

48 LOOK TO YOUR *OWN* HEART

Don't let anybody steal your dream!
DEXTER YAGER

When you want to go beyond a dream, make sure it's *your* dream! There's a big difference between looking to your own heart's desires and those of other people. Whether it's your family, your spouse, your siblings, good friends, coworkers, or your boss, those who know and care about you may have a completely different vision for you and your life. We often fall into the trap of accepting others' ideas as to what we should do and become. To truly fulfill a dream, it has to be yours.

Is there something stirring and bubbling inside you that you've always wanted to do but assumed it wouldn't fit other people's expectations? Maybe someone has convinced you that your dream isn't practical or reasonable. Perhaps you have listened so long that even you believe you're not capable of achieving your dream. Since I wrote my book *When Your Past Is Hurting Your Present,* one comment I hear more than any other is, "If only I had followed my heart's desire instead of listening to other people, I wouldn't be where I am today." I am convinced from the overwhelming response I have received from that book that almost everyone has a dream lying dormant within them, a suppressed desire gone unfulfilled much too long. That's one of the main reasons I wanted to write *this* book. Now I encourage each person by giving him or her hope, reminding the person that "it's never too late to go beyond a dream." I didn't have my first book published until I was close to 50 years old. You can achieve your dream too!

Allison told me she had always wanted to act and pursue a career in the theater. From the time she was a little girl, she would put on plays, musicals, and variety shows for her family and friends. But when she expressed her desire to follow this path as a career, her mother and father told her it wasn't a practical dream. Her family felt that she couldn't make a living that way and encouraged her to get a college education so she could get a "real" job. She agreed to do that, and once she graduated, she had a hard time getting motivated to search for work. Then she realized the reason she was not seriously hunting for a job was that routine work had no appeal to her. At about that time, she started to attend a church that had a drama team, which she immediately joined. When the leader recognized that she had a definite talent in acting, he recommended she train at a school for theater arts. This experience led her to a career in acting and singing that she has pursued with passion. Now she blesses many people through the dramatized sermons she writes and produces. Allison's dream got diverted for a while as she tried to fulfill others' expectations instead of the desires of her own heart. Although she had achieved her parents' dream for her, in order to be fulfilled she needed to pursue a vision of her own.

If you have been following someone else's leading rather than your own dream, you can still benefit in the end. You may find yourself in a position where your natural gifts will be uncovered. When I was raising my family, I wanted to earn extra income and not be gone from the children for long hours. My family and friends all said to me, "You're tall. You should be a model." (As if that's the only requirement!) However, I did take a course at a local agency and went on to model professionally for several years. It was fun and the income was helpful, but I didn't feel truly fulfilled until I was given the opportunity to teach modeling classes at the agency. What I especially enjoyed were the segments on self-improvement for women and men who did not necessarily want to become models but wanted to have more confidence and poise. From that time on, I knew I was cut out to be a speaker and presenter. Although others saw me pursuing modeling as a full-time profession, that experience helped uncover my innate skills and talents.

Perhaps you have been occupied fulfilling the dreams other people have for you. It's time to find one of your own. What have you done that excites you? What do you do well? Do you have a special talent? Is there some interest you have that could become an occupation? Maybe it isn't what everybody else sees you doing. Perhaps up until now you haven't even seen yourself doing it. Your dream could be hidden somewhere in your keenest interests and former successes. Dig deep for it is definitely hidden in your heart's deepest longing.

PART 8

The Cost of Success

49 BE WILLING TO PAY THE PRICE

If I had eight hours to chop down a tree,
I'd spend six sharpening my axe.
ABRAHAM LINCOLN

A few years ago a business associate said to me, "Sue, you are one of those ten-year overnight success stories!" While even today I don't see myself as having *arrived* (I still have too many magnificent dreams stirring inside me!), I do understand what he meant. It probably seemed to outsiders that I appeared on the speaker and author scene overnight, even though I had been working hard to fulfill my dream for years. It was Michelangelo who said, "If people knew how hard I had to work to gain my mastery, it wouldn't seem wonderful at all."

Many people don't realize that success comes with a price tag attached. To achieve the dream, there is always a cost. Any worthy goal requires a huge investment of time, effort, hard work, sacrifice, and energy. My dream involved long hours of research, taking courses, reading books, and listening to tapes to acquire a solid knowledge base that I developed into a series of inspirational talks, seminars, and workshops. After that I had to fine-tune my presentation style, practice delivery techniques and mannerisms, and hone my business skills, which included learning how to be a top-notch salesperson, an office administrator, and a business executive all at once. Even though your dream may involve following your natural calling and fulfilling your God-given destiny, there is still a cost involved.

When up-and-coming speakers and authors ask me to mentor them, I am hesitant to tell them all that goes on behind the scenes because I wonder if they will get discouraged. Yet I believe they need to know the cost because without understanding there is a price to pay and what that entails, they probably wouldn't stand a chance of surviving the roadblocks and pitfalls that are sure to come along. On the other hand, when the dreams are truly their calling, I believe they'll be willing to pay that price.

Regardless of what career or personal aspirations you have, there are some steps you can take to ensure you'll be able to pay the price to reach your goal. Take these ideas and adapt them to your own dreams.

The first step for me as a speaker and author was to have a *sense of mission*. Every time I imagined sharing my message with audiences, I got excited about the potential for change and the positive results people would experience in their personal journeys to overcome barriers and discover their own destiny. I believed I had something to share with them that would impact them into eternity. To convey that message, I developed a series of powerful, concise talks I would eventually deliver. The same was true for writing books. I didn't want to invest a lot of effort to merely entertain people, although I love to know people are laughing while reading my books and attending my programs. And it wasn't my goal to earn a lot of money either, although the financial rewards enable me to give more.

With a dynamic message written, the next step in my investment was to *rehearse* and tape myself giving my best performance, as though I were on stage at a paid engagement. To make this exercise as authentic as possible, I dressed in a business suit, stood in front of a full-length mirror, and held a microphone. Well, it wasn't an actual microphone, it was a banana, but it worked! My goal was to replicate an experience as close to the real thing as possible. While the tape recorder ran, I gave my full address without starting over after tripping on my words or making a mistake, since there wouldn't be such luxury in a real-life setting. Then I played the tape back while reinputting the material, making corrections, tweaking, and modifying the content. I also decided whether my voice inflections and expressions needed to be altered. Then I went through the whole process again…and again…and again, until I had it down pat.

After weeks of fine-tuning my message and honing my delivery style to the best of my ability, I knew it was time to practice by trying it out on real audiences. I decided the best way was to speak for free. It would give me the opportunity to find out what worked and what didn't. I searched the yellow pages and called every organization I thought would need a speaker but may not have a budget. Sometimes Cliff would come home and ask me if I had any work yet. I told him I had worked for eight hours, which was true since I had been on the phone all day calling potential clients, asking, "Do you need a speaker for your group…at no charge?" After each engagement, I followed up by asking for feedback. It was all valuable, although some comments made me cringe. Even these were helpful as I continued to revamp and polish my presentations. When the remarks were exceptionally positive, I asked to have them in writing. Since I knew my request would probably fall to the bottom of a busy client's to-do list, I jotted down the comments they made while on the phone, then offered to write them in the form of a letter so all they had to do was transfer it to company letterhead. These clients were most grateful that I would be so helpful. In no time, I had a collection of fantastic referral letters to send out in promotional packages to future clients—the paying kind!

In the beginning, I put in countless hours without being paid. I went on to work for many months in exchange for an honorarium before earning a "real" income. But one thing I learned was if you are willing to pay the price in the beginning, you can reap the benefits for the rest of your life.

50 INVEST IN YOUR DREAM

Our greatest lack is not money for any undertaking,
but rather ideas. If the ideas are good, cash will
somehow flow to where it is needed.
ROBERT SCHULLER

Behind the accomplishment of every great dream is the story of some incredible investment, whether it's one of time, money, energy, or effort. There are a lot of sincere and gifted people out there who never quite achieve their dreams. Often one thing that separates them from those who succeed is a wholehearted dedication to making an investment. Whether you're investing your life savings, a lot of hard work to hone your skill, or the time to gain experience, it's a willingness to sacrifice and do whatever is required to reach the goal that makes the difference between an average life and one that is exceptional. To go from ordinary to extraordinary, it's your investment that will take you to the next level and enable you to endure the setbacks or face the challenges that go along with achievement.

At one time I was presented with an incredible opportunity to invest in my dream—and I nearly turned it down. I suffered a *poverty mentality* and always thought that once the money ran out there wouldn't be any more. In fact, whenever I ate in a restaurant, I was in the habit of looking down the menu at the prices first and then choosing my meal accordingly, based on the least costly item available. I'm sure this resulted from years of being in a position where I really had to order that way if I wanted to have a restaurant meal. To this very day, even though, thankfully, I can afford to enjoy most anything I'd like, I still catch myself ordering that way. With that mind-set, it's easy to understand why it was such a challenge for me to even consider taking a particular course that would give me the credentials I needed to pursue one of my dreams—to be a professional image and wardrobe consultant. The course was called "Image Improvement" and was taught by Joanne Wallace, who has since become a good friend. This new career direction seemed to be a great complement to what I was already doing as a speaker and trainer with a nutrition and cosmetic company, and it was something I strongly believed I would be good at. However, with the price of the one-week course, including flight and hotel costs, totaling thousands of dollars, I felt sick at the mere thought. Cliff and I were newly married, and he encouraged me to go for it. I took out a small business loan to cover the costs and went ahead. That short course was packed with tools and techniques that gave me what I needed to open up a whole new business! Eventually the acquired knowledge and skills catapulted me to another level in the speaking world that was beyond my wildest dreams. That experience truly helped get me over the fear of investing in myself and my goals.

What can you invest in to support your dream? For you, it may mean paying for help or hiring professionals to lighten the burden of your workload. If you have started a small company, it might mean investing in a bookkeeper or an accountant. If you work from your home, you may want to invest in your sanity by hiring an assistant or someone to manage your website. As a stay-at-home mom, it may be a good idea to have a mother's helper to keep the kids busy while you catch up on some chores, do some reading, or pursue a hobby.

Let me share with you one piece of advice I received that literally set me free to follow my dreams. One mentor suggested that I stop doing tasks and activities that were not contributing to my highest goals and aspirations, even though I was good at them. You may be good at washing windows or mowing the lawn, but maybe your time is worth more. While I love to paint and wallpaper my home, I had to ask myself if doing those things was contributing to the achievement of my highest goals. Now, if you really love to do those things and find them to be stress-relieving, and not stress-activating, then they *are* contributing to a major goal—living a stress-free life. So go ahead and do them. I am capable of cleaning my own home and don't mind doing it, but I have come to realize that this is not the best use of my time if I have even higher aspirations of speaking more often and writing more books. (Besides, I remind myself that I am creating job opportunities, and there is someone out there who appreciates having that work.) Recognizing where I should and should not be spending my time and energy has freed me to pursue my dreams. However, when I'm to take a casserole or cake to the next potluck dinner, you can be sure I will be making it myself because cooking and baking are my relaxing hobbies.

Maybe your investment is one of disciplined effort and hours of practice to excel at your chosen trade, sport, craft, or profession. Perhaps it's reading more books, building a success library, taking courses and seminars, attending conferences, or listening to educational CDs. Maybe it means hiring an assistant, delegating more, or training someone to help. Your investment may mean spending more time in prayer, reading from God's Word, or getting involved in a Bible-study course. Only you can decide what kind of an investment you will make.

What is keeping you from fulfilling the mission God created you for? Make the investment and see where he takes you!

51 STAY COMMITTED... NO MATTER WHAT

There's a difference between interest and commitment.
When you're interested in doing something, you do it
only when it's convenient. When you're committed to
something, you accept no excuses, only results.

KEN BLANCHARD, COAUTHOR,
THE ONE MINUTE MANAGER

I f you want the energy to create the show," says Dan Sullivan, Strategic Coach president and founder, "sell the tickets first." This is one of my favorite quotes because of an experience I had as a child. I was just eight years old when I inadvertently took on my very first business venture. It taught me a valuable lesson about commitment that has played a major role to this day when it comes to attaining my dreams. It began one summer afternoon when my school friend Diane and I decided it would be fun to present a talent show in the basement of my home for the people who lived in our neighborhood. I can still picture where we sat brainstorming that day—at a child-size picnic table in my backyard under the shade of an old pear tree. We eagerly planned our variety show with vivid descriptions of the entire event, including the other kids we would recruit to perform, the dazzling costumes they would wear, how the stage would be brightly lit and decorated, and who would be in the audience. Next we created some fancy tickets using construction paper, glue, and crayons. The price was to be two cents (well, it *was* 50 years ago!), and the production date was the following Saturday afternoon. With all necessary information on the completed tickets, we enlisted Diane's brother Denis and my sister Lois to help sell them, and for the rest of the day, we made our way through the neighborhood. People were so receptive and kind, and some paid for their whole family to come. By the time we were done, we had collected a big bag of pennies, and although they amounted to less than two dollars, it seemed like a lot of money to us kids. It also meant a lot of people would be coming to see our show.

When my mom came outside and found the four of us sitting on the front porch crying our hearts out, she asked what could possibly be so devastating. We explained to her what we had done and how we'd collected all this money. She thought that was good news, but we went on to tell her the problem. There really wasn't a show! We had become so engrossed in making and selling tickets and convincing people to come, that we had neglected to actually coordinate the program. Now, with the reality of all these people coming in a few days to see something that didn't really exist, we were panic-stricken.

My parents must have been the greatest parents on earth. Right away Mom enlisted Dad, and the two of them helped us finalize a great show. First they called all my aunts, uncles, and cousins and pleaded with them to be there—in case no one else showed up. Then they rented a projector and some movies just to add variety to the program. Dad put together a makeshift stage in the basement and hung a sheet for a curtain. The record player was brought down to play music for those of us who would be tap dancing, singing, and twirling batons. The others performers were called together and roles were assigned such as reading poetry and playing musical instruments. Then rehearsals began. Mom loved to sew and quickly made up some pretty fancy costumes and stage decorations with leftover fabrics. On the day of the production, we made popcorn and put it in paper bags to sell for a penny. By the end of the day, we had earned $3.87 and donated it to the Red Cross. The local newspaper did a small write-up, and I still have the clipping pasted in my scrapbook!

One very powerful lesson Diane and I learned was that when you finally decide to move forward with your dream, it's best to burn all your bridges so there's no chance of quitting. For us, once those tickets were sold it would have been worse to turn back and cancel the whole thing. We were committed and had to follow through. Too often, when people have the option, they turn back from pursuing their dreams before they have the chance to get rooted.

Choose to put yourself in a position where there's no turning around. Where you can't get your money back, and there's no way out of it no matter what you do. Whether you're committing to marriage, a new business venture, or a ministry opportunity, throw yourself into the dream wholeheartedly with no thought of getting out. As scary as it might be, once you're committed to that degree, you will get very creative in finding ways to make it successful. Paul Hogan, the actor who played Crocodile Dundee, said, "The secret to my success is that I bit off more than I could chew and then chewed as fast as I could."

I am so glad my parents didn't simply have us return all the money, but instead helped us go through with our original commitment. I know it would have been a lot easier for them, but what a valuable life lesson we kids learned. That experience has impacted nearly every aspect of my work and personal life.

What dream do you have waiting for you to commit to fully? What could happen if you burned all your bridges? Take a big bite and get chewing!

52 BE PREPARED FOR YOUR OPPORTUNITY

For tomorrow…the Lord will do a great miracle.
JOSHUA 3:5 TLB

*Be ready when opportunity comes. Luck is the time
when preparation and opportunity meet.*
ROY D. CHAPIN JR.

People with big dreams often sabotage their success because they are not ready when opportunities present themselves. Contrary to popular opinion, success doesn't depend nearly as much on whom you know or being at the right place at the right time as it does on being ready. We tend to think that we'll get everything in order once our dream happens. The truth is that when we're prepared for opportunity, God will open the door. Football coach Paul "Bear" Bryant said, "It's not the will to win, but the will to prepare to win that makes the difference."

When I had been encouraged to turn my dream into a mental movie, I saw myself as a national sales trainer wearing a red suit, carrying a leather briefcase, flying across the country, and speaking to large audiences. Since I had never done those things, I knew I would have to take steps to be better prepared when the opportunity came. I actually went to a store, tried on all the red suits, and modeled leather briefcases in front of a mirror to get a sense of what it would feel like. I put everything back on the shelf since I couldn't afford to buy them at the time, but told the salesclerk I'd be back. Then I began preparing my sales team with training programs that would enable them to increase their sales—the same types of presentations that I dreamed of offering to audiences nationwide in the new position. Eventually, because of the extraordinary results that my team produced, I was given the opportunity to speak at several conferences, which led to getting my dream job. When the phone call came I said, "I knew you'd be calling, and I know where the suit and briefcase are!" Also, I had perfected my sales presentations by practicing them so often in front of my own small sales team that I felt comfortable speaking to larger groups. My preparation was rewarded!

When I eventually started my own speaking company, I dreamed about writing magazine articles that would benefit business people. I decided to devote one entire summer to writing 12 articles, one for each month of the upcoming year, without knowing when or where they would be published. Early in the fall, I got a call from a business magazine asking me if I would consider writing articles for them. You guessed it! What they requested was one per month for the next year. If your dreams suddenly appeared, are you ready? Charles Kingsley said, "Have thy tools ready. God will find thee work." We tend to think we'll get ready once the dream happens. The truth is the dream will more likely happen once you have everything in place.

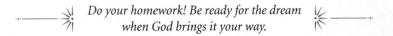

Do your homework! Be ready for the dream
when God brings it your way.

Professional performers—actors, entertainers, comedians, dancers, musicians—know that they have to do a lot of preparation. My niece Lee-Anne Galloway took tap dancing, jazz, and ballet lessons from the time she was four years old. Then, in her teens, she taught dance as a part-time job. Later on she started singing with a jazz ensemble and taking voice lessons. Eventually she attended the renowned Randolph Academy for Performing Arts to study many forms of dance plus singing and acting. She felt that learning more than just dance would give her more options. Through it all she discovered she had hidden talents in those other areas as well. She went on to take bit parts in musical productions, sing and dance at special events, and choreograph and teach children's programs at her academy. What she was doing was fine-tuning her skills until one day, at the age of 22 she was ready to accept the dream role she had waited for—performing on a cruise ship with a full-year contract to travel the world! Now it's exciting for us to receive photographs of Lee-Anne on the glaciers of Alaska, the beaches of Hawaii, the streets of Peru, and the Great Wall of China. After years of preparation, she is living her dream.

Abraham Lincoln said, "I will study and prepare myself, and then someday my chance will come." Whether being prepared involves groundwork, research, training, rehearsals, or buying equipment, successful dreamers prepare themselves in advance. Don't sabotage your dream by not being ready when your big break shows up. Make sure you have done your homework, investigated all your options, checked out needed supplies, honed your craft, and fine-tuned your skills. Then you'll be ready for the dream when God brings it your way.

53 TAKE ACTION

*Those who say it can't be done are
usually interrupted by others doing it!*

*Let your enthusiastic idea at the start
be equalled by your realistic action now.*
2 CORINTHIANS 8:11 TLB

In a rural community, a particular farmer was known for his magnificent vegetable gardens. Visitors would come from miles around to view his exquisite crops, and he would gladly take them on tours. One day a minister was standing in the middle of the farmer's field. As he looked up to the heavens, he proclaimed, "Isn't God good to give you all this?" The farmer replied, "Yes, I thank God every day. In fact, I happen to pray over my crops and ask him to bless them. I am very aware of his goodness to me. But I want to add something. You should have seen this place when God had it all to himself!" After all, "faith by itself, if it is not accompanied by action, is dead" (James 2:17). Success on earth is a partnership. It comes as a result of faith combined with action.

Some people think that with enough faith in God, everything will fall into place and dreams will drop from the sky. They never consider the hard work that must take place right along with their prayers. They refer to the passage in Matthew 6:25-26 TLB where Jesus says, "Look at the birds! They don't worry about what to eat—they don't need to sow or reap or store up food—for your heavenly Father feeds them. And you are far more valuable to him than they are." Some interpret this passage as meaning since God will take care of them, they don't need to act. They can sit back and watch to see how God will bring about results. I'm sure when these people have needs, they must believe that someone will miraculously come along to put food in the fridge, gas in their cars, clothes on their back, and pay all the bills. They simply wait for God to come and take care of everything.

While we know God does provide and perform miracles, let's take a good look at this passage. How does God provide for the birds? They aren't ordering worms through room service and waiting it out until God personally delivers each meal. It's true that God feeds the birds, but he does it by providing what they need. He makes the food available, and they go out and dig for it. He provides the supplies for a nest too, but the birds gather those supplies and build their own homes. In the same way, God looks after our needs. There is never a need to worry about our provisions; however, there are actions required of us to see our dreams fulfilled.

Instead of taking action, some people spend their time gathering knowledge, storing information, and talking about their dream project. While those are crucial steps in attaining any goal, knowledge is only potential success until it's combined with action. It's not what you know but *what you do* with what you know that makes the difference. For example, how much knowledge do you currently have about the importance of diets, nutrition, and exercise? In today's culture, we are bombarded with knowledge, but what we need even more is to take action! Dreamers who consistently produce extraordinary results have specific action plans. They know that an effective, productive life doesn't merely happen. Definite action steps produce definite results. "A dream comes through much activity, and a fool's voice is known by his many words" (Ecclesiastes 5:3 NKJV). Dreams come true when we spend more time praying and working toward achieving them than talking about what we plan to do.

Outline some steps you can take to get closer to seeing your dream happen. Maybe it's as simple as making a few phone calls or doing research at the library or on the Internet. Do you need to enlist the help of others? Perhaps there is someone you can ask to mentor you. Is there some training you need to get? Maybe you need financial backing to make your dream a reality. Do you need to apply for licenses, purchase equipment, or establish relationships with certain individuals? Write a detailed plan outlining all the steps required to accomplish your goal. Be sure to transfer those steps to your daily to-do list so you are doing something each and every day that brings you closer to the dream. Abandon all your excuses. Quit stalling. Stop procrastinating. There will never be ideal conditions, so take action now.

54 GET READY FOR HARD WORK

Success seems to be connected with action. Successful men keep moving. They make mistakes but they don't quit.
CONRAD HILTON

Work! Thank God for the swing of it, for the clamoring, hammering ring of it.
ANGELA MORGAN

An effective, productive life doesn't just happen, and dreams don't simply fall out of the sky. Great lives and great dreams require definite plans, strategic action steps, and lots of hard work. It's been said that opportunities come dressed in work clothes and that's why so many people miss them! You don't often get paid for what you know, but rather what you do with what you know. Knowledge is a great foundation, but it is only potential success until it's combined with hard work. For example, you may have knowledge about the importance of eating right and exercising, but until you take action, it won't do you one bit of good.

When I study the successful people in my audiences, I have noticed there is one attribute more than anything else that separates them from average people. Exceptional achievers take action and are willing to work hard at their dreams. They eagerly invest the necessary time and energy, tackle the tough tasks, and confront the challenging roadblocks. They stick with the difficult aspects of their work until the dream happens. Successful people are action-oriented. After discovering their vision; deciding on the dream; setting goals, objectives, and plans; breaking big steps into smaller ones; envisioning success; and expecting a miracle, they get to work.

I learned all about this during my early sales career. While working with a direct sales company, aside from selling products I recruited several hundred people as part of my division. This meant that I made a profit on products I personally sold and also earned commissions on the sales made by my team. Because I wanted my group to excel, I provided as much motivation for them as possible. About 20 of my top salespeople lived in my region, so I was able to meet with them on a regular basis. Monthly recognition meetings were combined with potluck suppers in my home. We'd have a great time acknowledging and celebrating successes. Balloons were prepared ahead of time with inspirational messages inside and one that read "Winner" for the door prize. There were games, additional prizes, good food, and lots of laughter. Everyone went home with an award for their accomplishments that month. While I included some sales training at each meeting, I realized my group needed something more intensive. So I designed an eight-week course with two-hour sessions to be held each Tuesday afternoon. The sessions included training on every aspect of success, from setting goals and closing the sale to product knowledge, handling rejection, organizing a home office, and maintaining life balance. I prepared a binder for every participant with sections for each of the topics, and typed out worksheets and handouts on my old typewriter. On the night I decided to announce this mandatory training, I knew I would be met with a lot of objections including "I don't have a car," "I'd need a babysitter," and "I don't have time." So I created a big sign with a list describing ten objections and added, "Please take a number and be seated." This let them know I was prepared for their concerns and had an answer. When the first Tuesday came around, I organized drivers to pick up those without their own vehicles. I hired a babysitter, picked up the children, and delivered them along with a box of cookies, a container of juice, and a bag of toys, to the sitter's house. Then I went to the restaurant where I had arranged to use the back room for free. Part of the deal was that at least one person would have a meal there, so I would eat lunch alone and occasionally a team member would join me. The program was ongoing so my team knew they could recruit new members at any point and, with the sessions being run consecutively, each new recruit would eventually get the full course. I kept this program going for two years. At the end of that time I was earning monthly bonus checks for thousands of dollars. After that, I was asked to do similar training sessions for the company nationally, which was a dream come true for me. The hard work paid off in many ways. As Booker T. Washington put it, "Excellence is to do a common thing in an uncommon way." There is nothing magical about achievement. If you always do more than is expected, you will be sure to meet with success. It's not about being a workaholic. It is about being innovative and creative in the way you work. It's more about choosing to "tackle every task that comes along, and if you fear God you can expect his blessing" (Ecclesiastes 7:18 TLB).

55 BE WILLING TO WAIT

For there is a proper time and procedure for every matter.
ECCLESIASTES 8:6

When it comes to fulfilling your dream, timing is everything. Sometimes it can seem as though your whole life is in a strange holding pattern. You may think because nothing is happening that God has stopped working in you to fulfill your purpose. But most likely you are being prepared for that purpose through the very process of waiting.

While I wrote my first book, my international speaking business was at its peak. There were weeks when I would fly to a different city every evening after presenting six-hour seminars to hundreds of people. This kept up for three or four days a week, two to three weeks each month. Sometimes I would wake up in the middle of the night and wonder which city I was in. Since rooms in hotel chains are usually similar, it was hard to tell. I would often have to check the phone book to find out where I was. Much of my book was written during those travels—in airports, on planes, and in my room. It was exhausting, but I loved both aspects of my career so I wanted to pursue both speaking and writing.

After it became clear that I would be writing more books, my business unexpectedly changed direction. After growing successfully over two decades, speaking engagements started falling away one by one. Conferences were being cancelled, funding for speakers was cut, and event planners were choosing to have members of their organization speak instead. The more I tried to finalize contracts, the more they disappeared, and the more frustrated I became. I cried out, "God, I love what you have gifted me to do, and I don't understand why you are taking it all away!" One day, I felt God instructing me to stop promoting myself, and more than that, to burn all my promotional materials. I also felt he wanted me to destroy my huge file full of hot leads. People in sales know the value of hot leads. These are potential clients who will most likely do business with you in the near future. I had worked hard to get them, and they represented the future of my business. Now I felt God telling me to get rid of all that and wait on him for direction.

I wish I could tell you I trustingly followed his instructions, but the truth is I went kicking and screaming all the way. Not only did I fight the idea of waiting, but I disobeyed, continuing to call potential clients. I would wake up early and think, "I'll just make that one call before God gets up!" Usually I would get the booking, and then just as quickly, the whole thing would fall through. My emotions were all over the place, always being swayed by the circumstances. One day I felt God gently tap my hand and say, "Sue, put down the phone. Can't you trust me?" When I persisted, I eventually heard, "Okay, my daughter, go ahead and have your way. When you are burned out, come to me and see what a glorious future I have in store for you." What I had to learn was to "stop quarreling with God! If you agree with him, you will have peace at last, and things will go well for you" (Job 22:21 NLT).

For over a year I was disappointed with the sparse bookings and wondered why God wouldn't restore my business. All I could do was turn to my Bible day by day, praying, waiting, and trusting that there was a new plan for my life. I was learning that I couldn't fulfill God's purpose while I focused on my own plans. Every sermon, every book, every television and radio message spoke to me about waiting. Scripture verses would jump out at me: "Wait on the LORD; be of good courage and He shall strengthen your heart; wait, I say, on the LORD" (Psalm 27:14 NKJV). "But if we hope for what we do not see, we eagerly wait for it with perseverance" (Romans 8:25 NKJV); "I waited patiently for the LORD; and He inclined to me, and heard my cry" (Psalm 40:1 NKJV).

Then one day Cliff helped me burn a huge pile of promotional materials and those hot leads. Tears streamed from my eyes as I watched pictures of my face, printed on all those flyers and brochures, surface and then burst into ashes. I knew God was refining me in that fire. Until then I had based my success on how full I could get my calendar. It was not so much about earnings, but more about how much work I had secured because with my old *poverty mentality,* I always thought, *Sure I have success today, but what about tomorrow?* If my calendar was sparse, I lived in fear that there would be no more work. But God took that fear away. I watched as he opened doors for me to write more books. That led to a less stressful speaking schedule. Until that happened, I didn't fully realize how burned out I had become from my previous hectic lifestyle.

Waiting on God is key. There is no instant way to get to your dream. God has a plan for our individual lives, and he often brings it to pass in a gradual way. Often at the time we get the dream, we are not ready to live it out. Then we're placed in situations, positions, and jobs along the way that prepare us. The process of moving toward the dream develops our character and produces responsibility in us. Sometimes God tells us where we are going with the dream, but he rarely tells us how long it will take. Be assured, the dream you have been given will come to pass. Until then, wait, be occupied, and walk in faith.

> *They that wait upon the LORD shall renew their strength;*
> *they shall mount up with wings as eagles; they shall run,*
> *and not be weary; and they shall walk, and not faint.*
> ISAIAH 40:31

PART 9

*From Roadblocks
to
Stepping-Stones*

56 DREAMING IN SPITE OF DISAPPOINTMENTS

And we know that all that happens to us is working for
our good if we love God and are fitting into his plans.
ROMANS 8:28 TLB

While I was speaking on a cruise ship in the Hawaiian Islands, there was something wrong with my foot. I was in pain most of the time. It got so bad Cliff encouraged me to see the doctor and have X-rays. The doctor on the ship treated it the best way he could, and I knew I'd have to see my own doctor when we got home. We returned a month later, and by then I had learned a whole new way of walking so that I didn't put pressure on that part of my foot. Although I was limping, I contemplated not seeing my doctor after all because I had become so accustomed to hobbling around in a way that protected the injury. But not going would have been foolish since, by getting proper treatment, I would be able to walk normally again.

Sometimes when you have been let down after your dreams have fallen apart, and you've lived with disappointment for a long time, you get to the point where you accept defeat and go through life limping along. You learn new ways to cope with failure and heartache and almost get used to hobbling around. You become numb to the thought of new possibilities and opportunities. You wonder if it's worthwhile to seek a better way or to dream new dreams. You feel stuck in your situation and are convinced that renewing a dream is hopeless. A daunting whisper in your ear says, "Things aren't going to be any different"; "Your life is never going to change"; "Your finances will always be like this"; or "Your marriage won't ever improve."

The first thing you need to do is get rid of these thoughts and change the way you talk to yourself! Start expecting a miracle. Believe that your life can have a total turnaround and that this can happen suddenly.

The best way to bounce back after any disappointment or defeat is to look for the lesson. What you might have viewed as a handicap, a setback, or a stumbling block may have actually been a valuable step in the development of a future goal or gift...and a blessing in disguise. A young Thomas Edison had a job selling candy on trains. One day a man lifted him and his entire box of candy onto the train—by his ears. That was the beginning of his hearing loss. Eventually he became fully dependant on a hearing aid. When someone asked if his deafness was a terrible handicap, he replied: "Deafness has been a great help to me. It saved me from having to listen to a lot of worthless chatter and has taught me to *hear from within!*" Here is someone who could have spent his life dwelling on a cruel and damaging experience. Instead, he learned to tune into the voice of God and received miraculous guidance and direction in his future work.

Defeat comes not so much from disappointing circumstances as from an *attitude of defeat,* which we carry from our past experiences. If you listen to the language of a person without a dream, it is usually in the past tense. Not only have these people failed to achieve their dreams, but they continue to live with the failures. They live in the past, reliving the pain of what happened. Listen to those who are succeeding in their dreams and goals, and you will notice they talk in the present tense with a future focus. You won't hear them talking a lot about their past other than to be an encouragement to others, even though it may have been checkered with loss, heartache, regrets, or disappointments. These people have a "whatever it takes" outlook and are determined to move forward.

Recall a dream you once had that left you disappointed. Perhaps it was failing in school, an unexpected divorce, or being let go from your position at work. Or maybe it was a stock market crash, having to declare bankruptcy, or finding out you have a debilitating disease.

How has God used your pain or heartache to bring good into your life? Did he draw you closer to him or teach you to listen for his voice? Are you filled with empathy for others in similar situations? Did you end up taking a risk or going in a new direction that you would not have taken? Maybe your disappointing circumstances protected you from even greater harm! Maybe you now have new understanding and wisdom that you can apply to your future dreams. God can use your heartaches and disappointments to build your character, draw you close to him, and prepare you to fulfill your ultimate purpose on earth. He says, "I will repay you for the years the locusts have eaten" (Joel 2:25). In the midst of the disappointments, watch for God to act. Start expecting your miracle.

57 OVERCOMING OBSTACLES, BREAKING DOWN BARRIERS

Success is to be measured not so much by the position one has reached in life as by the obstacles which he has overcome while trying to succeed.
BOOKER T. WASHINGTON

Obstacles are those frightful things we see when we take our eyes off the goal.
HENRY FORD

In his book *The Dream Giver,* Bruce Wilkinson states: "Your dream lies in the direction of an overwhelming obstacle. If you go toward it, you will experience a life marked by miracles." Now, I believe most of us long for a life marked by miracles, but our natural tendency when faced with an obstacle is to run *from* it rather than *toward* it.

Whenever you come up against an obstacle or confront a stumbling block, you need to stop and face it, then generate a few potential strategies for overcoming the hurdle. "When you come to a roadblock, take a detour," said Mary Kay Ash, founder of Mary Kay Cosmetics. There are always solutions to getting over, around, or through the barriers, but you'll only find them if you become solution-minded. If you spend time looking for answers and persevere in your search for them, you'll find them. Likewise, when you are in the habit of looking for problems and difficulties, that's what you'll see. When we are problem-oriented, we notice obstacles everywhere. They become examples of "See I told you I wasn't meant to succeed" or "I knew everyone was out to get me." Solution-minded people, on the other hand, view negative situations and roadblocks as opportunities to grow, change, and develop new and better methods for succeeding.

Life has a strange way of giving us what we expect. Maybe you've had this experience. You're driving around in your new car and suddenly you notice at every turn the same car—same make, model, and color. Were they there all along? Of course they were. You just didn't notice them until you had one too.

If you work for a company that downsizes and you suddenly find yourself without a job, you could tell yourself it's the worst thing to happen...or that now you just might find your dream job with more opportunities for advancement and higher income. Maybe the car in front of you insisted on going slower than the speed limit, making you late for an important appointment but saving you from getting caught in the radar trap up ahead. Was there a time in your life when something disastrous happened and later you saw it as a blessing in disguise? I call those times the "best–worst" times of life. I am sure you can think of times in the past when you thought what was happening was the worst thing in the world, and it turned out to be the best because of the person you became as a result. One time I was diagnosed with a serious blood disorder, but through the recovery process, I discovered how to create a more nutritious diet and a healthy, balanced lifestyle. Maybe you were passed up for a promotion, stuck in traffic, stood up at the altar, or had to say no to a business opportunity because of poor timing or lack of funds. Later, when you looked back, you realized it turned out to be for the best.

It's been said that an optimist sees an opportunity in every obstacle and a pessimist sees an obstacle in every opportunity. What if you were to start looking for the potential opportunity in every obstacle? Successful dreamers approach every experience and face every challenge as opportunities, believing something good will come from them.

St. Francis de Sales encouraged us with this thought: "We shall steer safely through every storm, so long as our heart is right, our intention fervent, our courage steadfast, and our trust fixed on God." If you take the approach that nothing is an accident and everything shows up in your life to serve a greater purpose, you'll begin to see even the tough, demanding, challenging events as a chance for enrichment and advancement. "Great things are done," said William Blake, "when men and mountains meet."

58 HOW TO TRIUMPH OVER FAILURE

*For every failure, there's an alternative course
of action. You just have to find it.*
MARY KAY ASH, FOUNDER, MARY KAY COSMETICS

Success is never final and failure never fatal.
WINSTON CHURCHILL

I f at first you *do* succeed, try to hide your astonishment!" Succeeding on the very first attempt of most new ventures is rare. There are very few success stories that are not marked with at least one major failure and several minor ones. Whenever we dream of doing something new, step away from the status quo, or attempt to stretch beyond our comfort zone, our endeavors will probably result in some frustrations, disappointments, or failures. That's simply part of the price we pay for following our dreams. The only way to be completely protected from failure would be to do nothing. "Far better it is to dare mighty things," said President Theodore Roosevelt, "to win glorious triumphs, even though checkered by failure than to take rank with those spirits who neither enjoy much nor suffer much, because they live in the grey twilight that knows neither victory nor defeat."

Failure isn't really the problem anyway. Failure is actually a very real part of success. The true problem is when we stay down, fail to learn from it, or identify ourselves with the failure. We are not failures. Failure is something that happens *to* us. Negative reactions to mistakes, setbacks, and blunders are what cause us to give up on our dreams. A positive reaction allows us to capitalize on failure as a valuable learning tool. Thomas Edison attempted to perfect one of his inventions more than a hundred times. When asked if he was discouraged, he replied that he now knew one hundred ways that don't work.

Many people never move forward with their dreams because of their fear of failing. Of course, no one wants to fail. We'd like to succeed every time. But we can learn more from our failures than we will from our successes. Rather than label your setbacks and blunders as failures, choose to say you have learned a lot of ways *not* to do something next time. It was Al Bernstein who commented, "Success is often the result of taking a misstep in the wrong direction." You can benefit from every failure, mistake, or embarrassing experience by asking yourself the following important questions:

- What did I learn from this experience?
- What will I do differently next time?

I often confess to my audiences that one reason I am able to do what I do today as an international speaker is that I've made every mistake you could possibly make from the platform at least twice—and God redeemed the misstep every time! After each embarrassing experience, I picked myself up, again and again, and kept going back to try out new ways until I got it right. If I had let humiliation keep me down, I'm not sure what I'd be doing now! I also learned to keep a "next time" file in which I itemize all the things I'll do differently when a similar situation arises in the future. This file becomes my "recipe for success"!

In most cases you can't go back and fix or change something. If you could, you would. The worst thing you can do is to keep bashing yourself about something that is over and done. You may have to deal with the consequences and possibly make apologies or offer regrets. Do the follow-up needed to resolve unfinished business brought about by the upset. Once you've done that, close the door to the past and never look back. Get mentally tough with yourself and refuse to let the failure stand between you and what you want to accomplish. Instead, look forward to your next opportunity to excel now that you know so much more than you did before. Sometimes we forget that God is a miracle worker. He is well able to take our failures and work them into his plans for our future.

Whether you've felt like a failure as a parent, had to declare bankruptcy after starting your own business, gone through a devastating divorce, or failed an important exam, remember you did the best you could with the knowledge and skills you had available at the time. After all, you did survive! Now you know you can cope with the results of failing.

To get yourself up and running once again, focus on past successes. Remind yourself you've had more victories than defeats. Try to spend time with positive, caring friends and family who can validate your worth and help you refocus on your goals. Once you've created a new plan of action, pick yourself up, brush yourself off, and move in the direction of your dreams. It was the comical George Burns who said, "I honestly think it is better to be a failure at something you love than to be a success at something you hate!"

59 CONQUERING YOUR FEARS

Fear is that little darkroom where
negatives are developed!
MICHAEL PRITCHARD

Do not let your hearts be troubled
and do not be afraid.
JOHN 14:27

When I was a child, I was terrified to go into the basement of our family home alone. In those days, basements were not as they are today—extensions of the living area, decorated and fully functional.

Instead, they were dank and dreary dungeons. Cobwebs hung down from the rafters, letting me know spiders lived there. We called it the cellar, and it was a spooky place to be. I was convinced some mysterious being was down there, lurking in the darkness, waiting to attack me. When I was sent there to fetch something, I would race as fast as my little feet would take me because I was certain someone was about to reach through the opening in the stairs to grab hold of my ankles! It was almost as bad going to sleep at night since there was certainly some creature hiding under my bed. The light switch was by the door, so as soon as it was shut off, I'd make a flying leap from the doorway to the bed. Those childhood fears were unfounded, and there never was a monster in the bedroom or an ogre in the cellar. The Bible says when you live in fear "you will even run when no one is chasing you!" (Leviticus 26:17 TLB). It wasn't until years later that I could say with the psalmist, "In God I have put my trust; I will not be afraid. What can man do to me?" (Psalm 56:11 NKJV).

Thoreau said, "Nothing is so much to be feared as fear." Fear paralyzes us. It keeps us stuck in one place so we don't move ahead with our goals and plans. People hold themselves back all the time from realizing their visions because of all types of fears. "What if I fail?" "What will people think?" we ask ourselves. Terrors that affect our ability to go beyond a dream range from fear of the unknown and uncertainty over our future to the fear of making mistakes, humiliating ourselves, not being capable, or looking foolish in the eyes of others. There are also more serious and debilitating phobias of every nature that people suffer from, some of which cause them to stay locked inside their homes, enduring each day alone, afraid to even venture outside.

Fears rob us of our ability to fully enter into life with abandon. They hold us back from reaching our potential, fulfilling our purpose, and receiving all the blessings God wants to pour out on us. In our society and culture, it's understandable that we would be afraid of such things as being a victim of food poisoning or tainted water supplies; getting Alzheimer's, cancer, or AIDS; being in a car crash; not having enough money for retirement; being followed by a stranger or being attacked by killer bees or foreign viruses. However, most of the fears that keep us from pursuing our dreams are unfounded. Someone once described fear with the acronym: **F**alse **E**vidence **A**ppearing **R**eal.

We can expect to experience fear if we take our eyes off the goal. More accurately, fear comes when we take our eyes off our heavenly Father. The apostle Peter walked on water as long as he stayed focused on Christ. Now I know Peter sometimes gets a bad rap, yet the great thing about him is that he at least got out of the boat before fear overtook him! Where were the others? Where would you and I be?

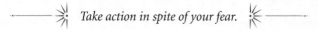 *Take action in spite of your fear.*

Another way fear manifests itself is in the form of *expected pain.* Aristotle put it this way: "Fear is pain arising from the anticipation of evil." Most of what we fear or worry about will never happen. However, focused fear can sometimes bring about exactly what we don't want. A student who fears failing an exam loses presence of mind, making it more difficult to concentrate and succeed. When someone fears criticism by a parent, spouse, or superior at work, he or she may make more mistakes than usual when that person is nearby. If we fear failure while attempting to accomplish our dreams, we may invite the very circumstances that would hold us back. As Job put it, "The thing I greatly feared has come upon me" (Job 3:25 NKJV). What he dreaded eventually happened. Yet even if the worst does happen to you, remind yourself that this too shall pass. A friend of mine says some of her favorite Bible verses start with "and it came to pass." In other words, it didn't come to stay!

Fear is a destructive force. It is the direct opposite of faith. Dispel all your fears by trusting and putting your faith in the one who made you and planted your dream inside you. "The one who calls you is faithful and he will do it" (1 Thessalonians 5:24). Take action in spite of the fear. Heroes and cowards all experience the same fears; it's just that heroes act differently. Mary Slessor, a respected missionary hero, said it well when she declared, "Why should I fear? I am on a royal mission. I am in the service of the King of kings!" She believed God when he said, "I am holding you by your right hand—I the Lord your God—and I say to you, Don't be afraid; I am here to help you" (Isaiah 41:13 TLB).

60　FACING THE FEAR OF SUCCESS

Our doubts are traitors and make us lose the good we oft
might win by fearing to attempt.
WILLIAM SHAKESPEARE

It may surprise you, but the fear of succeeding holds more people back than the fear of failing. I once heard a comedian say, "What is this—the fear of success? We must be running out of things to be afraid of. I think we're scraping the bottom of the barrel!" While his comment made me smile, I agree that the fear of success is hard to figure out. Fear of failure is at least understandable. But why would anyone be afraid to succeed? Isn't that what having a dream is all about?

For one thing, we can get so accustomed to not succeeding that achievement can seem as unfamiliar as failure is comfortable. One reason success is uncomfortable is that it always costs us something. Either we will end up with less energy because of an increase in demands or less time to do some of the things we really enjoy. So we hold ourselves back, often unknowingly. Once you realize that's what you've been doing, only you can decide whether the sacrifice truly is a worthy one and whether it lines up with your God-given calling.

Aside from that, fear shows up when we wonder whether we have what it takes to achieve the dream and, if so, whether we are equipped to maintain it. Many people have achieved high levels of success yet face each day fighting what's known as the *impostor syndrome.* They believe they've miraculously landed a great position or a wonderful relationship, but they doubt their capabilities and whether they deserve the success. The result is they live in fear that they'll be "found out." They're afraid someone will discover they are not really qualified to do what they're doing. They believe they were simply in the right place at the right time, whether by luck or fate. This is especially true for someone who is living his or her dream without having the customary education, training, or credentials. I know what that feels like. Many times when I speak at conferences I am aware that some of my audience members have much higher levels of education than I do, and many have degrees and letters behind their names. With only a high school education, I could be intimidated and feel like an impostor both as a speaker and author. I might think, *Who am I to teach others how to achieve success?* I've had to come to the place where I realize the information, principles, and strategies I offer my audiences and readers come from years of intense research and studies, from overcoming personal life challenges, and from specialized instruction in areas that are different from the training most of my audiences have received. In my field, I am an expert. It took some time before I stopped feeling like an impostor. Many artists, musicians, dancers, and comedians confess to feeling fraudulent too. They are not alone. I have interviewed professionals of all levels, including presidents of large corporations, managers, teachers, and business owners, who admit to feeling less than adequate when it comes to their job descriptions. Sadly, when we suffer the impostor syndrome, we never get to fully enjoy the success we've achieved.

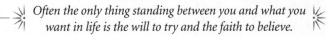

Often the only thing standing between you and what you want in life is the will to try and the faith to believe.

We might also question, "Sure, I'm successful today, but what about tomorrow? Will I be replaced? Will my dream suddenly go down the drain? Will my new relationship end?" With fears like that, we tend to sabotage our own success. We consciously or subconsciously impair our productivity and impede our effectiveness in order to quash a worthwhile effort. This assures us that we won't feel let down and disappointed if we do fail. It also guarantees no one will expect too much of us, including ourselves, and we will not be able to live out our dreams. Then we can conveniently blame outside circumstances or other people for the failure. Does this sound familiar? You stay up late and then blame exhaustion for not being able to fulfill your obligations the next day. You allow yourself to be disorganized and then miss crucial deadlines or misplace valuable documents, undermining your own success. You strive for perfection and then set impossible standards for yourself and others so you are always upset and dissatisfied. You incite an argument and then rationalize that you must not be meant to have a healthy relationship. You eat too much sugar, which leaves you touchy and irritable. You wreak havoc for yourself and those around you without realizing you are doing it to yourself. By chalking up your lack of success to all these things, it's less stressful than following through with your dreams for success.

Reaching your dream is a continual process of growing and changing. All transformation is uncomfortable for a season. Because of the fear of achievement, you may be tempted to hold yourself back. Instead, choose to focus on the long-term gains as well as the life purpose you are fulfilling. Success begins with a willingness to step away from what is comfortable. You can be assured that it is always God's will that you prosper in all good things and become everything you were designed to be. Often the only thing standing between you and what you want in life is the will to try and the faith to believe.

61 FACING THE FEAR OF REJECTION

It's not whether you get knocked down.
It's whether you get up again.
VINCE LOMBARDI

At some point in following your dream, you are going to endure rejection. Whether applying to a university, submitting a proposal for a new product idea or invention, asking someone to marry you, or asking for someone's order, there will be times when you'll have to deal with being turned down. People get rejected all the time: they don't get the raise they've requested, are passed over for a promotion, don't get elected, have their application for membership or a loan denied, have a manuscript turned down, or get stood up at the altar. Whether you didn't get chosen for the team, didn't get a part in the play, had your fund-raising request denied, or watched as your plans for a new business were thwarted, rejection hurts. The fear of being turned down can cause us to hold back from trying again.

Rejection is part of life. Whenever you have to ask anyone for anything, there is always a chance you'll be turned down. Basically, it's a numbers game. When a young salesman was going door-to-door selling kitchenware, his sales manager prepared him for rejection by letting him know that on average, nine out of ten potential customers would say no. When he knocked on one particular door and was given a flat out no, he started to laugh and jump up and down on the porch. The man at the door said, "Didn't you hear me? I do not want what you are selling!" The young man replied, "Yes, I heard. But you are number nine. That means your neighbor's going to buy!" Although in real life it may not be the tenth person who buys, when you get turned down remember the letters SBDWN. They stand for "So Big Deal…Who's Next?" When one avenue doesn't work out, you can be sure, if you are in God's will, he has something better waiting down the road. It's your job to turn the page to the next chapter.

When I first started marketing myself as a new speaker, I had to make nearly 100 phone calls in order to get 10 bookings. It was a 10 percent success ratio, which is not bad for making cold calls. What's interesting, though, is that the 10 bookings generally came in the last 10 or 15 phone calls. What if I had become discouraged with all the rejections and quit after the first 85 calls? When rejection takes its toll, we tell ourselves, "It's just not working. I might as well give up." But as Henry Wadsworth Longfellow put it, "If you only knock long enough and loud enough at the gate, you are sure to wake up somebody!"

One key to rejection is to not take it personally. Everyone who has ever fulfilled a dream has endured rejection. When you present your dream idea to someone and they do not respond positively, remind yourself it's not you they are rejecting. Either they are not in the market for what you are proposing or they don't understand the benefits of your idea. In that case, it would be a waste of time to continue pursuing the "sale" or to blame yourself.

Many authors wanting to be published submit their manuscripts to hundreds of publishers before being accepted. One rejection slip for *The Diary of Anne Frank* read: "The girl doesn't, it seems to me, have a special perception of feeling which would lift that book above the 'curiosity' level." The submitter had to rise above rejection. So did Elvis Presley, who was fired after one show at the Grand Ole Opry and told, "You ain't goin' nowhere, son." Colonel Sanders, of Kentucky Fried Chicken fame, had his secret recipe turned down more than 300 times before he found someone who believed in it. Now his restaurants are in more than 80 countries! A newspaper editor fired Walt Disney, saying he lacked creativity. When Alexander Graham Bell presented his telephone invention to Western Union, the president asked, "What would this company make of an electrical toy?"

If you have been rejected, you are in good company. The key to succeeding with your dream is to not give up. Don't get stuck in fear, resentment, or bitterness. Keep going. You can choose to see rejection as your enemy and allow it to defeat you, or you can view it as an opportunity to grow stronger. Face the future head-on with confidence in spite of being rejected. Get good at rejecting rejection! Most of all, accept God's divine direction for you. He will take you beyond the rejection and into the promised land.

62 WHEN DREAMS ARE SHATTERED

Our God, make us strong again!
Smile on us and save us.
PSALM 80:3 CEV

If you feel that your life is on an even keel, that you have dared to dream and the dream has been successful, you may not read this chapter. However, if you are like so many of us, you've had to overcome a variety of setbacks and obstacles where it seemed your dreams were crushed. Besides, success doesn't mean you are immune to other challenges such as feelings of low self-worth and difficulty in relationships. Most of us have some dream that needs to be repaired.

Is it possible that you can follow all the steps to accomplishing your dream—have a vision, decide on a goal, get it in writing with action steps, envision the outcome, believe it's possible, and expect a miracle—and still end up having your dream shattered? Could it be that earlier circumstances took us down the wrong path or our own poor choices led us astray? The poet Robert Frost wrote:

I shall be telling this with a sigh
Somewhere ages and ages hence.
Two roads diverged in a wood, and I—
I took the one less traveled by,
And that has made all the difference.
"THE ROAD NOT TAKEN," 1916

Somewhere along the way we have been faced with two paths in the woods and have had to choose which one to follow. Some of us were pushed down a path by parents who were living out their own dreams through us. Others took the easy path or the secure one, when we could tell exactly where we were going without any risk. You may have followed in the family business rather than stepping out on your own. Maybe you followed a dream but didn't have any guidance or direction and, as a result, made poor choices that left you with regrets and remorse. Some of us got lost on the path and are still trying to find our way. For whatever reason, if your dream is shattered, it can be renewed...or perhaps it's time to end that one and start over with a fresh vision.

Sheldon is a man who had always dreamed of owning his own restaurant. Since he was a boy, he enjoyed cooking and experimenting with gourmet recipes, and he wanted to go into business for himself. After receiving an unexpected inheritance, he invested in his dream by going to college where he studied to become a chef. After graduating, he rented a building in a high-class part of town. He and his wife decorated it together. He purchased the best possible furnishings and equipment and hung out a sign. They advertised in local newspapers and magazines and on the radio. But the few customers they had didn't bring in enough to pay the rent and other bills, and soon the money ran out. Sheldon went into a deep depression and, to make matters worse, his wife reminded him what they could have done if they had invested the inheritance another way. Eventually, Sheldon made an effort to move beyond the depression and started studying psychology courses and listening to self-development tapes. He discovered that he had a knack for teaching and went back to school to earn a degree. Now a successful high school teacher, he is making a difference in the lives of many young people. He truly enjoys his work. Sometimes it is our own choices that end the dream. Other times, like Sheldon, the dream has to die so we can find our new path.

To overcome the devastation of shattered dreams, we must face the problem and move to action. When we do, God comes to our aid. It had been 25 years since rhythm-and-blues singer Fontella Bass had a number one hit on the charts. Her dreams had been crushed. With no career to speak of, she was broke, worn out, and freezing. The only heat in her small home came from a gas stove in the kitchen. She had also left the church where she started singing gospel songs as a little girl. One day, at her lowest point, Fontella decided to pray. No sooner had she said "amen" than she heard her hit song "Rescue Me" on a television commercial. She said it was as if God had stepped right into her world that moment. She had no idea that American Express had been using her song as part of a commercial and officials had not been able to locate her to pay her royalties. Aside from receiving back royalties, new opportunities began to open up for her to start singing again!

Maybe your dream needs to be rekindled. When we cry out to God with our shattered dreams and broken hearts, and we recognize the futility of our own efforts, he renews our dreams and brings us blessings greater than we could ever imagine.

> *I've dreamed many dreams that never came true*
> *I've seen them vanish at dawn,*
> *But I've realized enough of my dreams, thank God,*
> *To make me want to dream on.*
> MARGARET NICKERSON MARTIN

63 SUCCESS IS JUST AROUND THE BEND

> *Just about any dream grows stronger,*
> *If you hold on a little longer!*
> MARGO GINA HART

> *It's always too soon to quit.*
> NORMAN VINCENT PEALE

Being totally committed to a dream doesn't mean it's going to be easy. Occasionally you'll be tested by obstacles you never imagined could happen, and no amount of planning could have prevented them. There will be times when you're going to have to persist in the face of overwhelming odds. "Success seems to be largely a matter of hanging on long after others have let go," said William Feather.

When we study successful dreamers, one quality they almost always have in common is persistence. They never give up. They know that the longer they hang in there and the more they persist, the greater the chance that something will happen in their favor. In following your dream, the going may be tough, and you'll have to make a choice to refuse to give up. Quite often the challenges you face will help you learn new lessons, get good at making difficult decisions, and develop your character.

It has been my experience that the closer I come to having a dream fulfilled, the more obstacles and problems I encounter. Because I know this now, I am more likely to get excited about pushing through difficult times because it's an indication that success must be near. With this in mind, it becomes easier to persist in spite of the challenges. If you can start to see your setbacks, roadblocks, and difficulties as signs that you are on the right track, you'll more likely have the endurance to press on until you reach your goal.

When my husband and I moved to our home in the country, we would often give our guests preprinted maps and directions when we invited them to visit us the first time. In the days before cell phones, we would regularly get calls from the owner of the country general store down the road saying our guests were lost. Usually we'd find out later that they had driven a certain distance and then turned around thinking they'd gone too far. When we asked them where they were when they decided to head back, invariably they were within walking distance of our home. If they had continued around one more curve, they would have succeeded in finding us. When we feel like quitting, victory is often just around the next bend!

When I first had the dream to leave my full-time position to build a business in direct sales with commissions, Cliff and I had just invested in our first home, based on having two full-time incomes. After several months of struggling to get my new business off the ground, Cliff came home from work one day, sat me down, and said he was sorry but we just couldn't keep up the expense of owning our country property on his income alone and I would have to get a "real" job. That night I was restless and couldn't sleep with the thought of having to work 40 hours a week again for a limited income when I knew that once my sales business was off the ground I could earn so much more. Besides, I preferred the idea of being my own boss. With all my tossing and turning, Cliff woke up and asked me what was keeping me awake. I told him I really thought I could make it in this business and just needed a bit more time to get it going. Eventually he agreed that I should go for it, and for the next few weeks, I made phone calls for nearly eight hours each day, introducing myself and my product, booking home demonstrations in the evenings, and recruiting salespeople into my group. While the struggle continued, we ate out less often, went without vacations, and cut back in as many ways as possible. Within months I started to earn what I would have in a regular job. By the end of the year my group sales and bonuses were so high it caught the attention of the president of the company, and he asked me to share my success principles at a series of annual company conventions. The sacrifice and persistence had paid off, and those opportunities began leading me in the direction of what I do today.

Former U.S. presidential candidate Ross Perot said, "Most people give up just when they're about to achieve success. They quit on the one-yard line. They give up at the last minute of the game, one foot from a winning touchdown." Never give up on your hopes and dreams. If you hang in there long enough, you will eventually reach your goal.

History has demonstrated that the most notable winners usually encountered heartbreaking obstacles before they triumphed. They won because they refused to become discouraged by their defeats.
B.C. FORBES, FOUNDER OF *Forbes* MAGAZINE

PART 10
Keep on Growing

64 STUDY SUCCESS

Let all things be done decently and in order.
1 CORINTHIANS 14:40 NKJV

Success leaves clues.

Whether your goal is to self-publish a book; become the top sales-person in the company; open your own country inn, spa, or gift shop; be the host of a television show; plan a surprise party; or improve your relationships, there are success stories you can study and inspiring people to model after. Most likely, anything you could possibly dream of doing has been done in one form or another by somebody at some point. And that person has probably written a book, taught an online course, or offered a seminar about it. Study the achievements of others. Success does leave clues.

What creates a leader, a true achiever? One thing about successful dreamers is they always have a plan. In the same way a contractor has a blueprint, a seamstress has a pattern, and a chef has a recipe, your plan helps you get on track and take action. When Dave Clarke was inspired with an idea for inventing a fun and informative family board game, he knew he needed a set of action steps to make it happen. The first was to invest hours in extensive research, after which he was able to create the trivia game Numaro. The answer to every question is a number, and there is always a winner since the guess closest to the actual number gets the point. Dave knew that aside from having an innovative and promising concept that he and his family and friends were excited about, he needed a marketing plan. Sometimes when we are trusting God with our dreams, we believe that if it's meant to happen it will.

But faith always requires work. Dave's plan included specific ways to further develop the idea, design the finished product, and promote it to the world. Today Numaro is sold in stores internationally and on many websites. What's really incredible about Dave is that, aside from being an inventor, he is a young family man with a beautiful wife and four young daughters, and is also living with a debilitating disease. You'd think it might hold him back, but with his great outlook, the prayers and support of family and friends, and complete faith in God, Dave is not only a dreamer and a planner, he is an overcomer. By having a definite plan, he has learned to keep his dreams alive while facing trials and adversity head on.

Another trait common to people who achieve excellence is they expect more from themselves than anyone else ever would. When publisher and editor Ethel Rowntree wanted to start her own magazine designed to creatively speak to those who do not yet have a personal relationship with God by presenting a balanced-life message, she worked diligently on her idea for more than a year. Her investment of time was spent researching the market, developing a detailed business plan, investigating potential advertisers, and seeking out regular contributors and columnists. She put in long hours, for which she was not being paid, and now her motivating and inspiring magazine, *Beyond Ordinary Living*, is distributed across Canada. Successful achievers willingly go the extra mile and know their efforts will be rewarded down the road.

Winners are dedicated and willing to persevere through the challenges that accompany achievement. My daughter, Sheila Cutler, wanted to give her life a total makeover. A talented and vivacious young wife and mother of three, Sheila decided to go back to college to become an educational assistant. Every evening she did homework right along with the kids, and though it was tempting to throw in the towel at times, she stuck it out and eventually graduated with honors. She applied for and got a job working in the public school system.

Her next dream was to get physically fit, so she started walking outdoors one hour a day and working out at a gym several times a week. She also persevered with kick boxing and aerobics classes, did weight training, and followed a particular weight loss plan for several months until she had lost more than 90 pounds, which she has kept off for over a year. While it may have been tempting to give in at times, Sheila had stick-to-itiveness and chose to persist regardless of the cost. She is a great role model to her family, friends, and coworkers.

The most successful people are always the most committed, dedicated, and persistent.

Successful dreamers also start with a clear vision. They can see the outcome of their dream in their mind's eye. For a long time Betty Boyd could envision an exquisite and fanciful "Princess Tea" for little girls and their "Queen Mothers" and "Fairy Grandmothers." She pictured a whimsical afternoon affair at her church where young girls could dress up as princesses and be treated to the delights of a luscious afternoon tea party. With a clear vision of how it would unfold, who would attend, what fanciful decorations she would use, which scrumptious tea goodies would be served, and the fun activities she would offer, Betty successfully presented her first tea party. It was an astounding success and is sure to become an annual event!

Look around and you will spot others who are leaving success clues. Study these people. Seek out those who have done what you want to do or something similar. Interview people about their dreams and how they achieved success. "This is what the Lord says: 'Stand at the crossroads and look; ask for the ancient paths, ask where the good way is, and walk in it'" (Jeremiah 6:16).

65 TAKE INVENTORY OF YOUR LIFE

If we could first know where we are, and whither we are
tending, we could better judge what to do and how to do it.
Abraham Lincoln

If you don't know where you're going,
you'll probably end up someplace else!

I f someone asks me how to get somewhere, with my dreadful sense of direction I usually feel safer telling them you can't get there from here. In amusements parks or shopping centers, you've probably noticed the big maps designed to help you out. They usually have an arrow printed on them with the words "You are here." The creators of those maps know you can't go someplace else until you know where you are now. That makes a lot of sense when it comes to your life, your future dreams, and your plans. You need to know where you are now. You won't be able to take your life in a new direction or see your dreams through to fulfillment until you have a clear understanding of what's currently happening. To decide which direction to move, it's necessary to take inventory of what's going on now to better determine what's working, what you like about it, and what you want to see changed.

The easiest and quickest way to find out what is or isn't working for you is to notice the results you are experiencing. Results speak for themselves. You are either in a healthy relationship or you're not. You're either financially secure or you're struggling to make ends meet. You're either in a job you enjoy or one you tolerate or even detest. You're physically fit or out of shape. Either you're satisfied and content, or you are disappointed, unhappy, or frustrated. It's quite straightforward. The outcomes you're experiencing are your reality. You can make all the excuses you want as to why things are the way they are, but if you're out of shape or not enjoying your home, work, or relationships, the best reasons in the world won't change a thing. You may be able to rationalize your situation, but justifying it won't stimulate new ideas or solutions. The only starting point is to face the truth about where you are now and what got you there.

One effective and fun technique for taking inventory of your life is called a mind map. This is a brainstorming technique that helps you think more clearly and become solution-oriented about any issue or concern that's holding you back. It works because you will have something tangible to consider and act on.

Start with a large sheet of blank paper. In the center, write your name and draw a circle around it. Next, draw lines out from that circle, similar to the spokes of a wheel. At the end of each spoke, identify the various areas of your life: health and fitness, spiritual growth, relationships, work and career, finances, recreation and free time, and contribution to your community.

Now put a circle around each of those with more spokes and label them with all the various aspects of each one, including what results you are experiencing, which aspects you like, and what areas you want to change. This will describe in detail what your current situation looks like.

Mind-mapping is an incredibly effective and valuable tool for finding out where you are now and where you want to go. Be sure to be ruthless with yourself. If you are not truthful, you are only kidding yourself. Be completely honest.

The only way to change results is to change behaviors. Is it time to alter your eating patterns or start an exercise program? Do you need to consult a financial expert to pay off bills, clear up credit-card debt, get a mortgage, or start planning for your retirement? Are there ways you can spend more time with the people who are important to you? Your life will always send you messages about the effects of your actions and behaviors through the results you are getting. Pay attention. If you're failing in school, if you're missing out on new business opportunities, if your house is always disorganized, if you're consistently exhausted or sickly, if you have no joy—these are the consequences of ineffective behaviors that need to be changed. Your results are letting you know something is wrong.

There are things you can do that will make a difference. But first you have to take a long, truthful look at the outcomes you are now producing. Then, make a practice of doing more of what's working, less of what's not, and developing some new and effective behavior patterns.

66 COMMIT TO ONGOING LEARNING

He who stops being better, stops being good.
OLIVER CROMWELL

God stands as it were a handbreadth off,
leaving His creatures room to grow in.
ROBERT BROWNING

Successful dreamers in any field, whether business, education, industry, arts, sports, homemaking, or community involvement, know the value of committing to ongoing learning. They are always ready and willing to investigate ways to make something better, to do it more efficiently, or to make it more profitable. They commit to enhancing their skills, improving their behavior, bettering their relationships, or refining their business practices. They are willing to invest time, money, and whatever it takes to make it happen.

There are numerous ways to continue learning, including finding an extra hour per week to volunteer your services in your chosen field, taking a night class at a local community college, attending a public seminar, listening to educational or motivational CDs in your car, watching training DVDs or reading books on the subject of your dream. At work, if you have a vision for your company to improve the area of customer service, you may decide to engage a consultant or professional trainer to conduct seminars for you and your team. Professionally, you may want to learn new computer skills, sales techniques, or negotiating strategies, so seek out a good course or seminar on those subjects. At home, if you want to clear out the clutter that has accumulated over the years, you can hire an organizational expert to come in and get you started, and then have him or her teach you the systems you'll need to maintain the new order. There are courses and books available on all sorts of home-related topics such as decorating, gourmet cooking, and gardening, or you may want to take a course on communication in marriage, parenting skills, or raising teens. Personally, you can learn new ways to get into shape, stay fit, eat healthy foods, and cook more nutritional meals for your family. You could also focus on learning more about money management, investing strategies, and retirement planning. You might want to learn how to play a musical instrument or paint with watercolors. Maybe you want to find out how to experience greater joy and inner peace through a Bible-study course about prayer and meditation.

In today's world, continued learning is essential just to keep up with the rapid pace of change. New technologies and manufacturing techniques are being introduced on a regular basis. Words and phrases are born as quickly as a fad or trend catches on. Even what we learn about human nature—our inner potential, our physical condition, and our capacity to bring about change through the choices we make—is astounding.

To stay dedicated to ongoing learning, ask yourself:

- What one thing could I learn today?
- Where can I go to gain new skills and information?
- How can I discover ways to do something better than before?

Remember that mastering new skills, perfecting your abilities, and becoming proficient at any new venture takes time. It's easy to become discouraged when success doesn't happen right away, considering that so many of today's products and services promise instant results. But there are no microwave miracles or drive-through breakthroughs. Real success comes as a result of honing your new skills through practice and refinement. Athletes exercise, musicians practice, and actors rehearse. Teachers go back to school to earn advanced certifications, and mechanics take courses to learn new procedures. They are all engaged in continuous learning.

Whatever your dream, decide what you'd like to learn about it and what steps you'll need to take to achieve that goal. Every seminar you attend, every book you read, every class you take can contribute in some way to your ultimate dreams and goals. Make a commitment to keep learning in small ways each day and to getting better and better in all you attempt. When you do, you'll see little efforts add up to huge results!

67 QUESTIONS ARE THE ANSWER

Ask and it will be given to you; seek and you will find;
knock and the door will be opened to you.
For everyone who asks receives; he who seeks finds; and to
him who knocks, the door will be opened.
MATTHEW 7:7-8

Questions are the creative acts of intelligence.
FRANK KINGDON

Since the days of Socrates, questions have been used as learning aids. Jesus loved to use questions as a great part of his teachings. What happens when someone asks you a question? Your brain immediately goes into gear, attempting to work out an answer. The senior pastor at my church is known for asking questions of his congregation without necessarily having an answer himself. It may seem to us that he always does, but his aim goes beyond discovering the answer. His goal is to get people thinking. Questions can set us in a new direction and get us to ponder, suppose, and consider various avenues and unique possibilities outside the box.

If we ask enough questions about what we truly want to accomplish in this life, we will eventually find answers. As a child I would lie on the grass and watch the birds fly from one treetop to another. It stirred in me a sense of freedom, and I asked myself what it would take to experience that same sensation. That question led me to doing what I do today as a writer and speaker. A Bible verse reminds us that we *have not* because we *ask not*. Often, by merely asking the right questions, feasible and realistic solutions miraculously appear to us. Many years ago, one particular seminar leader at an event I attended knew the power of asking questions of ourselves and suggested to the audience that we consider two powerful questions. The answers eventually played a role in transforming my life:

> First, if you could do, be, or have anything in this world and you knew it would be impossible to fail, what would it be? Would you start your own business, be the manager of your department, compose music, write or illustrate children's books, go on a mission trip, be the president of a company, start a charitable organization, go to school and graduate with honors, build a cottage by the lake, marry the person of your dreams, travel to an exotic island, open an antique shop, play a musical instrument in a philharmonic orchestra, or sail around the world? Would you build a house, a boat, or a houseboat?
>
> And second, if you could create your ideal life, what would you dare to dream? Consider what your everyday existence might look like. Where would you live, who would share your days with you, what would your job be, where would you vacation, which type of car would

you drive, and what recreational activities would you be involved in? Would you read more books, start a new hobby, take up a sport, go fishing more often, have regular massages, or learn to golf, oil paint, or play tennis? Would you relax more in a rocking chair by the fireside, a hammock in the backyard, or a candlelit bubble bath? Imagine what each day would be like if you were living the life you've only dreamed about.

Thought-provoking questions like these get you contemplating a more fulfilling way of life and considering new possibilities. After all, everything ever created began with a single thought, and all change begins in the mind.

Aside from asking yourself these powerful questions, develop the habit of asking others too. For instance, get someone close to you to answer the following questions: "How do you see me fulfilling the vision God's given me? What do you believe are my greatest assets and strengths that would contribute to it? How about my weaknesses and shortcomings that are holding me back? Which areas of my life do you think would have to change and what would have to take place before I could achieve my dream?" Still other questions will help you acquire the information, assistance, time, support, and money required to fulfill your vision. Most of all, ask in prayer of your heavenly Father, trusting that he hears and answers. "You can get anything—anything you ask for in prayer—if you believe" (Matthew 21:22 TLB). God has promised us, "I will answer them before they even call to me. While they are still talking to me about their needs, I will go ahead and answer their prayers" (Isaiah 65:24 TLB).

Considering all possible aspects of your life, what do you really want to see happen? This is such a basic question, but one that must be answered by anyone who wants to turn their dreams into realities. There's an old adage: "If you don't know where you're going, any road will get you there." So before you go further, ask yourself, "What is most important to me, and am I on the right pathway to get to it?"

68 BUILD YOUR SUCCESS LIBRARY

Leaders are readers.

*I find television very educational. Whenever
someone turns the set on, I go to
another room and read a good book!*
GROUCHO MARX

One way to get your dream off the ground is to read good books about the topic. Is there something related to your dream that you could study? Which aspects do you want to know more about? What are you interested in accomplishing through your vision? When I wanted to write my book *When Your Past Is Hurting Your Present,* I spent nearly a year preparing by reading books on many aspects of the matter, including forgiveness, getting unstuck, bouncing back after adversity, letting go of emotional baggage, and building hope for the future. While I have not been specifically influenced by those books, they did provide background information, brought to memory my own stories and examples, and acted as a reservoir of knowledge. Once you decide on a topic, you will begin to notice books and articles everywhere that will inspire and instruct you, and your research can fill a lifetime. The books you read will expand your knowledge and increase your motivation to continue your dream.

When I pick up a book, I use a highlighter pen to mark ideas that stand out and are especially meaningful. I also keep a spiral-bound notebook or journal handy to make summary notes of points that are pertinent to my dream or goal, as well as to record any thoughts and insights that come to me as I read. I put the title on the cover of my notebook and end up with a condensed version of the book I can refer to containing the ideas that I plan to adapt to my situation. Another habit I have is that I often read the end first—that way I know if the book is worth my time.

My passion for reading started as a small child. I liked to get up very early in the morning and, because I was awake, I felt everyone else should get up too. So my parents came up with a plan. Each night they would place a stack of books at the end of my bed. They told me it was all right to be awake as long as I stayed in my room to read. Soon reading became a delightful habit. On weekends, after school, and during summer vacation, books provided me with friends, imaginary travels, mystery, suspense, and laughter. It's a pleasurable pastime that has stayed with me all my life.

I am glad to know that in spite of the popularity of television, DVDs, and CDs, there are more books being purchased today than ever before. There is hardly a subject we could think of that doesn't have a volume or two telling us all about it or instructing us on how to do it. Never was there a time when more books on success were available. By building a personal success library, you'll have a reliable source of help and inspiration you can turn to concerning a variety of topics, including stress survival; time effectiveness; getting along with difficult people; dealing with change; building a business; making financial investments; improving marriage, family, and other relationships; understanding personality styles; goal setting; confidence building; and health and wellness techniques, to name a few. For pleasure reading, you can round out your library with biographies and autobiographies, travel books, and novels in a variety of genres. For sheer enjoyment, add a little comedy, mystery, and romance too. For years the bulk of my reading was related to my speaking and writing topics. But when I spoke in England, I decided to read some mystery novels by Agatha Christie. It was fun identifying with the local towns, tourist attractions, and train stations mentioned, and I was intrigued by the way the detective gathered clues to solve each mystery. I became so captivated that I lost all track of time, and when I returned to reality, I felt refreshed and renewed because I'd had so much fun.

I believe the most important book you will ever read is the greatest bestseller and most-read book of all times—God's Word. When I first discovered the powerful truths of the Bible, I placed one in every room of my home. Then I copied out scriptures on notecards and posted them where I could read them every day. I kept a Bible in bed with me so that I could read it before falling asleep and as soon as I woke up in the morning. In those days, I was going through such a difficult time that I found it impossible to even function without reading from God's

Word consistently. The Bible is unlike other books. Its words are alive! Whether you are facing the despair of hopelessness or are living each day with a heart full of joy and peace, the Bible can bring you closer to your dreams than any other book. And remember, the one who does not read is no better off than the one who will not read.

69 FEEDBACK IS VALUABLE

*We can chart our future clearly and wisely only when we
know the path which has led us to the present.*
ADLAI STEVENSON

A farmer spoke kind words to his horse one day. "Over the years, you have been hard-working, dependable, and reliable. I have always been able to count on you for a good day's work. For your age, you look pretty good too." The hungry old horse was annoyed and replied, "No, not feed*back*. Feed*bag!*" Although this horse was more interested in a good meal than an evaluation of his performance, most of us would benefit from some honest critique when pursuing our dreams and visions. Whether it's positive or negative, outside data can help us get back on target and reach our dreams.

"The time to repair the roof," said John F. Kennedy, "is when the sun is shining." If you can catch mistakes and glitches early in your plans, while there is still time to revise and make alterations, you'll save yourself from traveling too far down the wrong path. Getting feedback is one way of knowing whether you are doing the right thing while helping to determine when and where to tweak your plans. When you are following your dream, you most likely won't be doing everything perfectly at all times so you'll want to rectify problems quickly. According to a friend who works as an airline pilot, a plane is off course much of the time it is in the air. Although this is a scary thought, he assures me the autopilot does have a clear target and knows its destination, but it must continually make mid-course corrections while it's flying in order to get back to the original goal. We must make adjustments as we go too. One way to do that is to pay attention to the data we receive from outside sources so we keep doing the right things—such as honing our skills, expanding our knowledge, and catching snags before they become problems.

Feedback comes to us in a number of ways. One type that affirms our actions is when we're experiencing positive outcomes—we get results with our diet or exercise program, win an award, or get a raise or promotion on the job. That feedback tells us we are doing something right. Harmony, inner peace, intimacy in relationships, joy, and a balanced life let us know that what we are doing is working and we should continue. Negative feedback comes when we aren't getting the results we're after. The money's not there, the weight isn't coming off, our marriage is unfulfilling, and there's no joy, peace, or contentment in our lives. Those indications mean it's time to make adjustments.

Feedback also comes from other people. You'll often get it even if you haven't asked for it. Some people just feel free to offer their opinions, views, suggestions, advice, and criticism concerning your dreams whether or not you're interested in hearing it. They may pass judgment based on their own experiences or their perception of you and your qualifications to achieve your dream. While they may be well meaning (or not!), it's up to you to weigh their comments and determine if they're valid. Some remarks may be worth investigating, some may not. Valid critique will be encouraging and point you toward ways you can make positive changes. Plain criticism, on the other hand, tends to be insensitive and discouraging. It may come from someone who is negative about a lot of things—and you happen to be one of them. When you suspect it's coming from a negative attitude, take a position of curiosity and say to yourself, "Isn't it interesting that someone could be so negative about me and my goals? I wonder what it's based on." Remind yourself that it may stem from envy or jealousy, or the person criticizing you could be struggling through some difficulties in his or her own life. When someone is especially cruel in their criticism of me, I find it helpful to tell myself that they may have just come from divorce court, or maybe their feet hurt, or perhaps they have hemorrhoids!

Be not dismayed nor be surprised
If what you do is criticized.
Mistakes are made, I'll not deny,
But only made by those who try.

Although most of us appreciate constructive criticism, we seldom seek feedback for fear that the answers will be derogatory and hard on our self-esteem. Usually other people won't volunteer feedback either, other than the most affirmative comments, since they are uncomfortable with the possibility of disappointing us. They don't want to risk hurting our feelings. So if you really want to know how you're doing, you'll have to ask for an honest evaluation. When you do, the information can be invaluable. Make it comfortable for others to be honest by asking, "Do you see ways I might be holding myself back from achieving my dreams?" Most people find this an easy invitation to offer their comments. Once you have this new information, you'll be equipped to create a plan of action for moving away from limiting behaviors and developing more constructive and creative ones.

Sometimes you can get constructive feedback in advance. When I get hired to speak at an event, the first thing I do is have my clients complete a preprogram questionnaire. The answers they provide give me valuable information about the audience members and their average workday, any concerns, challenges, and fears they face, and their greatest strengths and victories. By the time I arrive to speak, I am able to capture the attention of the group by addressing their immediate interests, problems, and issues. Clients think it's brilliant. It's simply a result of their helpful response. Feedback is critical to success.

70 SEEK WISE COUNSEL

Wisdom knows what to do. Skill knows how to do it.

Where no counsel is, the people fall; but in the multitude
of counsellors there is safety.
PROVERBS 11:14 KJV

Dreaming big doesn't mean we forfeit being sensible and cautious when making decisions concerning our futures. There is one thing that distinguishes sensible dreamers from imprudent ones. Sensible dreamers realize they don't know all the answers and are willing to get good counsel. Those who are impulsive and overly spontaneous, or think they have all the solutions, don't even consider getting advice. They thoughtlessly rush into new ventures that eventually end in disaster. Never learning from the tragic results, they prefer to continue blundering on in their own direction than to succeed based on the recommendations of others who have more expertise and experience. Wise dreamers want to gather all the facts and data, and get the best advice, guidance, and suggestions possible before going ahead with any project.

Getting wise counsel was a tough lesson for me to learn. A number of years ago, after the release of my first book, *With Wings, There Are No Barriers,* I was approached by a businesswoman who said she had been following my career path and was very interested in supporting the work I was doing. She introduced herself as the owner of a company that promoted large motivational events and claimed to have worked for a number of other well-known speakers doing the same thing. What she proposed was that she would organize a series of inspirational events across the country where women at all stages of life could come to be inspired, motivated, and learn courage, confidence, and positive risk-taking skills. She won my confidence, and I was thrilled that someone with her expertise, background, and apparent experience would tap into my own dream and be as excited about it as I was. I was thankful she had caught my vision to take this program to women all across the nation. We agreed to go ahead, and she let me know she would need a cash advance in order to pay deposits on conference halls, promotion materials, and advertising. She said it was urgent that these be paid promptly, and it made sense to me logically, although I had a gnawing feeling deep down inside that cautioned me about handing over thousands of dollars. My initial response was to consider terminating this plan until I could get some professional advice. But I ignored my gut reaction and went ahead. Later she came to my house to pick up the check. As soon as I placed it in her hand, I had the terrible realization that I had done the wrong thing. After that, I lost all contact with her. By the time I tracked her down again she explained that registration had been so low that the events had to be cancelled, and subsequently, we had lost the deposits. What she didn't explain was the beautiful tan she had or how she afforded her three-week vacation in Jamaica!

Rather than beating myself over the head with the invisible baseball bat that so many of us carry, I asked myself, "What did I learn, and what would I do differently if I found myself in a similar situation in the future?" Now I know the importance of getting all the advice I can in order to make more informed choices. Here are some practical safeguards against being deceived and defrauded while vigilantly following your dreams:

- Always investigate other people involved and the potential opportunity. Any product, person, or organization that cannot stand to be investigated should be avoided.
- Don't rush into a decision. When you sense you are being forced into something with a great sense of urgency, be on guard. Any offer that is legitimately good today will still be good tomorrow, or next month. Sleep on every proposition. You may see it in a different light in the morning.
- When you are being flattered—for your ideas, insights, former successes, or expertise—postpone your decision. Dreamers can tend to be more susceptible to flattery and, therefore, more easily taken.
- Don't expect something for nothing. There is always a price tag attached to success. Many dreamers are defrauded because they want too much for too little, and end up getting little for much.

Take your time and look for good, dependable counsel. Whether you turn to a trained professional or a trusted friend, talk over new ventures and big decisions with someone you can count on *before* taking action. Most of all, take your situation to God in prayer. Ask for wisdom above all else. Proverbs 4:7 says, "Wisdom is the principal thing; therefore get wisdom: and with all thy getting get understanding" (KJV). Nothing is comparable to the perceptive insight that godly wisdom gives. It empowers you to act wisely and will enable you to make your way out of an outrageous maze of potentially disastrous paths. In the long run you will always prosper in proportion to the quality and quantity of the wisdom you exercise.

71 CHANGING DIRECTION

Since the Lord is directing our steps, why try to under-
stand everything that happens along the way?
PROVERBS 20:24 TLB

While you are headed down the path of your dreams and traveling confidently in a particular direction, the road may suddenly veer toward another route altogether. When this happens, successful dreamers keep on trusting that God's best plans for them are being worked out. They maintain their faith and a positive focus even when things drastically change and they are not sure anymore where God is leading them. When he says, "I will instruct you (says the Lord) and guide you along the best pathway for your life; I will advise you and watch your progress" (Psalm 32:8 TLB), they take him at his word.

My daughter Lori Page is an energetic and ambitious young entrepreneur who found out what it means to see plans suddenly change direction in midstream. As she was making her way toward a particular career goal, she discovered God had plans to open up an entirely different pathway, one she never imagined for herself. After studying business and human resources in college and graduating with honors, Lori searched diligently for a position in her region but found there wasn't one. During one night she believes God woke her and prompted her to check into starting a business in the field of post-construction cleaning. She wasn't sure what this entailed, so she looked it up on the Internet, where she discovered this meant contracting with home builders to clean new houses once construction was completed. Before home buyers moved in, every room needed to be immaculate from top to bottom, including air ducts, windows inside and out, bathroom tiles, drawers, closets, floors, and walls...and also basements and garages.

Although this was a completely new concept to her, Lori says when she was sure this was God's voice directing her, she immediately took action. She named her company A.C.E. Cleaners (**A**ffordable—**C**onscientious—**E**fficient) and had it registered in the Niagara region in Ontario, Canada. Then she purchased the industrial equipment she would need, applied for all necessary licensing, and took the required safety training courses. As it turns out, her college education is exactly what she needed to hire and train the best employees and operate a successful company. Although it may have looked as though she was being led down a different path, it now seems clear God had a plan from the beginning. Lori's business is thriving. As a single mom, operating her own company gives Lori the freedom to spend quality time with her daughter and be home more often than if she worked full-time in her original career choice. She believes God gave her the vision as well as the inspiration, the strength, and the courage to see the process through, and he is still opening up new opportunities daily.

Business owner Bobbi Joan Lococo is also in the habit of praying about her dreams and listening for God's direction. She knows firsthand what it's like to walk in faith, unsure of what's coming next. Bobbi started out with a fun and gratifying hobby—making specialty chocolates in her kitchen to give as gifts to family, friends, and coworkers. Soon others wanted to purchase them, and her hobby turned into a small business. Eventually she started giving private demonstrations in her home at Christmas and Easter time. Her customers were invited to choose from a variety of delectable chocolates in unique shapes and whimsical designs. This isn't something Bobbi would have ever considered doing, yet the endeavor was evolving from a simple pastime into an interesting and profitable venture. As business grew, Bobbi felt customers would be more comfortable coming to a storefront location. After much prayer, she and her husband purchased a quaint little shop in the village of Ridgeville, Ontario, where she now operates her thriving chocolate business, Sweet Thoughts. Family members and friends assist her in the shop, and the backroom is a great spot for her children to play while she works. By opening up another room in the store, she has been able to add a variety of unique gift items and beautiful artwork. Now she is expanding to add a café so customers can enhance their shopping experience. Bobbi Joan had no idea that through this series of twists and turns, she would go from having fun with her hobby to earning a little extra money to becoming a successful chocolateer. Like Lori, she has found that although her business wasn't her first career dream, it has changed direction many times, and with each step she has trusted God's guidance as he leads the way and opens new doors.

Both Lori and Bobbi Joan are still not sure where they will end up as their businesses continue to evolve, but they believe whatever direction they go, it will be God's best for them, their families, and their customers. Have you had some twists and turns in the direction of your dreams? What might happen if you decided to go with the flow and see just where God is leading you next? He says he knows the plans he has for you, "plans for good and not for evil, to give you a future and a hope" (Jeremiah 29:11 TLB). Take him at his word and expect miracles!

 72 I'M NOT OFF COURSE, I'M JUST INVESTIGATING!

> *May [God] give you the desire of your heart*
> *and make all your plans succeed.*
> PSALM 20:4 NLT

Early on in my business career, I learned what many successful dreamers have discovered: that even when you can't move ahead, you can keep moving in one direction or another. Whether you turn to the right or to the left isn't the issue. The secret is to stay active, keep learning, continue exploring, and never stop. While it may look and feel as though you are off course, you can get stuck if you wait for "ideal" conditions. Here's a news flash for you: There will never be a perfect time to take that leap and move forward. An even bigger revelation is that circumstances don't *have* to be ideal for you to pursue your dream. You may not have your ideal job, the career of your choice, the hobby you want to pursue, or your dream relationship just yet, but there are steps you can take in the meantime that will keep you moving—steps that will eventually reveal the right direction.

Sometimes in our desire to reach our objective, we can get caught in the trap of believing there's only one way to satisfy the dream. But there are many potential pathways to accomplishing your goal! While I was working toward my speaking career, many well-meaning friends sincerely wondered why I was continually changing direction. It must have appeared that way because I had a new job position every couple of years. People asked, "What are you doing *now?*" While I'm certain many thought I simply couldn't settle in any one area or had lost my way, I assured them I was not off course. I was exploring new opportunities and learning every step of the way.

Although some of my earlier careers covered a hodgepodge of interests that didn't seem to have any correlation, including teaching self-improvement classes for a modeling agency, managing a cosmetic salon, selling water purifiers, training salespeople for an educational toy manufacturer, and recruiting sales managers for a women's clothing line, my true aim never changed. It was always to inspire, challenge, encourage, and motivate others to make the powerful, positive choices that would transform their lives. I had been so inspired by the teaching I had received in each of my previous positions that I was able to take steps to see my own life transformed. As a result, my goal was to offer the same to others. So whether I achieved that through motivating a team of salespeople to reach for the stars, leading a series of inspirational self-development workshops at a modeling school, sharing my personal testimony in churches about overcoming incredible odds, or presenting public seminars about projecting an effective personal or professional image, to me they were all methods of fulfilling that same purpose.

I may not have been living my ultimate vision of being on stage at a convention center speaking to thousands of people like I am today, and I may not have been a published author with my information available in bestselling books, but I was still able to achieve my calling in many different formats and venues. In fact, when I first started speaking, I presented my programs in living rooms, kitchens, church basements, libraries, community halls, and restaurants—anywhere I could.

As I shared earlier, later on when I wanted to leave my sales career and seriously begin building a full-time speaking and writing business, I sought out a number of groups and organizations that needed to book speakers but didn't have the funds in their budgets. I volunteered to speak for free or for a small honorarium to cover travel costs. My goal was to gain experience while having the chance to fine-tune my material in a nonthreatening environment. Eventually I charged $500 for one presentation. In those days, that amount seemed incredible to me! I also felt that by keeping my fee low, I could experiment with new methods and innovative ideas. When I got some rave reviews from audiences, I asked the leaders of those organizations to write referral letters that I could include in future promotional packages. Those letters were the beginning of a prosperous 20-year career that has allowed me to fulfill my utmost dreams! Now I've written several books, and I enjoy speaking all over the world.

You too can get from where you are now to where you only dreamed you could be by enjoying the freedom to explore. Choose one area of your life, whether career, relationship, contribution, health, fitness, hobby, or financial, and take action. Keep moving!

PART 11

It's About Time

73 PRIORITIZE YOUR LIFE

"Everything is permissible for me"—but not
everything is beneficial.
1 CORINTHIANS 6:12

Have you ever noticed how quickly your focus narrows during an emergency? There's an unanticipated knock on the door or you get a frantic phone call in the middle of the night and suddenly priorities change because nothing else matters except that immediate concern. Whether your teenager has been in an accident, your spouse has lost his job, the family dog has been hit by a car, or a neighbor needs to be rushed to the hospital, everything else fades into the background while you go into emergency mode. You put your time and energy and ability into concentrating on what must be done next.

When an urgent matter suddenly becomes top priority, you somehow find "extra" time. Yet we know, in reality, there is no such thing as extra time. There are 24 hours in a day, and we're not getting any more. When a crisis happens, we immediately prioritize our activities and temporarily drop the lower priority items.

Until now, lack of time may be the reason you've been giving for putting your dreams on hold. A more likely answer is that you probably haven't assigned them top-level priority—yet. While I hope achieving your dream never comes down to an emergency situation, simply being aware of how you'd react in a crisis lets you know that it is possible to narrow your focus and give certain matters your full attention. One powerful way to get your plans in motion is to create that same sense of urgency for each of your dreams. Here are several ways to do that.

GIVE YOUR DREAM A BOGUS DEADLINE

Most people seem to do their best work with the added pressure of a specific due date. Without a deadline, following your dream lacks significance and is continually pushed to the bottom of the priority list. Assign your dream a start date and a completion date. If your dream is worth pursuing, it's worth giving it a time limit.

LIST THE BENEFITS OF ACHIEVING YOUR GOAL

Be sure you know the reasons for going after your dream. Whether you want to renovate your home, organize a family reunion, learn to play golf, or take up oil painting, it's the reasons and benefits that fuel your plans. Oil painting may give you a much-needed sanity break from the long hours you devote to your job. Learning to play golf will get you outdoors and may provide business networking opportunities. Once you get your home renovations completed, you could have the family reunion there.

LIST THE COST OF NOT FULFILLING YOUR DREAM

If you dream of achieving a certain body weight, getting a new job, or starting your own business, ask yourself what your life will be like in 5, 10, or 20 years if you don't reach the goal. Just realizing you will be in a similar—or worse—situation often proves to be motivation enough to get most people moving. Seeing the answers to these questions, especially if they are in writing, will crystallize your thinking, and you'll have a better chance of designing your plan of action and staying focused.

If you truly want to fulfill your dream, you must fix your sights on it and not get caught up in anything that won't take you there. Rather than dedicating your time and energy to tedious, unproductive, unfulfilling time-stealers, devote your attention to those pursuits that will bring you a step closer to your goal. Cut back on television viewing and Internet surfing. Instead, dedicate those hours to activities that contribute to your highest dreams and goals. Be wary of all the new opportunities that come your way too. Successful dreamers determine whether new options and possibilities truly fit with their overall life purpose and passion or whether they will take them on a wild goose chase. Continuously make an effort to prioritize your life in a way that supports your dreams. If you want to know which is the best road to take, you have to first establish a connection with God, the "giver of dreams." When you do, he will reveal to you which road to take. Once you've committed to it, all those irrelevant and unnecessary things will fall away on their own.

74 MAKE TIME FOR THE DREAM

There is a right time for everything.
ECCLESIASTES 3:1 TLB

Time is like a circus, always packing
up and moving away.
BEN HECHT

M aybe you've had a dream for a long time. It's a big one, and you get a rush at the mere thought of achieving it. You believe you have the potential and feel that your dream would take you in the direction of fulfilling your life purpose. You can vividly envision the end result and desire it with tremendous passion. Yet you can't seem to get started. Days pass by, then weeks, months, and years…and the dream remains, hovering in the back of your mind as a constant yearning. The longing gets stronger, but there just doesn't seem to be time enough to take the next step. Besides, there are so many steps you are excited about that you're not really sure what the first one should be.

One primary reason we don't pursue our dreams is we keep them separate from our daily life activities. Sure, we have our goals itemized and our plans listed, but they are neatly filed away in a drawer somewhere. Our daily to-do list, on the other hand, is right in front of us because everything on it is urgent and must be done now. We know what we have to do each day, and those demands engulf us. No wonder our dreams get pushed to the back of the line! We start out each morning getting ready to face the daily grind…take a shower, brush and whiten our teeth, gargle, style our hair, make the bed, get dressed, take our vitamins, blend up a fruit smoothie and gulp it down, and fly out of the house to get to our regular job. On the way home we stop off at the bank, post office, grocery store, and dry cleaners. Maybe we pick up the kids and take them to music lessons or sports practice. Once we get home we've got dinner to make, laundry to do, car maintenance or yard work to attend to, and bills to pay. Evenings are filled with meetings, kids doing their homework and science fair projects, Bible studies, choir practice, or the work we've brought home from the office. Sometimes we just collapse into our favorite chair in front of the TV, occasionally nodding off until the late-night news is over, letting us know it's time to go to bed. With our hectic schedules and daily pressures, it seems enough for us to simply get through one day after another without even thinking about our future dreams and how we plan to get them off the ground.

My dreams didn't start to materialize until I learned two major secrets. The first was to narrow my focus by selecting three or four dreams from my list that could realistically be achieved. When you do this, you'll want to choose from a variety of categories in order to attain balance. For instance, you might have one goal to spend more time with family, one in the area of spiritual health, and another concerning improving or changing your career. Later, once those are realized, your three new categories might include financial goals, sports or hobbies, and physical wellness. Next you may want to renovate your home, plan a family vacation, and get involved in making a contribution to your community. Keep going until you have covered all the areas of balance in your life. By choosing this way, you won't be overwhelmed by the extent of your list.

The second secret made an even bigger impact on my ability to follow my dreams. Connect part of the dream to your daily to-do list. Every day there should be at least one action item that has to do with the fulfillment of one or more of your dreams. People normally fall into the trap of waiting until they have leftover time to do those things. Here's a news flash: There is never going to be leftover time! We are all given 24 hours each day. For some, it's enough to achieve great feats;

for others, there can never be enough time. One thing is for sure: There will never be *more* time. Johann Wolfgang von Goethe remarked, "We always have enough time if we will but use it aright." Time cannot be managed. But what we can manage is our activities and how we spend the time we have. Experts agree: Managing our activities begins with planning. So by knowing what's important to you, you'll make your dreams a priority.

> *The wise man will find a time to do what he says. Yes,*
> *there is a time and a way for everything.*
> ECCLESIASTES 8:5

 ## 75 CONQUER PROCRASTINATION

> *The secret of getting ahead is getting started.*
> *The secret of getting started is breaking your*
> *complex, overwhelming tasks into small manageable*
> *tasks, and then starting on the first one.*
> MARK TWAIN

Do you dream of a more fulfilling and significant life—but put off taking action? Do you long for a more rewarding job, a stronger marriage, a happier home—but can't seem to get started making changes? Maybe you wish for more meaningful relationships with your family members and friends or you want to accomplish more and leave a lasting legacy for future generations. If you are like many people, you have your goals written on tomorrow's to-do list. Each night you go to bed disappointed because your day was crowded with the demands of mundane routines and other people's priorities, making it impossible to pursue what really matters to you. If your top priorities keep getting pushed to the bottom of the list and you want to break out to experience the fullness of all God intended for you, you need to conquer procrastination. There's a simple yet exceptionally effective process to change the way you handle all the tasks and activities that will help you achieve what's truly important to you. Here are some steps you can follow.

JUST DO IT

Too many people waste time preparing to get started! They spend so much time getting ready to do something they have no time left to do it. Stop fretting over minute details at this stage and take the first step. Learn when to stop researching and when to act. Remember Parkinson's Law: Work expands to fill the time available for its completion.

USE THE SALAMI TECHNIQUE

Some dreams can seem overwhelming, so you just don't know where to begin. Break large projects into smaller, bite-size pieces. Then continue to slice each piece the way you would cut up a big chunk of salami. Eventually a segment will surface that you can deal with. You can slice your project according to functions or time frames.

THIRTY-MINUTE PLAN

This technique works when you are paralyzed by the enormity of your project. Whether you are devising a business plan for starting your own company, writing a children's novel, cleaning away all the clutter in your garage, organizing your photographs in albums, or filing the papers on your desk, set a timer and do as much as you can within the time limit. When the time is up you are allowed to stop and not feel guilty that the task is not completed. Pick up where you left off tomorrow with another 30 minutes. After each 30-minute session, give yourself a reward. Take a break, have a cup of flavored coffee, browse through a magazine or newspaper, or do a crossword puzzle.

DO THE LEADING TASK

Select one simple, low-effort, undemanding task and do at least that much. It might entail making a phone call, addressing envelopes, or researching material. Doing that much may generate enough momentum to continue, but nothing will happen until you take some form of action.

Do the Worst First

Often within any dream project there is one "nasty" task. If you don't do it and get it out of the way, it hangs on, nagging you for days. Do the worst thing first and get the most difficult task off your list. Mark Twain understood this technique when he suggested, "If you're going to have to swallow a live frog, don't look at it too long!"

Go Public

When your dream involves changing some major habit, whether it's to start a long-term exercise program, quit smoking, or lose weight, this "broadcast" technique is exceptionally valuable. The principle is simple: Tell everybody your plans. There are two reasons for this. First, you will be accountable to others, which helps put the pressure on and you'll be more likely to stay motivated. Second, if you tell the right people, you will have plenty of support. This also works if you've been postponing starting your own business, changing careers, submitting a manuscript, taking a course, working on your degree, or getting married.

Sometimes we procrastinate making decisions. When this happens, start by gathering all the information, facts, and data you can. Then create a balance sheet with a line drawn down the middle. List the pros and cons. Then pray over them, trusting God's Spirit to sway your mind in the direction of his will for you. He will guide you by presenting clear reasons to take action down one path over the other.

If procrastination is the reason you're not achieving your dreams, a great question to ask yourself is, "What is the best use of my time right now concerning my highest aspirations?" Write that out on an index card with a bold black marker, filling in your particular dream, and place it where you can see it daily. Written reminders are powerful motivators. You might also want to write the words: "Do it now!" Remember, the door to success is labeled *Push!*

76 JUST DO IT!

A daring beginning is halfway to winning.
HEINRICH HEINE

Something amazing happens in our hearts when we dare to take that first step. To see your dream miraculously materialize, the best strategy is to jump in with both feet. Remember the old Nike motto? *Just do it!* Conditions will never be ideal, and there is no perfect time to start, so quit waiting for a supernatural sign that it's okay to begin. There may never be a sign, and you may never feel completely ready. "If you wait for perfect conditions, you will never get anything done" (Ecclesiastes 11:4 TLB).

Planning and preparation have their place, but some people spend their whole lives *getting ready.* Your life is not a dress rehearsal; it's the real thing. This is the big one—don't miss it. Although planning, organizing, researching, training, studying, and perfecting skills are all necessary elements in pursuing your dreams, it's possible to get bogged down with trying to get everything in order. You don't have to know everything or have everything in place before you take action. God can direct your path once you are moving. For example, I can tell you there is a wonderful car sitting in my garage, and I have faith that this car can take me to all sorts of wonderful places all over the continent. But until I actually get into the car, open the garage door, turn the key, start the engine, put it in gear, and get my foot on the gas pedal, it isn't going anywhere. Once I get moving, God can show me when to go left and right and when to turn the corner or go in a different direction altogether. But as long as I sit there planning my route and hoping to go someplace someday, I don't have a chance of reaching my destination. When you start to move, all manner of things will begin to happen that will produce results and take you beyond your original dream.

> *The key to success is to take the 101 strategies and principles in this book and put them into practice.*

Most of what you need to know you will learn in the classroom of life anyway. Following your dream is a matter of lifelong learning and "on the job" training. Usually the most important things you need to know can't be learned ahead of time or while studying, but only while you are actively involved. After doing your homework, researching, asking questions, analyzing, and getting the necessary training, you will probably still not know all you need to know to be successful. Many entrepreneurs and creative inventors say reaching their dream was a matter of trial and error and more like a process of elimination.

It's scary stepping out when we don't feel fully prepared. When we are afraid, we come up with all kinds of excuses. My husband has taken up the sport of fishing, and I have noticed that fishers are great at inventing excuses to let themselves off the hook, so to speak. When they come home empty-handed, the reasons they give for fish not biting are enough to stagger the imagination. According to a fisherman friend, either the water is too cold or too warm, it's too early or too late, the fish are too deep or they just lowered the lake, they haven't stocked it yet, the fish are up the river spawning, the water-skiers have them stirred up, or there aren't any fish because they've all been poisoned by pollution. We can come up with just as many reasons for not pursuing our dreams and goals too. Excuses are just a way to avoid making a commitment to go ahead. If you are fearful, that's natural and to be expected. Take action in spite of the fear.

The key to success is to take the 101 strategies and principles you are discovering in this book and put them into practice. You can't do them all at once, but you can take one step at a time. If you make a little progress day by day, you will develop new habits of success and discipline and move closer to reaching your dreams.

Discovering and implementing your personal dreams and visions are processes of learning about yourself, growing in your relationship with God, and continually fine-tuning your understanding of the dreams you've been given. As your purpose becomes clearer, you will keep refining it over the weeks, months, and years to come. While you are experiencing personal and spiritual growth, it's a good idea to review your dreams and goals periodically. As you grow and change, they will too. Your dream is usually not written in stone. You may want to add or take away certain elements as God unveils his purpose for you and refines your understanding of it. Make a commitment now to implement all you have learned and discovered so far. "Many people die with their music still inside them," said Oliver Wendell Holmes. "Why is this so? Too often it is because they are always getting ready to live. Before they know it, time runs out." Don't die with your dream still inside you. Do it!

77 BREAK IT DOWN

*The idea is to make decisions and act on them—to
decide what is important to accomplish, to decide
how it can best be accomplished, to find time to
work at it and get it done.*
KAREN KAKASCIK

Mark Twain had a simple philosophy for achieving goals. He said, "The secret of getting ahead is getting started. The secret of getting started is breaking your complex and overwhelming tasks into small manageable tasks, and then starting on the first one." Once you discover the dreams God intended for you, it's your job to take action. The best way to do that is to break larger goals down into monthly, weekly, and daily action steps. To make them measurable, have a start date and a target date for when you want to finish each phase. By breaking long-range dreams and actions into bite-size intervals, your dream will seem less daunting and more manageable. And by completing individual segments along the way, you will get the positive reinforcement you need to stay motivated and keep on track.

One method that has always worked for me is to start with the end in mind. Once you know your desired outcome, the completion date, and all the actions required to make it happen, work backward until there is something you can do today and each day until you reach your goal.

Let's say you want to plan a family reunion in one year on the thirtieth of June. Start by making a list of every task and activity involved in organizing an event like this. Consider each aspect: a venue, the guest list, which family members will be helping out, what type of invitations you will send, what the menu will consist of, and what you will do for entertainment, games, and decorations. List them at random for starters and assign a completion date to each item. This way you will be able to prioritize the activities according to dates. Once they are in the proper order, tackle them one at a time. You might decide that your number one priority is to book the venue—do that right away. Next, if you decide invitations should be sent out by the beginning of February, you will have to have them designed and printed in January. There will be a number of things you can do right away, including selecting and organizing your committee, choosing a theme, making phone calls to get quotes for catering, and designing the invitations. Start a file or project workbook to collect ideas for fun activities, games, and decorating ideas. Don't rely on reminders scribbled on scraps of paper, notes held in place by magnets on your refrigerator, or Post-it Notes stuck on your computer or desk.

By placing time frames on all of these activities, you have checkpoints or guideposts to let you know if you are still on target. It also helps you say no to interruptions, when warranted, because there will always be a deadline coming up to which you can refer. Then your mind is freed up to solve problems and create new and better ways to do things.

If your dream is to go on a cruise vacation or renovate part of your house with a target date of six months from now, you will need to determine short-range and intermediate goals within the framework of the larger one. By listing all the action steps necessary to complete the project, from making phone calls to researching all your options and getting quotes, you will be able to prioritize them and assign a time span to each one.

Always commit your objectives and action items to paper. Writing them down makes them concrete and gives them validity. Amazing things happen when you get your goals and plans in writing. They crystallize and become real. A written goal is similar to a seed planted, and you'll always reap what you sow.

Once you have your objectives in writing, put the most prominent and current ones on notecards and place them where you can see them regularly or carry them with you in your wallet or briefcase. Remember to be specific when you itemize your action steps. It is crucial to be clear and accurate about each activity. Definite plans produce definite results. Fill in all the details rather than creating vague or fuzzy descriptions. Your mind needs specific and thorough instructions to work on. Imagine what would happen if you simply asked someone to take your clothes to the cleaners. Or what if you told the courier to deliver your package and left it at that. People need more comprehensive instructions. Directions to yourself have to be accurate and precise as well.

Whatever dream you are working toward now, take a few moments to break it down into bite-size chunks with start and completion dates. Then talk to God about your list. Pray about your productivity, your stamina and energy levels, your attitude about the dream and why it is important. Life is too short to focus on anything that doesn't fulfill your purpose and bring glory to God.

78 MAKE ROOM FOR THE NEW

The ability to eliminate the unnecessary
puts the dream within reach.

If the astounding numbers of attendees at my workshop, "Organized & Clutter-Free at Last" are any indication, we all have too much stuff and we're not sure what to do about it. In order to move ahead with our dreams, we have to let go of the clutter. We must clear out the old to make room for the new (see Leviticus 26:10). In other words, release your clutter and watch what can happen! A financial planner I know tells me that whenever he wants to bring in new business, he meticulously clears the clutter from his office, home, briefcase, wallet, car, and garage. Almost miraculously, within a short time, new business opportunities begin to open up. He understands the principle of getting rid of the old to make way for the new.

How many things do you need to let go of, clear out, complete, delegate, or get rid of before your dream can come to you? Whether you're dreaming of new opportunities, relationships, hobbies, activities, or material possessions, you must make some space before they will come to you.

Cleaning out the old is not as easy as it sounds because most of us have incredible emotional and psychological attachments to our belongings. Many homes and offices these days are spilling over with piles of papers, magazines, catalogs, clothes that haven't been worn in years, broken toys, old appliances, projects that were started but never finished, parts from projects we don't even have anymore, obsolete typewriters and answering machines, things we don't even remember we have, items we don't need anymore, and boxes that haven't been opened in years. We save keys on a ring even though we don't know what they open. We keep old stationery and business cards, hosiery with holes, outdated jewelry, and pens that don't work. Instead of clearing out the old, we build bigger backyard storage sheds, make additions to our homes, purchase larger file cabinets, and rent storage space. Why do we have such a hard time letting go?

Part of holding on is the fear that we'll never get more. We hang on to the old as though nothing new will ever come our way. Whether it's tangible or intangible—a relationship, a job, an old sweater, a broken blender—it boils down to the fact that we don't trust that God will continue meeting our needs and providing for us.

The biggest problem with clutter—inner and outer—is that it's always affecting us. Inner clutter creates outer confusion; outer clutter creates inner turmoil. Once you release your grip on the outer clutter, inner turmoil and chaos have a way of subsiding too. Start by devoting one weekend and, after that, 15 minutes each day to clearing out your clutter. You'll be making some mental and physical space for your dreams. To kick-start your declutter exercise, make a list of some of the areas you want to clear out. Also include projects that need to be completed. Your list might include:

- Closets, cupboards, drawers
- Garage, basement, attic

- Desk and file cabinets
- Unfinished projects
- Unpaid debts
- Bank accounts that should be closed
- Junk drawers
- Broken tools and appliances
- Car trunk, glove compartment, backseat
- Credenza with uncompleted tasks
- Stacks of filing and piles of papers
- Computer files not backed up
- Emails not deleted or stored
- Family photographs not in albums
- Mending or ironing
- Piles of clothes to be given away
- Projects needing closure

You'll also want to get rid of anything that irritates you. Consider those daily annoyances like the zipper that won't zip or the toaster that won't pop. They're not necessarily life-threatening to you or your family or urgent to your business, but if they aggravate or annoy you in any way, they are draining energy from you that could be devoted to embarking on your dreams. Getting rid of the irritants will add vitality to your life.

Keep this phrase in mind at all times: simplify, simplify, simplify. You might want to write it on a note card and keep it posted where you'll be sure to see it often. Develop the habit of having "a place for everything and everything in its place." Your heavenly Father is waiting to bless you with an abundant life. Free up some room and watch what he'll do!

PART 12

Be Here Now

79 ESCAPE THE "I'LL BE HAPPY WHEN..." TRAP

*I've learned by now to be quite content whatever
my circumstances. I'm just as happy with little
as with much, with much as with little.*
PHILIPPIANS 4:11 MSG

*It's not enough to reach for the brass ring. You
must also enjoy the merry-go-round.*
JULIE ANDREWS

One drawback to dreaming big is that it keeps us hanging in the balance, always waiting for the completion of some goal so we can finally experience happiness and success. There's an old adage that reminds us, "Success is not a destination; it's a journey." As much as we know and believe that in our heads, our hearts still long to arrive at someplace up ahead where we can count on being truly contented and fulfilled at last. We think our success is "out there." Reaching your dreams does not mean you can't fully enjoy life until you arrive.

Maybe you've been putting your happiness on hold until the journey is complete, the destination has been reached, and all your dreams are realized. If so, it might be time to redefine success. Be sure to do it in your own terms rather than allowing the media, your neighbors, family members, the Joneses, or anyone else to determine what a "good life" will look like for you. Leave the status quo behind. Free yourself from the stereotypical assumptions of what is a normal or acceptable lifestyle. How would you define success and achievement for yourself? Write it down and contemplate it.

You may be living in the fairy-tale kingdom of "I'll be happy when…" if you believe that real success is in the next purchase, the next relationship, the next venture, or the next project. Check out this list and see if any of these statements sound familiar:

I'll be happy when…
- I turn 16/21/65.
- I graduate from school.
- I find my ideal mate.
- I get married/divorced.
- I have children.
- the children sleep through the night/go to school/leave home/get married.
- I move into a bigger house.
- my skills and abilities are recognized.
- my talents are acknowledged.
- I get discovered.
- I get the raise/promotion/new career.
- my spouse/boss changes.
- the weather improves.
- I have more money/time.
- the mortgage is paid and I'm out of debt.
- I get the new ring/car/big screen TV.
- I win at golf.
- my ship comes in.
- there's an end to all injustice in the world.

Have you been putting your happiness on hold? Some of us are waiting until we hear God's voice booming down from the heavens, telling us, "Your life is now perfect. You may go ahead and start living."

Sometimes when we do manage to get the right job, a caring and attractive mate, a luxury car, the dream home, or all the material possessions associated with prosperity and success, we're disappointed because we find out that no matter how much we get, it's never enough. If you've just moved into a new home, there's always a bigger or better one out there. If you're driving a new car, you're already looking forward to next year's model. When you return from your dream vacation, you're eager to start planning the next one. Success in your job usually opens up yet another advancement to strive toward. Before you know it, you are locked into a lifelong struggle to move ahead while attaining material possessions, leisure activities, positions, and influence that will supposedly provide you with the happiness you long to experience. But it's really a trap…fortunately it's one you can be set free from.

Who decides whether you'll be happy or unhappy? The answer is *you!* So choose to enjoy all you have at this moment. Start living today with gratitude for all you have right now. After all, as Abraham Lincoln put it, "A man is about as happy as he makes up his mind to be!"

80 THE IMPACT OF CONTENTMENT

Contentment makes poor men rich.
Discontent makes rich men poor.
BENJAMIN DISRAELI

True contentment is found, not in having
everything you want, but in not
wanting to have everything.

There's a story of a wealthy businessman who went home to a small fishing village to visit his family. When he arrived at lunch time, he was disturbed to see his brother bringing in his boat and finishing up for the day. He asked, "Why aren't you out there fishing since the day is only half over?" "Because I've caught enough fish for the day, and I'm going home to be with my wife and children," was his reply. "We'll go for a walk on the beach, have a long, leisurely picnic supper together, and later I will play my guitar at the village square so our friends can sing and dance." "But why don't you catch more fish than you need?" asked the rich brother. "Then you could earn more money, buy a better boat, purchase nylon nets, go deeper, and catch even more fish. Eventually you could hire other fishermen and have a fleet of boats. Soon you could be rich like me." "Then what would I do?" asked the fisherman. "Well," said his brother, "you could take time off, spend it with your wife and children, go for long walks, visit with your friends and…uh, never mind."

Sometimes in our quest for success, we lose sight of our original motivation for the dream. Charles Spurgeon said, "It's not how much we have, but how much we enjoy, that makes happiness." When my two children and I first lived in our small apartment after escaping a violent and abusive situation, we were quite content with our new home. While our surroundings and belongings were modest, we felt safe and secure and had basically everything we needed to live comfortably. Friends and family helped us decorate and furnish the apartment, and it was a warm and cozy haven for us to begin our new life.

Shortly after we moved there, I was blessed with a wonderful job opportunity in which I was able to double my earnings. I will always remember the day I got my first paycheck and wanted to celebrate. As I stood looking around the apartment, I started to notice that the carpet was a bit frayed, the dining room table looked worn, and the living room furniture was faded. The artwork on the walls didn't quite coordinate with the rest of the furnishings, and the lamps didn't match either. I knew that I was now in a position to replace all these things. Why hadn't I noticed their paltry condition before?

We had been so thankful that God had provided all our needs that the state of our belongings didn't really matter that much. So what was the difference now that I could afford to make changes? I caught myself as I realized that I had been satisfied the day before, but today none of that was good enough. I dropped to my knees and prayed for forgiveness. That day I asked God to help me be content with little or much. I wanted to be in a position where I would always have enough but not so much that I would forget where my success comes from. In Philippians 4:11-12 TLB, the apostle Paul says, "I have learned how to get along happily whether I have much or little. I know how to live on almost nothing or with everything. I have learned the secret of contentment in every situation."

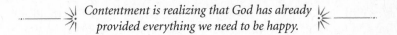

*Contentment is realizing that God has already
provided everything we need to be happy.*

The opposite of contentment is dissatisfaction, being disgruntled with your situation and unsatisfied with your surroundings. As a business speaker, I often get asked by corporations that are struggling in some way to speak to the people in their organizations who had the potential to be good managers and leaders but were falling below expectations. As we go through various exercises together, I am always struck by how dissatisfied these people tend to be with the company and their jobs. Some say that is to be expected since they know they're in trouble within the company. I wonder if it may work the other way. Perhaps with all the discontent, dissatisfaction, and grumbling, they became negative and their work suffered. One of the most powerful ways to turn things around in a situation like this is to find contentment within the current circumstances and to be satisfied with the way things are while working toward positive change in order to attain excellence. While dreaming big and having grand expectations is part of success, so is contentment and gratification that come with a job well done.

Contentment is realizing that God has already provided everything we need to be happy. Give up the striving and straining to make your dream happen, for "my God shall supply all your need according to His riches in glory by Christ Jesus" (Philippians 4:19 NKJV)

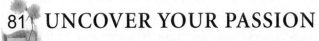

81 UNCOVER YOUR PASSION

He did it with all his heart. So he prospered.
2 CHRONICLES 31:21 TLB

*A strong passion will ensure success for the desire of the
end will point out the means.*
WILLIAM HAZLITT

Is there something in life you are deeply and enthusiastically passionate about? What makes it difficult to sit still because you can hardly wait to get to it? Because you are reading this book, I believe you probably have at least one thing that causes your heart to do giant flip-flops every time you think about it. Passion is the fuel that empowers you to follow even seemingly impossible dreams.

Maybe your passion is found in your job. If it is, you probably approach your work with energy and a sense of mission…or even as a type of ministry to others. I had the opportunity to see this in action after presenting a customer service workshop for a large hotel one snowy winter day. The next morning several of the employees were so motivated that, on their own initiative, they bundled up, went out to the parking lot, and removed snow and ice from the windshield of each guest's car just before check-out time. They left notes under the windshield wipers saying "Compliments of the hotel." Not only were those patrons dazzled and grateful, but the staff had a renewed sense of passion about their work. After that seminar, they began to approach their jobs with creativity, pride, and zeal. These days the level of service they offer their guests goes well beyond what is normally expected in most hotels. And with this attitude and sense of purpose, they are much more enthusiastic about getting to work each day.

Now, I have a confession to make about my own job. Although I don't make a point of telling this to my clients, I am so passionate about what I do that I'm sure I would do it even if I had to pay *them* to let me get up on stage and talk. (Please don't let the cat out of the bag!) One creative way to discover your passion when considering a career is to ask yourself: What would I do even if I had to pay someone to let me do it? When people approach me because they want to be professional speakers and want to know how to get into the business, I ask them two questions: *What do you have to say?* and *Who needs to hear it?* When you have a passion for a subject, it is so much a part of you that you *must* share it. People who sustain their success over long periods have a genuine zeal for what they do and believe wholeheartedly that their message, service, or product needs to be out there.

If your work isn't terribly fulfilling or rewarding just now, your passion might be found in other areas of your life, such as organizing fund-raising events for local charities, teaching Sunday school, or coaching Little League baseball. Maybe it's being a Big Brother or Big Sister, playing a musical instrument in a band or orchestra, acting in local theater, singing in a choir, or writing poetry. One man I know loves to create elegant and colorful gardens to treat passersby in his neighborhood. What you do isn't what matters. What does matter is that there is something in your life that you can become so completely immersed in that you lose all track of time and you're not concerned with what's in the refrigerator. You'll know it's a true passion when you totally forget the clock and your stomach!

When you dream, be sure to have at least one thing that is completely for your personal fulfillment. For example, watching a movie with the family, having dinner out with friends, or taking the kids bowling or ice-skating are great ways to spend time with those you care about. But passions that are completely separate from nurturing family and other relationships serve to give our life balance. The time we spend pursuing our passions is a precious, therapeutic commodity. Afterward, we return to our relationships and jobs with more zeal too.

A man who attended one of my seminars recently said he spends much of his spare time in his woodworking shop. His passion is creating unique pieces of furniture for family and friends. Although it's a time-consuming and fairly costly pastime, he says it is worth pinching pennies and blocking off certain hours because he likes the person he is when he comes back to his wife, his children, and his regular job. He has found to be true what I have noticed: The happiest people have at least one passion. If you haven't found yours, search for it…and keep looking until you discover it.

82 LOVE WHAT YOU DO

*Nothing is really work unless you'd rather
be doing something else.*
JAMES M. BARRIE

*It's not your position that makes you happy,
it's your disposition.*
AUTHOR UNKNOWN

Do you ever wonder why people who are financially independent continue to work when they really don't have to? And why do some people who are of retirement age keep working when they could be taking it easy without any external demands or expectations? The answer is that they love what they do. They have fun and it shows. In fact, they can't imagine *not* doing what they do. Perhaps they know they are fulfilling their greatest purpose here on earth. Maybe they are passionate about offering their God-given gifts to enhance the lives of others. In some cases, they are having so much enjoyment that they would feel deprived if they weren't able to do it anymore. Whatever the case, continuing in their line of work is most likely the fulfillment of their dreams, bringing them greater pleasure than almost anything else they could be doing with their time and energy. So why would they stop because they are wealthy? Why would they consider retiring simply because they've reached a certain age? These are people with a love for life and their calling, and nothing can hold them back!

If you want to discover what you'd really love to do, ask yourself these questions:

- What do you enjoy doing so much that you'd pay someone to let you do it?
- If you suddenly became a millionaire, would you continue to do what you do now?
- What are you working at when you find you laugh a lot with good, wholesome humor?

The answers to these questions will help you know whether you are pursuing dreams that are right for you. If being independently wealthy would cause you to change the way you spend your days, then maybe you should start considering that right now. Why stay stuck in a dreary position when you could be having some fun?

Over the years I have met many men and women who achieved success by society's financial standards, yet they are happy to continue in their chosen fields with or without compensation. Recently I was interviewed on television by a beautiful woman who is now into her seventh decade and could choose to retire at any time. She sees her work as a ministry—an opportunity to offer encouragement, comfort, and hope to viewers who are hurting or in desperate situations. She enjoys what she does and finds happiness in helping people. There are many speakers, authors, and entertainers I know who love what they do so much that they say if no one hired them, they would gladly pay for the chance to get on stage and perform.

So what's your pleasure? Loving what you do is one of the major keys to unlocking your personal passion. You will have a better chance at realizing your dream if you are filled with enthusiasm about what you plan to do. By analyzing pleasurable moments in your life, you will discover your inner strengths and positive attributes that will allow you to perform effortlessly and naturally, making your work pleasurable. Start by focusing on the times in your life when you were fully enjoying yourself. What were you doing? Were you alone or with someone? Was it work-related or did it have to do with a hobby or sport? Was there a time in school when you felt a sense of accomplishment that came from doing what you liked? How about extracurricular activities that fascinated you? Think about hobbies or special interests you have enjoyed so much that no one had to motivate you to be involved.

Were there times on the job or in a business you operate or in a relationship you're involved in when you were able to solve problems and have fun doing it? Are there memories of certain experiences you've had that make you smile just thinking about them? Looking at your most pleasurable experiences will give you a fresh sense of direction when it comes to pursuing new dreams. Most of us don't analyze our happy times, we just have them. Looking at them this new way will help you zone in on what you truly love and enjoy. Spontaneous, joy-filled times hold the key to the direction you will want to take with your future dreams.

83 FLAMING ENTHUSIASM

Nothing great was ever achieved without enthusiasm.
RALPH WALDO EMERSON

Flaming enthusiasm, backed up by horse sense and persistence, is the quality that most frequently makes for success.
DALE CARNEGIE

The word *enthusiasm* comes from the Greek word *entheos*, which means to be filled with God. Enthusiasm of a spiritual nature goes beyond a mere feeling. It's when you are brimming with inner zeal and fervor, and your spirit is inspired from deep within. When God inspires us, it means literally to breathe into and infuse with life. "Enthusiasm is a kind of faith that has been set afire!" said George Matthew Adams. Flaming enthusiasm provides the continual energy, focus, and zest you need to reach your target. With all your senses enlivened, you will approach your dream with gusto.

My prayer has long been "Lord, let me live as long as I'm alive!" Do you know people who are still breathing but there isn't much life in them? They lack enthusiasm and passion. Nothing fills them with delight. These are people who have "lost all their marvels."

When your work becomes touched by blazing fervor, you approach it with gusto, and it becomes as enjoyable as any pastime. Thomas Edison said, "I never did a day's work in my life. It was all fun." If your dream involves something you love to do and are enthusiastic about, you will be successful. There may still be occasional difficulties, problems, and trials, and your dream may cause you to stretch and feel uncomfortable. It may involve sacrifice, and there will probably be many hurdles, snags, inconveniences, and stumbling blocks along the way. There might be times when you have to exert yourself just to get up and face the world each day. But when you are enthusiastic about a project, you will have the energy and confidence to keep going. On the other hand, one thing that robs us of our enthusiasm is being unsure that what we are doing is actually what we are called to do. You'll find success eluding you if you are constantly haunted by the idea that you could—or should—be doing something else.

If your life has become one humdrum routine after another, get a fresh dream of God's will for your life. Get out of your rut and break away from your everyday routine. Leave old ideas and viewpoints behind. Try something different. Learn something new. You may find the spark of enthusiasm you need, giving you the incentive to change and grow again. Sadly, for many people, their only dreams are to earn a living, get the bills paid off, take a vacation or two, and buy more stuff. There is more to life than a dream like that. When you have accomplished these things, you will get to a point where you say, "Is this all there is?" But when you have a burning passion to fulfill a purpose, you'll have fire in your life!

Most people, at some point, get caught in the trap of simply preserving and maintaining what they have already accomplished. Their marriage is satisfactory, the kids are grown, the mortgage is paid, finances are adequate, and the business is running fine. Thinking they'll just coast and enjoy life for a while, they kick into maintenance mode. The problem is you cannot coast in life. You are always moving—either forward or backward. Life is like being in a river. If you don't keep swimming, you'll float downstream. Enthusiasm for a fresh dream is what keeps you from becoming stagnant.

Enthusiasm comes naturally when you follow your heart and discover what you were born to do. It comes from caring about what you do and what you have to offer the world. When you find your passion, you will be excited about getting up each morning. If you enjoy your work and look forward to each day, you are already a success! My dad played piano in a dance band for years. Although the group never cut a record, and they never went on to become superstars outside their own area, he felt successful because he enjoyed his art. He often commented on how he got a thrill from the joy and pleasure he was able to bring his audiences through his music every Saturday night. When what you do fills your heart with enthusiasm, and you approach it with zeal and vigor, it won't matter if you never hit the big time. Even if you failed at it, what does it matter anyway? You were having fun!

84 TAKE A POSITIVE RISK

People who never get out of the
boat can't expect to walk on water.

Do not pray for easy lives; pray to
be stronger men. Do not pray for tasks equal to your
powers; pray for powers equal to your tasks.
PHILLIPS BROOKS

Many people would choose security over risk if that were an option. But if you want to go beyond a dream, there's really not a choice. Turning goals into realities requires that you be a positive risk-taker. You have to leave security behind. Besides, as Helen Keller stated, "Security is mostly superstition. It doesn't exist in nature nor do the children of men as a whole experience it. Avoiding danger in the long run is no safer than outright exposure. Life is either a daring adventure or it is nothing."

Risking is when you take a quantum leap of faith that requires an enormous amount of courage. A *positive* risk is when you leap without abandoning your good judgment and common sense. It's those times when you have done your homework, investigated all your options, prayed for guidance, weighed the pros and cons, and then, based on your findings, decide to take action. Positive risk-taking isn't about being involved in something dangerous or doing something that infringes on the rights of others. It doesn't mean gambling, speeding in your car, or flirting with someone else's spouse. If it's a *positive* risk, it won't cause you to end up unpopular, in jail, or dead!

What is risky for one person may not be for another. While some people would be thrilled at the chance to go bungee jumping, white-water rafting, or roller-coaster riding, others might not find those feats at all risky. For them it may be riskier to attend a conference or social function alone or stand up at a wedding and give a speech in front of family and friends. Some of us might be secure eating by ourselves in a fast-food restaurant or deli, but we'd feel uncomfortable dining alone in a more luxurious or sophisticated spot. In business, we might be comfortable charging $50 an hour for our services but $75 an hour would make us cringe. For one person it would be risky to walk away from an unhealthy friendship or a dead-end job, and for another, it might be a risk to pay off all debts and stop using credit cards.

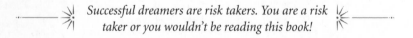

Successful dreamers are risk takers. You are a risk taker or you wouldn't be reading this book!

What is it for you? Would it be risky to initiate a friendship with someone you consider "out of your league"? Maybe you'd feel quite comfortable paying $30 for a cotton sweater but you'd be anxious spending $200 for a cashmere one. Would it be a risk to go to a professional counselor, let go of a life-threatening addiction or compulsion, or leave a harmful relationship or work situation? How about signing up for a night-school course, applying for a job in another part of the country, or running for president of an organization you belong to?

A true positive risk always has two primary elements: You'll be scared silly and exhilarated at the same time. I find it an interesting facet of human nature that we can experience both those emotions simultaneously. While you are scared at the thought of investing in a brand-new car, it is also exciting. Moving across the country, changing careers, planning a wedding, going off to college, starting your own business, or getting a promotion makes you nervous and exhilarated.

Does your dream require you to do something risky? Successful dreamers are risk takers. You are too or you wouldn't be reading this book! Emerson said, "Do the thing you fear the most and the death of fear is certain." Choose to take action even though you're afraid. Stop putting your dreams on hold until the fear goes away. Here's a news flash: Fear is not going away. "Quit thinking you must halt before the barrier of inner negativity. You need not. You can crash through!" said Vernon Howard. When we trust God, who is bigger than all our doubts, fears, and circumstances, we gain the courage necessary to win in spite of the obstacles. With the apostle Paul we can say, "I can do everything through him who gives me strength" (Philippians 4:13).

On the other hand, making a leap of faith on your own is not only frightening, it's unsafe. Only leap when you are God-directed. Then, although it's still scary, he will be there to catch you. When my children were small, they would stand at the top of the stairs with their chubby little arms outstretched and then jump with all their might right into my waiting arms. I am sure it was scary for them, but gladly I was able to catch them every time. A true leap of faith is like that. It means letting go of what's safe, secure, and predictable, and trusting God to catch you. And you know he'll be there with arms outstretched! Hebrews 11:8 TLB says, "Abraham trusted God, and when God told him to leave home and go far away to another land that he promised to give him, Abraham obeyed. Away he went, not even knowing where he was going." You may have a dream yet still not know exactly where you are going with it. If God is asking you to risk something in order to make your dream come true, and if he is the one calling you to leap, you can be sure he is ready to catch you!

85 UNWAVERING COURAGE

*All our dreams can come true—if we have
the courage to pursue them.*
WALT DISNEY

Being a risk taker requires courage. When you are brave and daring you have the ability to face the unknown, endure the fears, and overcome the difficulties that go along with achievement. The opposite is to be disheartened and held back by fear. The things you fear can be very real and understandable, as they may result from childhood trauma, unrealistic expectations set by adults in your life, or impossible standards presented through our culture or the media. If you grew up in a controlling environment, you may still be lacking the courage to take risks. You may be doing things a certain way because you believe they're supposed to be done that way. You'll be afraid to step away from the status quo if, for instance, you were raised to believe that buying a particular model of car, voting for a specific political party, following certain holiday traditions, or living in a particular part of the country because your family lives there is the only acceptable way.

Your old beliefs, thoughts, and mental habit patterns could be keeping you stuck and preventing you from pursuing new dreams. Maybe it's time to analyze some of your past views and opinions and clear out those that are not working for you. As Gilett Burgess remarked, "If in the last few years, you haven't discarded a major opinion or acquired a new one, check your pulse. You may be dead!"

With lack of courage, you eliminate entire areas of possibilities to enjoy the freedom God wants you to have and minimize your potential. Whether you are inhibited by painful memories, haunting fears, doubts and uncertainties, or even unconscious harmful beliefs, letting go is never easy—but it's worth the effort.

One way to gain courage and get unstuck is to purposely put yourself into uncomfortable situations that cause you to stretch and take risks. Try calling someone you've been intimidated to call. Volunteer to help out with a project even though you have no prior experience. Apply for a promotion or a job that you are not yet quite qualified to do. You can grow into it! Enroll in a course or sign up to take lessons in something that interests you but is outside your realm of expertise. Take a risk each day by doing something that causes you to stretch. Ask yourself: What's the worst that can happen if it doesn't work out? There will be other opportunities, and you will have grown in many ways.

Courage means doing courageous acts before you are feeling courageous. Mark Twain put it this way: "Courage is resistance to fear, mastery of fear—not absence of fear." When I was asked to give talks at various functions before I began my professional career, I had a terrible fear of public speaking. But since I believed the message I offered would inspire others, I kept saying yes to the invitations in spite of my fear. Each time I saw my name on an agenda, I felt myself getting sicker and sicker as it got closer to the time I would have to go on stage. I remember hoping that if I mysteriously became deathly ill they would let me off the hook and excuse me from speaking! But I persevered, and there did come a day when I actually got excited about being introduced as the next speaker. I clearly remember the moment it happened. I was thinking, "Come on...get on with the program and introduce me. I have something encouraging, helpful, and fun to share with everyone!" That day I realized how far I had come. Although I still had butterflies in my stomach, now they were flying in formation. When I was finally in my comfort zone, God said, "It's time to stretch again!" Next came writing books and doing media tours, with autographing events, television interviews, and radio call-in shows. I am still being challenged to this day—and that is okay!

Think about your most magnificent dreams and ask yourself some important questions:

- What are the biggest risks you'll have to face in achieving the dream?

- What are the greatest opportunities opening up ahead of
  you?
- What inner strengths and other resources do you need to
  develop that will help you capture those opportunities?

Courage is having what it takes to tackle obstacles in the face of
fear. If there were no challenges in reaching your dreams, there would
be no need to be courageous. To have courage is the opposite of being
discouraged and comes from a certainty more powerful than outside
circumstances. When we recognize we serve a God who is bigger than
all our obstacles, we gain the courage necessary to win. He says, "Be
strong and courageous and…you will be successful in everything you
do" (Joshua 1:7 TLB). Either we remain safely ensconced in our limited
world of the possible or we trust God and step into the "impossible"
realm. I'm praying for you, my friend, that just as it was no accident this
book has come into your hands, by the time you've finished reading it
you will accept the challenge. Be a courageous dreamer and step out.
Leave the possible and join the risk takers in the roller-coaster realm
of the impossible. Sure it's scary out here. But believe me, it's worth it!

86 KEEP YOUR CHILD HEART

I was a fourteen-year-old boy for thirty years.
MICKEY ROONEY

The great man is he that does not lose his child's heart.
MENCIUS

When a newspaper reporter interviewed a man celebrating his one-
hundredth birthday, he questioned him on his incredible good
health. The reporter tried to find out if his energy and vitality could be
attributed to a positive mental outlook, wholesome upbringing, a healthy
diet, or a regular fitness routine over the years. But the old fellow kept

saying he didn't really know. Finally the reporter asked, "Well, how was your childhood?" At last, with a big smile, the man replied, "So far, so good!"

Here was someone who knew the value of keeping a "child heart." The most creative dreamers I have ever met are like that. They have an air of playfulness about them. They know how to escape the "daily-ness" of routine and see the fun side of everyday situations. They make plans to play often—whether it's with children, a group of friends, or alone. They're the ones you'll see swinging on a tree swing, using the slide and teeter totter, or taking a dip in the wading pool. They love to blow bubbles, fly kites, tell jokes and riddles, catch fireflies, and study the stars. In summertime you'll see them sharing water squirt toys or pails and shovels with kids at the beach. In the winter, they'll be tobogganing or ice-skating on an outdoor rink or making snow angels. It's in their playfulness that their most creative and innovative ideas come to them. They never have a shortage of exciting and fulfilling projects on the go.

When my grandchildren came along, I learned all over again the joy and value of play. Suddenly there was an opportunity to splash in puddles and jump in piles of autumn leaves. I had an excuse to build sandcastles and ride the merry-go-round. It's too bad we need an excuse to play. Sometimes our inhibitions hold us back from leaving our serious side behind, and we have a hard time doing something silly or outrageous just for the fun of it. Fortunately, it's never too late to learn the *art of playfulness!* As Mae West put it, "You're never too old to become younger!" We need to play in order to stimulate our imaginations if we are going to dream bigger dreams and recognize everyday miracles.

How often do you go out to play? Everyone needs to get away from life's challenges every now and then. Whether you play at home or go on a retreat, let loose and be a kid again. Men are often better at this, maybe because they often go away on fishing trips or golfing weekends. My husband enjoys attending car races several weekends out of the year. My sisters and I caught on to the importance of this exceptionally restorative practice a while ago. There are five of us, and our homes are scattered across the continent. Getting together involves a good deal of advance planning plus an investment of time and money. But we discovered that the rejuvenating benefits are priceless and well worth the effort. We will soon celebrate our twenty-fifth annual "Augustine Girls Weekend Getaway." Each year a different sister takes the lead and plans the entire retreat. We have traveled to many interesting places. And while we are together, we enjoy everything from pampering spa days and attending live theater to biking, canoeing, playing tennis, and horseback riding. Everyone's favorite time is our late-night pajama parties when we play board games into the wee hours, eat way too many snacks, and laugh until our faces hurt. The best part? We get to be kids all over again!

So capture the spirit of play. Whether you are eating a cherry Popsicle, riding a roller coaster at an amusement park, wearing a red clown nose, or rolling down a grassy hillside, you'll soon be able to go beyond a dream in more ways than you've imagined.

There's a big difference between being childlike and childish. The Bible tells us to become like little children. Maybe that is because they are more likely to be the dreamers. Jesus recognized that little children had great comprehension and a grasp of the things of heaven. He prayed, "O Father, Lord of heaven and earth, thank you for hiding the truth from those who think themselves so wise, and for revealing it to little children" (Matthew 11:25 TLB). Do you remember having unwavering faith as a child, where no dream was too outrageous? Rainer Marie Rilke put it well when she declared, "And even if you were in some prison, the walls of which let none of the sounds of the world come to your sense—would you not then still have your childhood, that precious kingly possession, that treasure-house of memories?"

PART 13

Healthy, Wealthy, and Wise

87 AIM FOR BALANCE

Show me the way I should go, for to you I lift up my soul.
PSALM 143:8

To achieve harmony in your life, plan to have dreams and goals in a variety of areas. For starters, you'll want to strive toward wellness in your body, mind, and spirit. Then bring balance into your life in the areas of personal growth, relationships, home life, and work. In order to maintain harmony in all your life goals, consider your answers to the following questions covering various facets of your life. Your answers could lead you to making profound changes toward your future.

MENTAL WELLNESS

Which books would you like to read and courses could you take to expand your knowledge base? Are there ways you can develop your mind through memory training, public speaking, or learning a new language? Which games, puzzles, brainteasers, and creative projects could enhance your problem-solving capabilities? Which ventures could you undertake that would cause you to stretch and take risks?

PHYSICAL WELLNESS

What can you do to increase your energy, strength, and stamina? How can you trim and firm up your body? Which foods could you add or eliminate from your diet to feel healthier? What exercise programs can you become involved in to be more fit? How can you get more rest and relaxation? How can you minimize the negative effects of stress in your life? What hobbies or crafts would you find relaxing or stimulating?

SPIRITUAL WELLNESS

How can you make time each day to sit quietly, read from God's Word, and meditate? What other inspirational books and materials could you read? What Scripture verses could you memorize, and how do you plan to do that? What groups could you join and events could you attend to celebrate with other believers? How can you remind yourself to think about God and talk to him during the day? In what areas could you volunteer your time and talents to contribute to your community?

Aside from these areas of balance in your body, mind, and spirit, goals in other areas can bring balance to your daily life. Consider these focus areas and answer the questions.

PERSONAL GROWTH

Which character traits do you want to develop or improve? What attitudes and behaviors representing those of your family or heritage may be keeping you from fully reaching your potential? Who could provide valuable feedback to help you make the necessary changes to reach your dream? Are there ways you could cultivate your sense of humor, including taking yourself less seriously?

INTIMATE RELATIONSHIPS

Does your spouse look forward to being with you? Are you the type of person *you* want to be around? What are some ways you can express your appreciation for the one you love? How can you show affection, including physical intimacy, that isn't necessarily sexual? How can you let your spouse know he or she is the most important person on earth to you? How can you be sure your past is not affecting your current relationship?

FAMILY AND FRIENDS

What are some ways you can demonstrate love to your children, parents, siblings, and other family members? Who uplifts you when you are down? Which of your family members and friends are fun to be around? What can you do to show your appreciation to special people?

Who can be part of your support team, and how can you strengthen these relationships? Which negative or critical people do you need to associate with less often?

CAREER OR OCCUPATION

What do you want to accomplish on the job within the next year, five years, ten years? What needs to happen in your life before you will consider yourself successful? How could you create a career from something you have a passion for? What can you do to have a more positive attitude toward the job or position you currently have? When you reach your goals, what will it take to stay at your new level?

EDUCATION

How can you continue to be a student of new skills and knowledge? What three things could you learn that would contribute to overall achievement? What type of information that is supportive of your highest aspirations do you expose yourself to on a regular basis?

FINANCIAL

What are some ways you could earn extra money if you were willing to invest your time and effort? What steps can you take to ensure financial freedom? What books can you read or courses can you take regarding financial planning?

TRAVEL AND LEISURE

How much do you need to save monthly for your next vacation? Which gallery exhibits, local theater productions, lunchtime concerts, or lecture series are available in your area? What cultural events can you attend that you have never experienced before?

MATERIAL POSSESSIONS

What external assets and belongings can help you feel fulfilled? What can you do to surround yourself with the things that make you feel comfortable, inspired, and at peace? What must you let go of internally to be free from the need for more stuff?

CONTRIBUTION AND CHARITY

In which organizations can you volunteer your services? What possessions that you are not using can you give to someone else to enrich his or her life? How can you donate regularly to a worthy cause?

The answers to these questions will reveal the desires of your heart. And those desires are quite simply God's way of giving you a compass for the pathways he wants you to take. By fulfilling dreams in each of these areas, your life will stay balanced and healthy.

88 CAN YOUR BODY KEEP UP?

If you are going to try cross-country skiing, you should start with a small country.
AUTHOR UNKNOWN

Would you like to stay young and live a long, vibrant life? God says he wants you to do well and be in good health even as your soul prospers. Yet so many people today complain of being overworked, overwhelmed, overextended, and overtired. They feel stretched to the limit and are physically exhausted most of the time. It's no wonder they don't dream big dreams for themselves! It's difficult to get excited and enthusiastic about doing anything extra when you are worn out. That is precisely why it is so important to have a vision for your future. Often when physical problems do surface, they are merely symptoms of the inactivity in a person's life. When we become stagnant, our bodies break down and we slowly die. Lack of vision is also why so many people pass away early in their retirement years.

The opposite is also true. Lethargy and illness can be the result of having too many dreams and failing to care for ourselves properly as we pursue them. The result is we become imbalanced. To experience vibrant health, energy, and vitality requires effort and planning.

First of all, we need to get our focus back in perspective. Although many people do have heavy workloads during the week and not nearly enough time off on weekends to recuperate, much of the stress we experience doesn't come from our work. Instead it comes from getting our wants mixed up with our needs. Our desire for material gain and the drive to have more tangible possessions cause us to work overtime, take second jobs, and live in such a rush that we no longer have time to renew and recharge our bodies. When we are worn out and every bone in our body aches, it's difficult to be thrilled about anything, let alone following a dream. When you can barely drag your body through the routines of each day, fulfilling a life purpose can seem like a grueling task. If this sounds like you, it may be time to slow down and reevaluate your priorities.

Second, sometimes we simply have to get away from it all. Getting out, especially spending time in nature, can infuse our bodies and souls with new life. While in Chicago on a media tour, I had the opportunity to visit the Dwight L. Moody Institute and museum. There I learned that one strong characteristic of Mr. Moody's was his yearning to spend time in the country. He was born there, and for him the hills possessed miraculous recuperative powers. An inner prompting, he said, drew him back there periodically, away from the crowds of the city where he lived and worked. Then, after a little reprieve, he would return feeling refreshed and invigorated, ready to face the challenges of his work and ministry once again. You and I need to retreat now and again to get recharged.

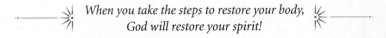

When you take the steps to restore your body,
God will restore your spirit!

Third, when you lack energy, start to recognize your body as an energy system that functions with efficient food fuel. Maybe you don't attempt to dream because you know you don't have the energy to fulfill your vision. However, you were created to experience vibrant vitality. Radiant health and boundless energy are your birthright. Health is natural; disease is not. We fall into the trap of believing lethargy and sickness are inevitable. Even medical science supports that our bodies were created to be self-renewing, self-cleansing, and self-healing…with the right fuel.

What type of fuel have you been providing for your system? When we are exhausted, we make poor food choices dictated by impulse, moods, or convenience, but this is when it is even more critical to focus on balanced nutrition. Switch to drinking water and juice over soft drinks and coffee. Cut back on sugar, which is like poison in your system and one of the main culprits of fatigue. To feel lighter and more energetic, add more high-water content foods—fresh fruits and vegetables—and whole grains to your diet.

When you are feeling hopeless because you have no dream or vision for your future, do you go to the refrigerator for junk food? Or maybe you take refuge in a drink from the liquor cabinet, or smoke cigarettes, or pop pills. Escaping is a dangerous game and provides only momentary relief. Your body is a temple of the Holy Spirit and deserves to be treated royally. Whether you spend time outdoors, go for a walk every day, exercise more often, get more rest, or change your eating patterns, get serious about your health. It is not something to take for granted. When you take the steps to restore your body, God will restore your spirit!

89 BE STILL

Teach me the art of creating islands of stillness in which I
can absorb the beauty of everyday things.
MARIAN STROUD

One of the ways in which man brings the most trouble upon himself," said Pascal, "is by his inability to be still." It is also one of the major ways we hold ourselves back from pursuing our dreams. If we would stop regularly and immerse ourselves in times of complete stillness, our minds and spirits would be more open to receive the insights we so earnestly pray for when it comes to fulfilling a vision. Stillness is a rare commodity in our fast-paced world. Ponder the word *stillness*. When I looked it up in my thesaurus, I found words such as *tranquil, calm, serene, composed, unruffled, unflustered, unflappable,* and *unperturbed.* Reading those words made me realize there really isn't much stillness in a typical day for most of us. The opposite is more like it—to live in a state of constant commotion and flurry, feeling agitated, restless, frantic, frenzied, or harried. It's no wonder that people don't even have a dream, let alone take action and see one through to completion.

In days gone by, when people ran into each other and asked, "How are you?" the answer was invariably, "Fine, thank you. And you?" Today the response is more likely to be, "I am so busy. It seems like I'm always on the go. If only there was more time" or "I can't seem to get caught up. I wish there were more hours in a day." Most of us feel as though our daily lives are too demanding to spend time and energy on following our dream. We are always on the move and spend our days literally running. We attempt to cram far too much into too little time. We juggle home, family, work, and volunteer activities, and we get pretty good at it. What we are not good at is being still, and that is a crucial element to becoming a visionary. Tim Himmel, author of *Little House on the Freeway,* says, "We have a love affair with haste. We call it convenience, and there is no doubt that many modern conveniences have made some of the mundane duties of life more tolerable. But there is a subtle programming that goes on at the same time. It's not long before we drive our lives the same way we drive our cars—too fast." Jesus knew the value of getting away from it all. He said,

> Come to me. Get away with me and you'll recover your life. I'll show you how to take a real rest. Walk with me and work with me—watch how I do it. Learn the unforced rhythms of grace. I won't lay anything heavy or ill-fitting on you. Keep company with me and you'll learn to live freely and lightly (Matthew 11:29 MSG).

Imagine how different your life would be if you created periodic islands of stillness in your day. At the very least, you may have the chance to absorb the beauty of everyday things around you. You may reclaim your life with renewed vision, passion, and dreams for an exciting future. Our heavenly Father says, "Be still, and know that I am God" (Psalm 46:10). God knows we need to experience stillness in order to clearly recognize his voice and receive divine direction when it comes to discovering and pursuing new dreams.

Think about how much better we would be at tuning into our true life purpose and vision if we would slow down and even pause in our hectic schedules to catch our breath, to get lost in the moment, to be alert to the miraculous. Several times a day, consciously choose to move in a slow, unhurried, laid-back pace. Create an environment of stillness and peace for yourself. Purposely slow yourself down when you drive, walk, talk, and eat. Make time to be still and meditate. Even indulge in a midday snooze once in a while.

Rather than always talking about how busy you are, capture moments of stillness and focus on those. A few years ago, I chose to eliminate the phrase "I'm too busy" from my vocabulary. I realized it implied I was out of control and that outside circumstances had more influence over my life than I had. Instead I say, "I have a full schedule," which is saying I'm in charge of how occupied I will be. When someone asks me to commit to yet another activity and I tell them I am not able to at this time, the reason might be that I'm going to spend some time alone being still—meditating, praying, walking in the country, or reading. Perhaps I'll be having a quiet picnic with my husband, a relaxing lunch with my daughters, or on a play date with my grandchildren. Maybe the reason I am not available is because I am going on a weekend retreat with my sisters; spending an afternoon at the park with friends to use the swings or teeter totter; going for a massage, manicure, or facial; working on a favorite hobby; or pursuing a current dream. Having a full schedule doesn't mean I am *too busy*. It means I have taken back control of my life. You can do it too. Eliminate all the busyness and hustle and bustle from your days. Plan special times of stillness. You are the one who ultimately decides how frenzied or still you will be.

90 PRACTICE SILENCE

In quietness and confidence is your strength.
ISAIAH 30:15 TLB

If you are like many creative dreamers, at least once in recent weeks you have probably caught yourself saying, "If only I could have some peace and quiet" or "It's so noisy around here I can hardly hear myself think." Silence is golden. These days it's a rare commodity, not just because of everyday noisemakers—nerve-rattling alarm clocks bellowing first thing in the morning; pagers beeping; telephones ringing; televisions, radios, and car horns blaring; lawn mowers and leaf blowers roaring; or the incessant chatter that goes on all around us, but mainly because we forget the purpose of silence and neglect to chase after it. "True silence is the rest of the mind," said William Penn. "It is to the spirit what sleep is to the body: nourishment and refreshment."

When you are having a hard time focusing on your dreams and goals because of the noise around you, try this experiment. Periodically during the day, stop what you are doing, seek out the most serene spot you can find, and focus on the silence. For some it may simply be a matter of turning off the television or getting away by yourself during your lunch break at work. For others it might mean book-ending your days with silence by waking up half an hour before the rest of the family or going to bed a bit early. Providing a quiet interlude for your spirit first thing in the day and last thing at night could be the pauses or breaks in routine you need to provide time for introspection and reviewing your dreams and goals. It will be a chance to lift up your vision to God, suspend all your own plans, and ask him to guide and direct you. Envision your dreams and imagine ways they might evolve more smoothly. In the silence picture yourself as productive, energetic, and stress-free. See quietness, harmony, and orderliness unfolding in your future rather than the noisy mayhem and confusion that's been part of your past.

Wherever your quiet spot is, whether out in nature or indoors in a sunny corner of your favorite room, immerse yourself in the silence. The goal is not to be aware of your surroundings but to listen within. When you are pursuing your dreams, silence allows you to discover your deepest passions, catch your unique vision, be aware of your true purpose, and devise the most creative plans and solutions to organize your best strategy. Thoughts that come to you in the silence will be meaningful, insightful, and even profound. To hear from God on this deep, internal level, we must periodically escape the external cacophony of sounds that invade our space. "We need to find God," said Mother

Teresa, "and he cannot be found in noise and restlessness. God is the friend of silence."

One time of day when you can be assured of experiencing complete silence is in the middle of the night. If ever you find you are wide awake and can't fall back to sleep no matter how hard you try, remind yourself that it may be God's plan to speak to you with a fresh dream, a change in direction for an existing one, or some spectacular new vision. God tends to whisper to us in the silence. The psalmist said, "I lie awake at night thinking of you—of how much you have helped me—and how I rejoice through the night beneath the protecting shadow of your wings" (Psalm 63:6-7 TLB).

We have grown so accustomed to noise that it sometimes seems as though the silence could swallow us up. On those rare occasions when no one is talking or we're home alone, we have the tendency to fill the hush with background sounds. Automatically we turn on the television or radio, pop in a DVD, or put on a CD. Don't let silence threaten you. Once you become at ease with it, you'll be aware of the tremendous influence it can have on your ability to dream bigger dreams and concentrate on how you will fulfill your visions. Jesus said, "Here's what I want you to do: Find a quiet, secluded place so you won't be tempted to role-play before God. Just be there as simply and honestly as you can manage. The focus will shift from you to God, and you will begin to sense his grace" (Matthew 6:6 MSG).

91 SEIZE SOME SOLITUDE

> *I love to be alone. I never found a companion that*
> *was so companionable as solitude.*
> HENRY DAVID THOREAU

Solitude energizes us. We are physically, mentally, and emotionally restored when we get alone for a much-needed respite. Lack of energy is one of the main reasons so many people don't attempt their dreams. They know they simply don't have the strength to fulfill the vision. But it's "'not by might nor by power, but by my Spirit,' says the LORD" (Zechariah 4:6). Taking time to be alone with God helps you trust him for your strength. When you do, you will be equipped to conquer burnout, overcome mental and emotional fatigue, and maintain your sanity while handling the new obligations that go along with achieving every dream.

Solitude has been referred to as a divine retreat. Have you felt lately that you need a retreat, a heavenly haven where you can withdraw from the world to mull over current goals and future dreams? I'm sorry to tell you that no one is going to come along and offer it to you. You'll have to seize some solitude for yourself. It's crucial to your dreams because time spent alone can refresh your soul and revive your imagination. Getting away from everything is an essential element in discovering and living out your vision.

How often do you spend time alone? I mean really alone. You may feel you have too many responsibilities and people counting on you to get away and be by yourself. Relinquishing some of your commitments may feel foreign and uncomfortable to you. You may feel as though you are being selfish. The truth is that taking time alone to be restored and renewed is one of the kindest things you can do for the people you live and work with, care about, and love.

Spending time in solitude is a skill that can be acquired and enhanced—one that is worth obtaining and refining. At some point today take time to be alone with just a journal and pen. On a blank page write the words *solitude, privacy, seclusion,* and *isolation.* Think about how they are different from loneliness. Being alone and being lonely are two different things. Periods of solitude for your personal refreshment are essential if you are going to continue on the path toward your dream. Make a list of the ways you could experience solitude. Whether you can get away alone to a nearby park, go for a hike on a wooded trail, or escape into your own backyard for a few minutes with a cup of coffee, take a break outdoors to allow nature to nurture you and your dreams. Study the trees, the birds, and the flowers. Hear the rustle of the breeze in the leaves. Notice the variety of colors and textures. Examine the sky, the clouds, and the stars. The psalmist said,

> The heavens are telling the glory of God; they are a
> marvelous display of his craftsmanship. Day and night

they keep on telling about God. Without a sound or
word, silent in the skies, their message reaches out to
all the world. The sun lives in the heavens where God
placed it and moves out across the skies as radiant as a
bride-groom going to his wedding, or as joyous as an
athlete looking forward to a race! (Psalm 19:1-5 TLB).

Scripture is full of examples of people who seized moments of solitude. Abraham wandered and worshiped alone. Isaiah was alone in the
temple when a live coal touched his lips. Daniel dined and prayed alone.
Joshua walked in solitude under the stars by the wall of Jericho when
the captain of the Lord's host stood before him. It was when he was
alone in the desert that Moses was shown the burning bush. Paul sent
his companions along the shore by the sea while he chose to go alone.
Mary was alone when the angel brought her the message of the Lord. It's
recorded throughout the Gospels that Jesus withdrew from the crowds
to be alone with his Father. Communing was his consuming passion.
Everything Jesus did when he returned to the crowds, the Father first
revealed to him during times of solitude. Henri Nouwen, priest and
psychologist, made the statement that solitude in God's presence is "the
place of the great encounter with him. It is the place from which all
other encounters derive their meaning." When you are alone with God,
he can get your attention and speak to your heart.

For most of us, choosing to spend time in solitude can be challenging and requires deliberate planning, but it's well worth the effort.
When we make the effort to get away and be alone with him, God takes
our dream and works all things together for good. It's in solitude that
you will discover the destiny God has in mind for you.

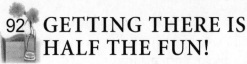

92 GETTING THERE IS HALF THE FUN!

This is the day the Lord has made;
let us rejoice and be glad in it.
PSALM 118:24

Success is not a destination but a journey.

With our hectic schedules, most of us are running full throttle, pursuing our dreams and climbing the ladder of achievement at top speeds. We might be exhausted, frustrated, or close to burnout, and we're not even totally certain what's at the top, but we sure are in a rush to get there so we can move on to the next big dream. We have fallen into the trap of believing that speeding up and doing more faster than ever before is what following a dream is all about. But for successful dreamers, the *process of getting there,* the researching and developing a new idea and watching it evolve, is an intriguing and satisfying end in itself. They know how to truly enjoy the journey. They've discovered that watching the dream unfold, progress, expand, and advance toward its ultimate completion is often one of the best parts of having dreams.

When you think about it, most of us are much happier getting ready for an event or planning to go somewhere than we are afterward, whether it's going out for dinner, taking a vacation, rehearsing a play we are in, arranging a holiday celebration, or organizing a party. After eating a delicious dinner in a restaurant, it's no fun anymore. We're too full and we have to pay the bill. When the vacation is over, we have to make the trip home, unpack, do laundry, and catch up on all that's happened while we were away. After a holiday celebration, a party, or a wedding, there is the cleanup and the letdown once it's over. As much as we enjoy the event, it is rarely as much fun as the anticipation and expectancy that's part of the preparation. So instead of rushing through that stage of development like a child who can hardly wait to be grownup, slow down and enjoy each step of the way.

I often get asked to mentor speakers and authors, which I love to do. The best part for me is seeing the passion, zeal, and freshness in someone who is new at building their dreams. I find myself reliving the beginnings of my own dreams as I take them through the various stages of constructing their vision. I remember all over again the excitement of starting out with a mere concept, then planting the seed of an idea, watering it, and eventually seeing the dream blossom.

The process of getting ready for the very first public seminar I ever held is still one of my fondest memories. It was a professional development program I offered to local businesses and professionals in the city where I live, teaching goal-setting, time effectiveness, organization, and sanity secrets for stress survival. After designing and circulating the promotional flyer, the registrations started to come in quickly. I was also invited to do a series of radio, television, and newspaper interviews. As a result of all this marketing, the meeting room I had booked soon filled up. I had invested so much effort and energy into promoting the event and filling the room that I had left little time for actually preparing the program. At the last minute my assistant and I needed to stay up until well after midnight photocopying handouts, three-hole punching them, and inserting them into binders for the more than 200 participants who would attend the next day! We drank coffee, ate donuts, laughed until our sides ached, and worked until the sun came up. The anticipation and excitement that built in us kept us going through most of the night and the next day. Although I have conducted many similar events over the years and now have a systematic approach in place to prepare more smoothly and efficiently, it's those beginning days that stand out in my memory as being the most fun, challenging, and exhilarating.

We do not remember days; we remember moments. So enjoy the moment and capture the sheer joy of fresh starts and new beginnings as you head down pathways you have never explored. The expectancy, hope, and eagerness you experience will keep you energized and hopeful. Then say a prayer of thanksgiving for your dream and the journey you are traveling to reach it, however slow it may seem to you. Gratitude and achieving big dreams go hand in hand. Counting your blessings generates a feeling of abundance. Thinking grateful thoughts reminds us of past dreams and other goals that have become realities too.

When you are progressing toward a worthy goal and following your heart's desire, it's not work. It's a way of life. You enjoy yourself because you are making a contribution to the world around you through your involvement in relationships, your job, your community, and your church, Life is an ongoing process, a gradual growth into the talents and gifts and the dreams and visions God has placed within us. You have a lifetime to develop them. Don't be in a hurry to arrive. Enjoy each step of the way. "There is a time for everything, and a season for every activity under heaven" (Ecclesiastes 3:1). God's ways are not our ways, and neither is his timetable our timetable. Yesterday is finished; tomorrow is a vision of hope. Look to today for it is life.

I have no Yesterdays,
Time took them away;
Tomorrow may not be—
But I have Today.
PEARL YEADON McGINNIS

PART 14
The Principle of Giving

93 GIVE YOURSELF AWAY

The highest of distinctions is service to others.
KING GEORGE VI

Whoever wants to be great must become a servant.
MARK 10:44 MSG

The best portion of a good man's life are his little, nameless, unremembered acts of kindness and of love," said William Wordsworth. You will probably find as you look back on your life that the times which stand out, those moments when you have truly lived, are likely the moments when you served others and did things in a spirit of helpfulness, compassion, and generosity. The greatest levels of true inner joy are experienced by those who have found some way to be of service to others. In addition to the contentment and satisfaction created by serving, it is a well-known principle that you cannot give something away without it coming back multiplied. Although it is not our primary motive for giving, the truth is that it's impossible to give too much away. "Give away your life; you'll find life given back, but not merely given back—given back with bonus and blessing" (Luke 6:38 MSG). It's simply not possible to out-give God.

Giving is at the heart and soul of true achievement. All great men and women became successful because they gave some talent, ability, or skill in the service of others. And no matter how limited our time or talents, or how small our dream, we too can contribute to others in some way. Ralph Waldo Emerson said, "It is one of the beautiful compensations of this life that no man can sincerely try to help another without helping himself." Zig Ziglar, renowned author and motivational speaker, put it this way: "You can get anything in life you want if you will just help enough other people get what they want."

When I began writing my book *When Your Past Is Hurting Your Present,* I found many people with servant hearts who were willing to contribute to this project. Aside from their prayers, they provided me with powerful stories and examples of how they felt their own past experiences were impacting their lives today. Equipped with information about what they believe is affecting their current relationships, health, jobs, and futures and what was holding them back from leading a rewarding life today, I believed I could effectively address those issues in the book. I also felt these real-life examples would make it easier for readers to relate to the principles and guidelines in a practical way. So I designed a short but in-depth questionnaire for individuals of diverse backgrounds and circulated copies to friends, business associates, and acquaintances. I found people were more than glad to support my project by completing the surveys. This technique turned out to be one of the most beneficial forms of research I was able to do. The participants were willing to serve not only me, but the future readers of the book by offering their heartfelt stories and examples. I am convinced that the success of the book came about partly as a result of hard work and lots of prayer, but also due to the deep desire of so many others to be of service and to contribute to the healing of past wounds of hurting people by giving as much constructive, practical, and beneficial information as possible. The stories and examples in *this* book came about in the same way.

 Givers live longer, lead healthier lives, have higher self-esteem, and experience a deeper sense of purpose and worth.

Anything you can give away that benefits others is a form of ministry. When you care for and comfort others, your focus is on giving rather than getting. And although your motivation is altruistic, in the end you will receive back more than you have given. "And whatever you do, do it heartily, as to the Lord and not to men, knowing that from the Lord you will receive the reward of the inheritance" (Colossians 3:23-24 NKJV).

There are other benefits too. Research on unselfish and charitable generosity shows that givers live longer, lead healthier lives, have higher self-esteem, and experience a deeper sense of purpose and worth than those who do not give. And those who start to give—of their time, talents, and energy—in their younger years will more likely land more influential positions and higher-paying jobs throughout their lives.

Take some time to consider what worthy causes and issues are important to you. What special groups are making a difference in areas that matter to you? There are many charitable organizations that could benefit from your skills, expertise, and devotion. When you are passionate about an issue, you can make dreams come true and get a lot done in this world.

94 SOW ACTS OF KINDNESS

It is more blessed to give than to receive.
ACTS 20:35

Acts of kindness enhance your journey to realizing your dreams. The Bible says, "The liberal man shall be rich! By watering others, he waters himself" (Proverbs 11:25 TLB). Each time you sow seeds of thoughtfulness by making an effort to enrich someone's life, you can't help but nurture your own soul.

When you start to develop the habit of giving to others, you will notice countless opportunities in everyday occurrences—someone needs a hand carrying an armload of parcels, a waitress needs a word of encouragement, a friend needs a hug, a coworker needs to be reminded he is doing a great job, or someone in traffic needs to be let in line. You could stop in and chat with a patient in the hospital who may not have any visitors or take a meal to your neighbor who is elderly or always seems to be alone. Maybe there's someone close to you who would appreciate a single rose or a love note on the windshield of his or her car.

Successful dreamers know acts of kindness have tremendous power.

We never know when our action, whether it's a warm smile, an encouraging word, a compliment, or a small gift, could be just what it takes to offer people hope and a way out of the despair they may be experiencing. One time when I was hired to speak at a retreat, my topic was "Living Stress-Free in the Midst of Chaos." Whether it's at a resort or on a cruise ship, I'm always impressed with the number of registered guests who choose to attend a personal development course while on vacation. Now I realize these people know they have to go back home and face the same old issues they left behind before taking the trip. There is no such thing as running away from our problems. My mom used to remind us kids, "Wherever I go, there I am." At this particular event, a gentleman came to me after the presentation, took my hand in both of his, and when he looked me straight in the eye, I noticed his eyes were watering. He said, "You don't know me, but I am the CEO of a large corporation. When I go home, I have a very difficult task ahead of me and some challenging letters to write. When I came in the room today, I was feeling pretty hopeless and despondent. As you shook my hand, a warm, calming sensation flooded through my entire being. Then, during the session, at least ten of the principles you presented were ones that I know I can apply in this situation that will make it easier for me to handle. I just want to say thank you and that I think you are a God-send." Miracles really do happen! I told him I would pray for him and his situation and encouraged him to trust God for further inspiration, guidance, and peace. Without even knowing it, through my actions and words I was able to make a tremendous difference in someone's life.

One day I was feeling frustrated with some business challenges I was facing. When I answered a knock at the door, I was surprised to see the florist delivering a huge, brilliant arrangement complete with flowers, ribbons, and multicolored balloons. It was from a very special friend and given for no particular reason. This gift couldn't have come at a better time, and I will always be grateful for her thoughtfulness. Can you think of some innovative ways you can practice acts of kindness in your daily life? Be on the lookout for opportunities. You never know when you will be entertaining angels unawares. The interesting thing about giving is that we nearly always get back something much better than what we've given. As George Dana Boardman declared, "The law of harvest is to reap more than you sow."

95 FIND A NEED AND FILL IT

No enterprise can exist for itself alone. It ministers
to some great end; it performs some great service,
not for itself, but for others; or failing therein, it
ceases to be profitable and ceases to exist.
CALVIN COOLIDGE

One of my first full-time jobs was when I worked with my mother in the retail store she owned. I learned many valuable lessons during that time, but one principle that impacted me more than the others is the foundation of success in any venture: Discover a need and fill it. In our boutique we sold skin-care products and cosmetics and offered complimentary makeup lessons to women and teens. Eventually a big part of the business involved makeup applications for weddings on weekends. Each Friday and Saturday, bridal parties would come to the shop after visiting the hair salon. Once we applied their makeup, they'd rush home to have lunch, finish doing their nails, and change into their gowns. Then we thought brides might appreciate being able to have this service at home. That way, while each one was having her makeup done, the rest could be taking care of other things in preparation for having photographs taken. This was a service not being offered in our area, so we were the first to try it. It soon became immensely popular. Eventually working with bridal parties became solely my job. I was able to do several weddings on a Saturday and earned more in a day than I once had for an entire week.

Is your dream to achieve success in the business world? Then be on the lookout for some problem and work out a solution. Do you want to start your own company? Identify a need that isn't being met and determine a way to fill it. Do you want to be more successful in your relationships? Perhaps you know someone who has never been encouraged to follow his or her dreams. There's a need you can fill!

Many of the entrepreneurs and innovators in our world have become successful by identifying a need in the marketplace and providing a solution for it. Whether it's developing a new product, enhancing an existing one, or providing a service to support a current trend, there are always needs you can find to build a business or service around. Many of the services, inventions, and gadgets we now take for granted were at one time "unmet needs." Back in 1914, a woman named Mary Phelps Jacob was tired of being bound in corsets with their stays and laces. She stitched together two lace handkerchiefs and attached some pink ribbon and the modern day bra was born. Minor frustrations can stimulate our imagination. One person got tired of looking for a lost eraser and out of desperation finally glued one to the end of a pencil. It solved the problem, and we've been using the idea ever since. Direct sales companies came about as a result of our hectic lifestyles because they offered people the chance to shop at home. Everything from the ballpoint pen, Hallmark cards, Post-it Notes, Scotch Tape, and pop-up toasters to eBay, the Jolly Jumper, and dating services came as a result of people discovering something they needed in their own lives or identifying the needs of others.

What need do you have that hasn't been met? Is there some annoyance or missing element that could be solved with a new service or product? Needs are all around you, and solutions are hovering nearby, just waiting to be discovered. During my goal-setting seminars where I share my own story of reaching an impossible dream, I realized people were being held back by their imperfect past, and, as long as they were stuck there, they would never be free to pursue their dreams. That's when I decided to write *When Your Past Is Hurting Your Present*. What I didn't know was how deep this need really was until the book sold out shortly after its release and within months went to several more printings. That book continues to sell well around the world. Thomas Edison said, "I find out what the world needs and then I proceed to invent." Ask yourself, "What does my family, my company, my employer or employees, my community, my church, or the world need that I can

provide or supply?" The answer may be just what you need to accelerate
you toward your dream!

96 GIVING BACK TO GOD

I will give you back a tenth of everything you give me!
GENESIS 28:22 TLB

Bring all the tithes into the storehouse so that there will
be food enough in my Temple; if you do, I will open up
the windows of heaven for you and pour out a blessing so
great you won't have room enough to take it in!
MALACHI 3:10 TLB

A bundance and prosperity are part of God's plan for you and your
dreams. Jesus said that he came to give us an abundant life and that
means *beyond sufficient* or *more than adequate!* Once we recognize that
everything we have comes from God, we can clear up some myths about
money and finances and mistaken beliefs concerning giving and tithing.

First of all, there's nothing wrong with having money. Without it
we can't survive, let alone realize our dreams. God's Word tells us that
money is not the problem; the *love* of money is the root of evil. Besides,
"he who loves money shall never have enough" (Ecclesiastes 5:10 TLB).
Yet we also know that many of our dreams are wrapped up in dollars and cents. So much of what we long for and yearn to accomplish
requires financial support. Nothing robs us of the joy of pursuing a
dream more than financial hardship, debts we can't seem to get rid
of, and lack of funding or provision. You may be in a position where
you are wondering if you have enough money to get the education or
training you need to fulfill your vision. If you are starting a business,
you may need financing for equipment, employee wages, and living
expenses while you're building the dream. If your vision is to take music
lessons, produce live dramas, open a fishing resort, operate a tea room

or a country inn, buy a farm, or start a breakfast program in schools, you know that you'll need some type of investment up front.

So is money a blessing or a curse? Years ago, I heard Zig Ziglar make an amusing comment about finances. He said in his career there have been times when he's had money and times when he hasn't had money, and he's decided he'd rather have it! I have also heard it said that one of the best ways we can help the poor is to not be one of them.

When I lived with my two small children after leaving a devastating situation in my first marriage, we lived at poverty level. We barely had enough money to buy food, pay the rent, and make car payments. But I had received good teaching about tithing and knew that ten percent of my income belonged to God. Because we didn't want to rob God of what was already his, we tithed to our church regularly. "The purpose of tithing is to teach you always to put God first in your lives" (Deuteronomy 14:23 TLB). We also gave to those who were less fortunate than we were whenever we had the opportunity, and my girls tell me they never figured out that we were poor as well. We also found out the Bible promises that "those who seek the Lord shall not lack any good thing" (Psalm 34:10 NKJV). Well, we were seeking the Lord in every area of our lives. We believed God was our source, and that he would provide everything we needed. He did that and more!

So many financial needs can be solved when we trust God for everything. That means if you give when he says to give, he promises to bless you, protect you, and prosper you. "Cheerful givers are the ones God prizes. God is able to make it up to you by giving you everything you need and more so that there will not only be enough for your own needs but plenty left over to give joyfully to others" (2 Corinthians 9:7-8 TLB). "Yes, God will give you much so that you can give away much" (2 Corinthians 9:11 TLB). In other words, you can never out-give God. His shovel is always bigger than yours.

Giving is not a magic wand you wave whenever you have a financial need. We know that many successful entrepreneurs and wealthy businesspeople in our world have used the principle of tithing and are prospering even though they do not have a personal relationship with God. Because giving and sowing is one of God's principles, it will always be true. But God also says, "Who wants your sacrifices when you have no sorrow for your sins?" (Isaiah 1:13 TLB). Jesus said, "You should tithe, yes, but you should not leave other things undone" (Luke 11:42 TLB). He was talking to the Pharisees about how careful they were to tithe even the smallest part of their income, and then completely forgot about showing the love of God through generosity, fairness, and integrity. "Learn to do good, to be fair and to help the poor, the fatherless, and widows" (Isaiah 1:17 TLB).

When you follow God's direction and tithe your finances, time, energy, and talent, you'll be content to live within your means and not always strive for more. It doesn't mean you won't continue to reach for new dreams and visions that could increase your income, but you will know that your blessings come from the hand of God and will never run out.

PART 15
Keep on Dreaming

97 RELEASE THE PAST
TO EMBRACE THE FUTURE

Forget the former things; do not dwell on the past.
See, I am doing a new thing!
ISAIAH 43:18-19

Dreaming and successfully living out your vision involve getting yourself prepared for the future. One thing you can't do is move into the future while dragging the past around like a heavy chain. People who are stuck in the heartache, pain, and unforgiveness of past experiences rarely see the fulfillment of their dreams. Letting go of the old baggage is crucial to receiving all God has in store for your future.

Anger, resentment, remorse, regrets, bitterness, and the desire for revenge can drain you of the very energy you need to take positive action in pursuing your dream. Until you are able to break the cycle and let go of past hurts, you will most likely attract more of the same into your life. In *When Your Past Is Hurting Your Present,* there is one chapter called "Ready. Set. Let Go." Letting go is one of the major cornerstones of being liberated from your past, and being set free is a decision only you can make.

Letting go often involves forgiveness. Forgiving others is difficult for most of us because it *seems* to condone the actions of others. For you it might be the ex-spouse who was unfaithful or arranged some things that were unfair during the divorce proceedings or who wants custody of your children. Maybe it's a coworker who started nasty rumors about you or took credit for a project of yours. Or perhaps it was a thief who robbed you of precious valuables in your home. Whatever the case, forgiving others is not a matter of letting them off the hook. In reality, you are letting yourself off the hook by saying, "Yes, I was wronged, but I am not going to let this offense keep harming me. I will not allow it to prevent me from becoming all I was created to be."

From my own personal experiences, I know it is not easy to forgive and let go. I was physically abused by a now ex-spouse for a number of years, had a business associate embezzle me out of thousands of dollars, and have been taken advantage of in other business situations numerous times. In each experience, I had to learn what it meant to forgive because I knew if I didn't, those experiences would keep me from living out my future dreams and goals. And besides that, the principal reason to forgive is that Jesus forgave us and commands us to forgive too.

Each of my situations was a learning experience. I had to ask myself: "What did I learn, and what will I do differently next time?" I started keeping a "next time" file I could refer to if I was ever in a similar situation. My notes will help me make better choices to protect myself and others and my financial interests. Whatever hurts you are dealing with, please know that I understand. We all may have reasons to be the way we are, but none of us has a valid reason to stay that way. What can hurt you even more is holding a grudge, harboring bitterness and resentment, and wanting others to pay for their actions. It was Nelson Mandela who said, "Resentment is like drinking poison and then hoping it will kill your enemies." When you hold a grudge, it eventually holds you.

Each time you release a hurtful experience, you will feel lighter and freer to forge ahead with the vision God has revealed to you for your future. Although it may not seem like it, with the help of the Holy Spirit it is possible to forgive anyone of anything, no matter how atrocious, cruel, or heartbreaking. One thing that has helped me more than anything else is to view others from a heavenly perspective. When I asked God to help me do that, I came to realize that the other people involved were doing the best they could with the abilities and tools they had available to them at the time. What they did in most cases was not personal. It was not against me. It was usually done as a result of what was going on in their own lives and spirits.

Releasing a painful past and the hurts you have endured along the way puts you on the path to total freedom while you reach forward to fulfill your highest dreams and aspirations. Letting go and forgiveness are choices. You can decide to say, "I forgive myself, and I forgive others. I am choosing to be free from the baggage that's been keeping me stuck. And I am freeing others to become all they were created to be in God's almighty plan." Jesus said, "Even if he wrongs you seven times a day and each time turns again and asks forgiveness, forgive him" (Luke 17:4 TLB).

98 IT'S NEVER TOO LATE

Teach us to number our days and recognize how few they are; help us to spend them as we should.
PSALM 90:12 TLB

I am always astounded by the people at my speaking engagements who come up and tell me that because they have arrived at a certain stage in life, they think the principles I'm presenting about having a dream do not apply to them. They say, "It's too late for dreaming big dreams. I've done all I can do." Because of their age, they aren't even considering the possibility of taking their lives to new heights. I think they have forgotten that with all their years of learning and growing and overcoming, they have so much to say and offer. Besides, history is full of examples that prove it is never too late to live out your dreams and fulfill the purposes for your life:

- Strauss was still composing music until after his eightieth birthday.
- Michelangelo was nearly 90 years old when he painted the Sistine Chapel while laying on his back on a scaffold.
- Benjamin Franklin was serving his country in France at the age of 78 and wrote his autobiography when he was over 80.
- When John Wesley was in his eighties, he was annoyed that he could not write for more than 15 hours a day and felt ashamed that he could only preach twice a day.

Obviously these people never stopped using their minds, imaginations, ingenuity, and creativeness. They did not let age interfere with their motivation to reach new dreams and undertake innovative and demanding challenges. And neither should we!

Creative development is a lifelong endeavor. Ecclesiastes 3:1 says, "There is a time for everything, and a season for every activity under heaven." As in nature, our lives seem to go through four seasons. The first is birth and a time when we are completely dependent on others for our survival and growth. It is a period of learning, a time when we receive training in right and wrong and find out what is important in life. During the next season we are more independent when it comes to others, although we are fully dependent on God as our source. This is when we first capture our vision and our purpose. We discover what we are born to do, and we live out those dreams and goals through our marriages, our families, our careers, our ministries, and our passions. In the third season we have achieved many dreams and visions so we can pass our learning on to the next generation. Our experiences are not only beneficial to others, but they make the pursuit of our own future dreams even more exciting. The fourth season is when we die and, as believers, go on to our true home with Christ in heaven. This is when our lives can become the sustenance for the dreams of future generations through the legacy we leave.

It could be said that aging and the passing of time is in the eye of the beholder. The psalmist said that to God a thousand years are like a single hour (Psalm 90:4 TLB). As for us, "we glide along the tides of time as swiftly as a racing river" (Psalm 90:5 TLB). Let's choose to serve and give with all our heart for as long as we can! John Wesley advised:

> Do all the good you can,
> By all the means you can,
> In all the ways you can,
> In all the places you can,
> At all the times you can,
> To all the people you can,
> *As long as you ever can!*

The truth is that soon we will all be gone from this earth. Even if we were to live to be 110, those years are like a tiny speck in time compared to eternity. Let's make the remaining years count! Discover the dreams God has placed in you and pursue them with your whole heart. His Word tells us "the godly shall flourish like palm trees and grow tall as the cedars of Lebanon. For they are transplanted into the Lord's own garden and are under his personal care. Even in old age they will still produce fruit and be vital and green" (Psalm 92:12-14 TLB).

99 THE ROCKING CHAIR TEST

Let us endeavor so to live that, when we come to die,
even the undertaker will be sorry.
MARK TWAIN

You don't want to end your life full of regrets, nothing but
sin and bones, saying, "Oh, why didn't I do what they told
me? Why did I reject a disciplined life? Why didn't I listen
to my mentors, or take my teachers seriously? My life is
ruined! I haven't one blessed thing to show for my life!"
PROVERBS 5:11-14 MSG

Imagine for a minute that you are 99 years old and sitting in a rocking chair on your veranda. As you ponder your life and think back over the years, is there anything you wish you had done or said or attempted? Are there journeys you contemplated but never embarked upon? Do you have regrets about any of your relationships? Are there dreams that still lay hidden deep in your soul? Now go ahead and put those things in writing. Turn them into your current and future goals, and start to pursue them while there is still time. A great way to live a worthy and effective life is to envision what you'd like the end to be and then start living it out today.

Maybe you are reading this and you *are* sitting in your rocker! Perhaps you're well into your seventh or eighth decade or beyond, and as you look back over the last 50 years you ask yourself, "What dreams did

I achieve? What have I done to fulfill my purpose here on earth?" Are you thinking, *I'm too old now, and I probably don't have the time or the energy to make a difference anyway?* You might be thinking, *Why am I even reading this book?* From Bible stories we know that God recharged many people past retirement age. Stories about Abraham and Sarah in Genesis, chapter 18, or Elizabeth and Zechariah in Luke, chapter 1, let us know they were able to have a fresh start even though they thought their lives were almost over. I have a friend who didn't start to run 10K races until she was in her fifties and another who became a lawyer in her eighties. Uncovering your dream will give you renewed energy and strength and a fresh vision for the years you have left.

Once you have a long-term vision, there's a great way to maintain it. Imagine your loved ones have gathered together after you're gone. As you see them reminiscing about the past, what do you think they're saying about you and their lives with you? How would they describe your character or your attitude toward life? What will they say your top priorities were, and how would they describe your values? Which of your character traits, standards, and priorities do they hope their children will, or will not, develop? When you think about all your answers, is there anything that concerns you? Are there things you'd like to be different? This is your chance to make changes in the way you approach life today. If you suddenly found out that you had only five years to live, how would you choose to spend them? What would be the main focus of your life?

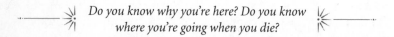

Do you know why you're here? Do you know where you're going when you die?

Another way to set new life priorities is to write out your own obituary or eulogy. A friend who died recently after a short illness requested that her family hold a "FUN-eral. When I saw how it was announced, I knew what a joyous time it would be for family and friends. How true this was to her character. It was meant to be a time of celebration as she went home to be with Jesus, and she wanted everyone to enjoy the experience with her.

Ask yourself, "What would my family and friends say was the driving force in my life?" and "What do I *want* it to be?" You were not put on earth to be remembered, but to prepare for eternity, and to serve, and to be a witness of God's great love. So answer with that in mind. Many people want to be remembered for doing some great work. They strive and strain, attempting to create a lasting legacy here on earth. What a shortsighted goal. A better dream would be to build an eternal heritage. Are you going to heaven? If so, who will you be taking with you?

We often fail to realize that all our efforts will be forgotten. Achievements we recognized as being great will eventually be improved upon or outdone. Records are broken and accolades fade. One of my dreams, to write a life-changing book for women, came true and when it was released in 1996, we all celebrated. But years later, I was with a friend at a yard sale and she bought a copy of that book for 50 cents! In the end, what really matters is not what others think of you or your dreams, but what God thinks.

A.W. Tozer said,

> The average person in the world today, without faith and without God and without hope, is engaged in a desperate personal search throughout his lifetime. He does not really know where he has been. He does not really know what he is doing here and now. He does not know where he is going. The sad commentary is that he is doing it all on borrowed time and borrowed money and borrowed strength—and he already knows that in the end, he will surely die.

Do you know why you are here? More importantly, do you know where you are going when you die? You can be assured of a home in heaven, my friend. There is a way. Jesus Christ made that way and paid the price for your sins by shedding his precious blood. He said, "I am the way and the truth and the life. No one comes to the Father except through me" (John 14:6). When you believe Jesus died on the cross for you and rose again on the third day, ask him to forgive you of your sins, dedicate your life to him, and he will save you and give you an eternal home in heaven with him. I encourage you to turn your life and all your dreams, aspirations, goals, and plans over to him today. Look to Jesus who loves you and accepts you just as you are. You can trust him with your dreams! "There has never been the slightest doubt in my mind that the God who started this great work in you would keep at it and bring it to a flourishing finish on the very day Christ Jesus appears" (Philippians 1:6 MSG).

100 LOVE EXTRAVAGANTLY— YOUR LIFE DEPENDS ON IT

You will find as you look back upon your life
that the moments that stand out, the moments
when you have really lived, are the moments when
you have done things in a spirit of love.
HENRY DRUMMOND

Go after a life of love as if your life
depended on it—because it does.
1 CORINTHIANS 14:1 MSG

With all our lofty dreams, worthy aspirations, and admirable ambitions, it comes down to this: "Let love be your greatest aim" (1 Corinthians 14:1 TLB). A life without love is empty. It's of no value. In light of all eternity, the dreams you fulfill here on earth will matter little apart from the love you have for others and the relationships you build with them. One million years from now, the career position you had, the car you drove, the house you lived in, the furnishings and other possessions you amassed, the money you invested, the vacations you took, and the hobbies you pursued will have no significance whatsoever. The exaggerated emphasis in our culture on fitness regimes, workouts, and dieting will not matter either. "Don't think of eating as important because someday God will do away with both stomachs and food" (1 Corinthians 6:13 TLB). In fact, when we die, even hope and faith will come to an end—but love will remain. Without love, our impressive gifts, extraordinary acts of generosity, and spectacular deeds may be little more than empty clatter. Our best efforts, devoid of love, will seem hollow. On the flip side, even the smallest loving act can hold eternal significance.

Beyond our achievements, accomplishments, acquisitions, and the sacrifices we've made, what matters most in life is love that shows itself in our relationships. If we're not careful, we'll tend to see relationships as part of our long list of things to do. We can view a blissful marriage, a happy family, meaningful friendships, and even opportunities to help the hurting, the lost, and the lonely as merely more goals we hope to achieve. But as the apostle Paul says, "No matter what I say, what I believe, and what I do, I'm bankrupt without love" (1 Corinthians 13:3 MSG).

When our lives are full of activities and we are caught up in following our dreams and aspirations, we can almost view the time we spend on relationships as something negotiable. Maybe we think we can cut back on time with others to free up more time for the "higher priority" activities. The truth is that there really is nothing more important than our relationships. The whole point of life on earth is to love—first God and then people. If we believe that God is love, then life must be all about love. Therefore, the most important dream you can follow, the biggest goal you can have on this earth, is to learn how to love.

TRUE LOVE

Listen to what God has to say about love:

> Love never gives up. Love cares more for others than for self. Love doesn't want what it doesn't have. Love doesn't strut, doesn't have a swelled head, doesn't force itself on others, isn't always "me first," doesn't fly off the handle, doesn't keep score of the sins of others, doesn't revel when others grovel, takes pleasure in the flowering of truth, puts up with anything, trusts God always, always looks for the best, never looks back, but keeps going to the end (1 Corinthians 13:4-7 MSG).

Learn to love as God loves us—unconditionally. Being loved without prerequisites is something everyone is searching for. "He loves each one of us," said St. Augustine, "as if there were only one of us." Love is truly the most important element. Without it, our lives resound with emptiness. With it, we radiate warmth, affection, tenderness, value, and significance. Our lives will be like magnets, and others will be miraculously drawn to us, to Christ's love in us. "We never live so intensely as when we love strongly. We never realize ourselves so vividly as when we are in the full glow of love for others," declared Walter Rauschenbusch. Even in difficulties and hardship, love can shine through.

So search for eternal love as though your life depends on it. Make it your grandest quest. Keep searching until you find it and it overwhelms you. Then, once you have learned to love, you will have learned to live. As Anna Louise de Stael put it, "Love is the emblem of eternity; it confounds all notion of time; effaces all memory of a beginning; all fear of an end."

There are three things that remain—faith, hope, and
love—and the greatest of these is love.
1 CORINTHIANS 13:13 TLB

101 PRAY YOUR HEART OUT!

You can get anything—anything you ask
for in prayer—if you believe.
MATTHEW 21:22 TLB

Thou art coming to a King
Large petitions with thee bring;
For his grace and power are such
None can ever ask too much.
JOHN NEWTON

There's a fable about a man who went to heaven and asked the angel Gabriel if he could go inside a big building he spotted in the distance. Gabriel answered, "I don't think you want to see inside. You will be very disappointed." But the man insisted, so the angel took him in and showed him room after room full of beautifully wrapped gifts of all sizes and shapes. When the man asked about the presents, Gabriel replied sadly, "We wrapped all these gifts for people on earth, but for some reason they've never asked for them!" What a shame that so many of our blessings are still wrapped and waiting for us to simply whisper a prayer in faith.

Christ emphatically taught his followers that they could have anything they asked for in prayer if they believed it would happen (Matthew 21:22). While it sounds pretty incredible, we know it's true because it's in the Bible. But when we look closely, there are a few things to consider. First of all, are you in prayer? The Bible says to pray without ceasing. Prayer means to have ongoing communication with your heavenly Father. You can only talk intimately with God and make your requests with confidence if you know him and have a relationship with him. Most of us wouldn't think of asking for something of any true significance from a stranger or approach a friend only when we have a serious need. Before you start asking for anything, no matter how much you believe it can happen, you need to have a relationship with the giver of all gifts. Get to know him personally!

Second, if you are in prayer, who are you talking to? When you ask for something, whom do you ask? Nowhere in Scripture does it say we are to pray to angels. Nor are we ever instructed to ask the saints to answer our prayers. Instead, the one we are to go to with our requests is God himself. The only way we can do that is to enter the Holy of Holies through Jesus Christ, who made a way for us. That is why we always end our prayers, "In Jesus' name." We pray *to* God the Father, *with* the Holy Spirit helping us to express what's in our hearts, and *through* Jesus Christ our Lord and Savior. In John 15:16, Jesus says no matter what you ask for from the Father using his name, God will give it to you.

Third and most important, Christ was talking to his followers. Are you a follower of Christ? He said, "I am the way and the truth and the life. No one comes to the Father except through me" (John 14:6). When we pray to the one true God, the Holy Spirit speaks to our hearts and reveals him to us. When you are a follower of someone, you become like that person. You start to have the same mannerisms, views, and desires. You have the same ways of expressing yourself. Eventually you start to think alike and even look alike. We know this happens to married people all the time, and that's why you want to choose your partner carefully! God is saying, "You need to think like I think and speak like I speak." He is also saying, "Why would you want to hang around with the turkeys in the barnyard when I have called you to soar with the eagles? Dream big and bring your big dreams to me in prayer."

"Prayer delights God's ear, it melts His heart, it opens His hand; God cannot deny a praying soul," said Thomas Watson. So why don't we pray about our dreams? Do we not believe in the power of our prayers? Don't we know the powerful impact praying about our dreams could make in our lives when it comes to fulfilling our purpose, reaching our potential, and living out the vision God has placed in us? "Prayer is a mighty instrument, not for getting man's will done in Heaven," said Robert Law, "but for getting God's will done on earth." Just think what a difference you could make in so many ways, with so many lives, if you were to pray passionately for the dream and believe your vision could become a reality. Dream big. And in all your dreaming, know that God is bigger than anything you could ever begin to imagine.

The word *amen* at the end of a prayer means "so be it" or "may this prayer come true." My desire for you, my friend, is that you see your prayers answered, discover your purpose, live your life with meaning and passion, and fulfill your ultimate destiny. And may all your dreams come true! Amen.

The Dream

Ah, great it is to believe the dream
As we stand in youth by the starry stream;
But a greater thing is to fight life through
And say at the end, "The dream is true!"

About the Author

Invigorating, captivating, stimulating describe Sue Augustine when she offers audiences the principles, skills, and inspiration they need to experience extraordinary results. Sue has a unique talent for inspiring and challenging men and women to make the powerful, positive choices that will transform their lives and careers. Through her keynote addresses, seminars, workshops, and books, she speaks internationally on personal effectiveness and excellence.

Due to her exceptional ability to influence men and women, and compel them to take action, Sue's services are sought after by numerous distinguished corporations, businesses, professional associations, school boards, shopping centers, hospitals, and not-for-profit groups. She has been featured in several business publications and regularly appears on international television and radio shows.

What is truly remarkable is knowing where Sue came from. After surviving a severe illness and a devastating personal situation, she became a successful entrepreneur and corporate trainer in sales before attaining her goal of speaking professionally. Sue knows firsthand what it takes to turn tragedy into triumph and dreams into realities.

Sue is the author of *When Your Past Is Hurting Your Present* and *With Wings, There Are No Barriers.* She is also a contributing author to the bestselling series Chicken Soup for the Soul.

Aside from her speaking career, Sue is married, mother of two daughters, grandmother of four, and actively involved in her community in Ontario, Canada. She serves on the Board of Directors for Niagara Life Centre, a nonprofit family counseling service.

To contact Sue Augustine or book her for an event, check out

www.sueaugustine.com

or e-mail her at

wings@vaxxine.com

When Your Past Is Hurting Your Present
Getting Beyond Fears That Hold You Back
Sue Augustine

Free from Your Past—at Last!

Is your past dictating your present? And your future? Do you want to break this destructive pattern and move on to a happier life, but find it impossible to do so?

Sue Augustine understands your situation. She too was once held captive by a painful past. With compassion, empathy, and a touch of humor, Sue shows you how to…

- identify, release, and change how you respond to the past
- overcome a "victim" stance
- trade bitterness and resentment for peace and joy
- set goals for the future with passion and purpose
- understand God's incredible timing and direction

If you're struggling with a difficult past that's harming your present and crippling your future, you can begin today to cut loose the baggage of the long-ago…and start to see your fears conquered, your dreams renewed, and your future become bright with new possibilities.

More Great Harvest House Books

FOLLOWING GOD ONE YES AT A TIME
Connie Cavanaugh

Jesus said, "Follow Me." Simple and straightforward, right? But like everything else today, following God has gotten way too complicated. Are you looking for a simpler path? A way to know what the next turn is? Author and dynamic speaker Connie Cavanaugh can relate! With humor and compassion, she shares insights and biblical truths that will help you

- hear God more clearly to discern your next step
- celebrate God's presence in your day-to-day life
- overcome six common barriers to following God

This book is full of inspirational stories from people like you who have discovered the best way to follow God is one yes at a time.

READY TO WIN OVER WORRY AND ANXIETY
Thelma Wells

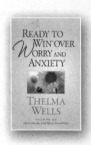

Are you anxious? Feeling concerned about your family, your job, your health, your finances? When author Thelma Wells discovered how to defeat worry and anxiety, she found a life of confident, joyful living. And she wants to help you experience more happiness too. Offering hope and compassion, she invites you on an interactive journey that includes questions to help you evaluate your worries, biblical wisdom to give you strength, and doable steps to kick anxiety out of your life. Together you will...

- evaluate the impact of big and little worries in your life
- explore how faith in Christ will help you conquer anxiety
- find ways to add upbeat, life-building thoughts to every day

Ready to Win over Worry and Anxiety reveals how you can eliminate worry and anxiety and choose freedom and peace in Christ.

WRESTLING PRAYER
Eric and Leslie Ludy

Martin Luther said, *"Prayer is that mightiest of all weapons that created natures can wield."* Do you long to pray more effectively? Are you ready to pray with real power and experience real results? Powerful prayer leads to powerful living. That's been confirmed by great spiritual warriors such as King David, the apostle Paul, Augustine, John Knox, David Brainerd, Hudson Taylor, Amy Carmichael, and others.

Did you know God desires to work through you in the same mighty ways He worked through them? *Wrestling Prayer* is the key that unlocks the supernatural strength that moves mountains and calms storms. It can radically transform your life and unleash God's power in ways beyond what you can even imagine.

This mightiest of all weapons is yours to use. Join Eric and Leslie as they lead you on an inspiring journey, and discover how wrestling prayer can alter every area of your life. You'll never be the same.

NORMAL PEOPLE DO THE CRAZIEST THINGS
David Hawkins

Do you ever wonder whether you're going just a little bit crazy? Sometimes life comes at you with so much, you become unsure of yourself and even begin to wonder, *Am I losing my mind?* You can trust this reassuring counsel from a seasoned Christian psychologist: You're probably a lot more normal than you think. Rather than allowing everyday problems to fool you into thinking you're a little off-center, you can…

- look at your problems from God's perspective
- open your life freely instead of keeping too many secrets
- learn to handle relational issues with biblical wisdom and compassion

Yes, life can be difficult. But with the right tools, you can handle it!

KEEPING YOUR COOL...WHEN YOUR ANGER IS HOT!
June Hunt

Add a *d* in front of *anger,* and it spells *danger!* Most people have been taught anger is bad. So they stuff it, disguise it, mask it, medicate it, numb it, and rename it. But that only fuels the fire within...making an explosion all the more likely.

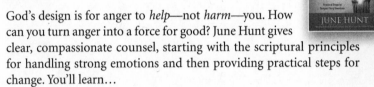

God's design is for anger to *help*—not *harm*—you. How can you turn anger into a force for good? June Hunt gives clear, compassionate counsel, starting with the scriptural principles for handling strong emotions and then providing practical steps for change. You'll learn...

- the four sources of anger and their triggers
- how to respond to angry people
- how to *act* positively rather than *react* negatively

You'll find this practical approach refreshingly effective. Soon you'll experience new freedom, power, and peace.